teach®
yourself

spanish

D0621962

teach
yourself

spanish
juan kattán-ibarra
advisory editor
paul coggle

For over 60 years, more than
50 million people have learnt over
750 subjects the **teach yourself**
way, with impressive results.

be where you want to be
with **teach yourself**

For UK order enquiries: please contact Bookpoint Ltd, 130 Milton Park, Abingdon, Oxon, OX14 4SB. Telephone: +44 (0) 1235 827720. Fax: +44 (0) 1235 400454. Lines are open 09.00–17.00, Monday to Saturday, with a 24-hour message answering service. Details about our titles and how to order are available at www.teachyourself.co.uk

For USA order enquiries: please contact McGraw-Hill Customer Services, PO Box 545, Blacklick, OH 43004-0545, USA. Telephone: 1-800-722-4726. Fax: 1-614-755-5645.

For Canada order enquiries: please contact McGraw-Hill Ryerson Ltd, 300 Water St, Whitby, Ontario, L1N 9B6, Canada. Telephone: 905 430 5000. Fax: 905 430 5020.

Long renowned as the authoritative source for self-guided learning – with more than 50 million copies sold worldwide – the **teach yourself** series includes over 500 titles in the fields of languages, crafts, hobbies, business, computing and education.

British Library Cataloguing in Publication Data: a catalogue record for this title is available from the British Library.

Library of Congress Catalog Card Number: on file.

First published in UK 1998 by Hodder Education, 338 Euston Road, London, NW1 3BH.

First published in US 1998 by The McGraw-Hill Companies, Inc.

This edition published 2007.

The **teach yourself** name is a registered trade mark of Hodder Headline.

Copyright © 1998, 2003, 2007 Juan Kattán-Ibarra
Advisory Editor: Paul Coggle, University of Kent at Canterbury

Typeset by Transet Limited, Coventry, England.
Printed in Great Britain for Hodder Education, a division of Hodder Headline, an Hachette Livre UK Company, 338 Euston Road, London, NW1 3BH, by Cox & Wyman Ltd, Reading, Berkshire.

The publisher has used its best endeavours to ensure that the URLs for external websites referred to in this book are correct and active at the time of going to press. However, the publisher and the author have no responsibility for the websites and can make no guarantee that a site will remain live or that the content will remain relevant, decent or appropriate.

Hodder Headline's policy is to use papers that are natural, renewable and recyclable products and made from wood grown in sustainable forests. The logging and manufacturing processes are expected to conform to the environmental regulations of the country of origin.

Impression number   10 9 8 7 6 5 4 3 2 1
Year   2010 2009 2008 2007

acknowledgements

The author wishes to thank Juan Luzzi for his assistance in the production of the manuscript. Thanks are also due to the following people for their help with recordings: María Catalina Botello, Carlos Riera, Elsa Ochoa, Leonardo Sánchez Gorosito, Sarah Sherborne.

Every effort has been made to obtain permission for all material used. In the absence of any response to enquiries, the author and publisher would like to acknowledge the following for use of their material: Revistas *Quo, Mía, Blanco y Negro de ABC, Guía del Ocio*, diario *El Periódico*, Oficina Municipal de Turismo del Ayuntamiento de Fuengirola, RENFE, from Spain; diarios *El Mercurio* and *La Tercera*, from Chile.

About the author

Juan Kattán-Ibarra has wide experience of teaching Spanish to adults at all levels and has written a number of very successful books. He is the sole author of *Teach Yourself Improve your Spanish*, *Teach Yourself Latin American Spanish*, *Teach Yourself Spanish Grammar*, *Conversational Spanish*, *Conversando*, *Panorama de la prensa*, *Perspectivas Culturales de España*, *Perspectivas Culturales de Hispanoamérica*, and co-author of *Teach Yourself Spanish Conversation*, *Working with Spanish*, *Talking Business Spanish*, *España nuevo siglo*, *Sueños – World Spanish Intermediate (BBC)*, *Modern Spanish Grammar*, *Modern Spanish Grammar Workbook and Spanish Grammar in Context*.

contents

introduction

Welcome to *Teach Yourself Spanish!*

Is this the right course for you? If you are an adult learner with no previous knowledge of Spanish and studying on your own, then this is the course for you. Perhaps you are taking up Spanish again after a break from it, or you are intending to learn with the support of a class? Again, you will find this course very well suited to your purposes.

Developing your skills

The language introduced in this course is centred around realistic everyday situations. The emphasis is first and foremost on *using* Spanish, but we also aim to give you an idea of how the language works, so that you can create sentences of your own.

The course covers all four of the basic skills – listening and speaking, reading and writing. If you are working on your own, the audio recordings will be all the more important, as they will provide you with the essential opportunity to listen to Spanish and to speak it within a controlled framework. You should therefore try to obtain a copy of the audio recordings if you haven't already got one.

Use it or lose it!

Language learning is a bit like jogging – you need to do it regularly for it to do any good! Ideally, you should find a 'study buddy' to work through the course with you. This way you will have someone to try out your Spanish on. And when the going gets tough, you will have someone to chivvy you on until you reach your target.

Where can I find real Spanish?

Don't expect to be able to understand everything you hear or read straight away. If you watch Spanish-speaking programmes on TV or buy Spanish magazines you should not get discouraged when you realize how quickly native-speakers speak and how much vocabulary there is still to be learned. Just concentrate on a *small* extract – either a video/audio clip or a short article – and work through it till you have mastered it. In this way, you'll find that your command of Spanish increases steadily. See the **Taking it further** section on page 283 for information on sources of authentic Spanish, including newspapers, magazines, websites and organizations linked to the Spanish-speaking world.

The structure of this course

The course book contains

- an introductory unit
- 25 course units
- self-assessment tests and a reference section at the back of the book
- 2 CDs (which you really do need to have if you are going to get maximum benefit from the course).

The course units

The course units can be divided roughly into the following categories, although of course there is a certain amount of overlap from one category to another.

Statement of aims

You will be told what you can expect to learn, mostly in terms of what you will be able to do in Spanish by the end of the unit.

Presentation of new language

You will find two or more dialogues which are recorded ▶ on the CDs and also printed in the book. Some assistance with vocabulary is also given. The language is presented in manageable chunks, building carefully on what you have learned in earlier units. Transcripts of listening comprehension exercises are at the back of the book.

Key phrases and expressions

xiii

introduction

All new phrases and expressions with their English translation are listed in the **How do you say it?** section.

Description of language forms

In the **Grammar** section you learn about the forms of the language, thus enabling you to construct your own sentences correctly. For those who are daunted by grammar, assistance is given in various ways.

Pronunciation

The best way to acquire a good pronunciation and intonation is to listen to native speakers and try to imitate them. But most people do not actually notice that certain sounds in Spanish are pronounced differently from their English counterparts, until this is pointed out to them. Specific advice on pronunciation is given in the **Pronunciation Guide** on page xvii, and in the **Pronunciation** section in the first half of the course.

Practice of the new language

In the **Practice** section you will be able to use the language that you have learned. Practice is graded, so that activities ('actividades' on the recording) which require mainly *recognition* normally come first. As you grow in confidence in manipulating language forms, you will be encouraged to *produce* both in writing and in speech.

Information on Spanish-speaking countries

At different stages in the course, you will find relevant information about aspects of life and customs in the Spanish-speaking world. This information, found in the 🛈 section, is given in English in the first part of the course, but later on in Spanish.

Testing yourself

A **Testing yourself** section, on pages 270–79, will help you to test what you have learnt in your Spanish course, and allow you to judge whether you have successfully mastered the language and if you are ready to move to a more advanced course.

Each activity in this section has references to the relevant units, so you can either do the tests at intervals, after every five units, or when you have worked your way through the course. If you are uncertain about how you perfomed with a particular test, you will be able to check your answers in the **Key to 'testing yourself'** section and revise that language point until you feel confident that you have mastered it.

Reference

At the end of the book there are sections that you can use for reference:

- a key to the 'testing yourself' exercises
- a 'taking it further' section
- a glossary of grammatical terms
- a grammar summary
- a list of irregular verbs
- transcripts of the listening comprehension exercises
- a key to the activities in each unit
- a Spanish–English vocabulary
- an English–Spanish vocabulary
- an index to the grammar

Online exercises

Online exercises linked to each unit of the course will be found on the website. You can either work through these activities at intervals, after each unit, or when you have completed a certain number of units or the full course.

How to use this course

Make sure at the beginning of each course unit that you are clear about what you can expect to learn.

Read any background information that is provided. Then listen to the dialogues on the audio recordings. Try to get the gist of what is being said before you look at the printed text in the book. Refer to the printed text and the key vocabulary in order to study the dialogues in more detail. If you want an explanation of new language points at this stage, study the relevant paragraphs in the **Grammar** section. All the dialogues include listening and reading activities and you can check your answers in the **Key to the activities**.

Don't fall into the trap of thinking you have 'done that' when you have listened to the audio a couple of times and worked through the dialogues and activities in the book. You may *recognize* what you hear and read, but you almost certainly still have some way to go before you can *produce* the language of the dialogues correctly and fluently. This is why we recommend that you keep listening to the recordings at every opportunity – sitting on the train or bus, waiting at the dentist's or stuck in a traffic jam in the car, using what would otherwise be 'dead' time. Of course, you must also be internalizing what you hear and making sense of it – just playing it in the background without really paying attention is not enough!

After you have gone through the dialogues, check the **How do you say it?** section for key phrases and expressions. Try covering up the English translations and producing the English equivalents of the Spanish. If you find that relatively easy, go on to cover the Spanish sentences and produce the Spanish equivalents of the English. You will probably find this more difficult. Trying to recall the context in which words and phrases were used may help you learn them better.

You can then study the grammar explanations in the **Grammar** section in a systematic way. We have tried to make these as user-friendly as possible, since we recognize that many people find grammar daunting. But in the end, it is up to you just how much time you spend on studying and sorting out the grammar points. Some people find that they can do better by getting an ear for what sounds right, others need to know in detail how the language is put together. At this stage you may want to refer to the relevant sections of the **Glossary of grammatical terms** and the **Grammar summary** for clarification and further information.

You will then be ready to move on to the **Practice** section and work through the activities following the instructions that precede them. Some of the activities in this section are listen-only activities. The temptation may be to go straight to the transcriptions in the back of the book, but try not to do this. The whole point of listening exercises is to improve your listening skills. You will not do this by reading first. The transcriptions are there to help you if you get stuck.

As you work your way through the activities, check your answers carefully in the back of the book. It is easy to overlook your own mistakes. If you have a study buddy it's a good idea to check each other's answers. Most of the exercises have fixed answers, but some are a bit more open-ended, especially when we are asking you to talk about yourself. We then, in most cases, give you a model answer which you can adapt for your own purposes.

Before you move on to a new unit, go through the **How do you say it?** section once more to make sure that you know all the key language in the current unit.

Spanish in the modern world

Spanish, **el español,** also known as **el castellano,** is an international language and more than 300 million people speak it as their mother tongue. Outside Spain, Spanish is an official language in nineteen countries in Latin America. It is also spoken in parts of Africa, by many people in the Philippines, and by over 30 million people in the United States. Speakers from across Spain and places as far afield as Mexico and Chile share a common language, and the different accents and local words are no obstacle to communication.

Other languages

Alongside Spanish, other languages are spoken by a large number of Spaniards in their own country: **el catalán,** in Cataluña, Valencia and the Balearic Islands; **el gallego,** in Galicia; and **el vasco** or **el euskera,** in the Basque Country, each of them having an official status in the regions in which they are spoken. In Latin America, Spanish is used by millions of indigenous people alongside their own native languages. Spanish has borrowed a number of words from these indigenous languages, some of which have found their way into Peninsular Spanish and even other European languages.

What kind of Spanish am I going to learn?

The language we have chosen for your *Teach Yourself Spanish* course is standard Spanish, which will allow you to communicate with speakers anywhere in the Spanish-speaking world. The audio recordings have been done mostly by speakers from Spain, but to get you acquainted with other accents, some have been recorded by people from Mexico and Argentina. Differences between Peninsular and Latin American Spanish are explained in some of the course units. The abbreviation *LAm* has been used to signal a Latin American term, but note that usage may differ from country to country so, with a few exceptions, only words used more widely have been given.

We hope you enjoy working your way through *Teach Yourself Spanish*. Don't get discouraged. Mastering a new language does take time and perseverance and sometimes things can seem just too difficult. But then you'll come back to it another day and things will begin to make more sense again.

▶ Pronunciation Guide

The aim of this pronunciation guide is to offer hints which will enable you to produce sounds recognizable to Spanish speakers. It cannot by itself teach you to pronounce Spanish accurately. The best way to acquire a reasonably good accent is to listen to and try to imitate native speakers. Listed below are the main elements of Spanish pronunciation and their approximate English equivalent. In addition to these, between Units 1-13 you will find further notes on some individual sounds and you will have a chance to practise them by imitating the speakers on the recording. Read the notes below, which include only those sounds which may cause difficulty to English speakers, and listen to and repeat the words that you hear.

Vowels

a	like the **a** in *cat*	**Ana**
e	like the **e** in *red*	**Elena**
i	like the **ea** in *mean*	**Rita**
o	like the **o** in *god*	**poco**
u	like the **oo** in *moon*	**luna**

Consonants

b and v	in initial position and after **n** are pronounced the same, like the **b** in *bar*	**Barcelona, invierno**
b and v	in other positions, more like the **v** in *very*	**Sevilla, Alba**
c	before **a, o, u**, like the **c** in *car*	**coche**
	before **e, i**, like the **th** in *think* (in Latin America, Southern	**gracias, Valencia**

xvii
introduction

	Spain and the Canaries, like the s in *sink*)	
g	before **a, o, u**, like the **g** in *get* before **e, i**, like the **ch** in *loch*	**Málaga** **Gibraltar**
gu	before **e, i**, like the **g** in *get*	**Guernica**
h	is silent	**Honduras**
j	like the **ch** in *loch*	**Jamaica**
ll	like **lli** in *million* (in parts of Latin America, more like the **j** in *jam*)	**paella**
ñ	like **ni** in *onion*	**mañana**
qu	like the **k** in *keep*	**que**
r	between vowels or at the end of a word, like the **r** in *very*; in initial position, strongly rolled	**caro, calor** **Roma**
rr	always strongly rolled	**Tarragona**
v	like **b** (see **b** above)	
w	(in foreign words) like Spanish **b** and **v** (see above) or English **w**	**wáter** **Taiwán**
x	between vowels, like the **x** in *box*; before a consonant, usually like the **s** in *some*, in Peninsular Spanish (like the **x** in *box*, in Latin American Spanish); in a few words, like the **ch** in *loch*	**taxi** **sexto** **México**
y	like the **y** in *yes* (in parts of Latin America, more like the **j** in *jam*)	**mayo**
z	like the **z** in *think* (in Latin America, Southern Spain and the Canaries, like the **s** in *sink*)	**Zaragoza, Cádiz**

The pronunciation of **c** before **i, e**, as in **gracias, Valencia,** and **z**, as in **Zaragoza, Cádiz**, both pronounced like an **s** in Latin America (as well as in Southern Spain and the Canaries), can be said to be the main difference in pronunciation between Latin American Spanish and that spoken in most parts of Spain.

(For the alphabet and how the letters are read see Unit 03)

Stress and accentuation

a Words which end in a vowel, **n** or **s** stress the last syllable but one: *na*da, *to*man, E*sta*dos U*ni*dos.

b Words which end in a consonant other than **n** or **s** stress the last syllable: Ma*drid,* espa*ñol.*

c Words which do not follow the above rules carry a written accent over the vowel of the stressed syllable: **allí, autobús, invitación.**

Abbreviations

The following abbreviations have been used in this book.

(m) for masculine, (f) for feminine, (sing) for singular, (pl) for plural, (inf) for informal, (adj) for adjective, (adv) for adverb, (esp) for especially, (LAm) for Latin America, (AmE) for American English, (S. Cone) for Southern Cone: Argentina, Uruguay and Paraguay, (Mex) for Mexico, (Arg) for Argentina.

antes de empezar

before you start

In this unit you will learn how to:

- greet people
- ask someone´s name and say your name
- seek clarification and help
- say goodbye

▶1 Hola, ¿qué tal?

In Part 1 of this unit you'll learn to greet people. You'll hear people say *hello* to each other and you'll learn the Spanish words for *good morning, good afternoon, good evening,* and *good night.*

1.1 Look at the drawings first, then listen to the recording and try to imitate the speakers as you hear them.

¡Hola!

Hola, buenos días.

Buenos días   Buenas tardes   Buenas noches

How do you say it?

Greeting people

¡Hola!	*Hello!, Hi!*
Hola, ¿qué tal?	*Hello, how are things?/how are you?*
Buenos días.	*Good morning* (literally, *good days*)
Buenas tardes.	*Good afternoon/evening.*
Buenas noches.	*Good evening/night.*

❶Greetings

Hola, used on its own, is familiar, but it may also be used in formal address when followed by other greetings, for example **hola, buenos días. Buenas tardes** is normally used after lunch and until early evening. After that use **buenas noches**.

1.2 Say it in Spanish!

a At a party you see your friend Rosa. Say hello to her and ask her how are things.

b It's 8.00 a.m. Greet the hotel receptionist at your hotel.

c It's 2.00 p.m. Greet the waitress who'll be serving you lunch.

d It's 9.00 p.m. Greet the barman before you order a drink.

▶ 2 ¿Cómo te llamas?

In Part 2 of this Unit you'll learn to ask someone's name and to say your name.

2.1 Listen to the expressions on the recording and try to imitate the speakers as you hear them.

How do you say it?

Asking someone's name and saying your name

¿Cómo te llamas?	*What's your name? (informal)*
¿Cómo se llama (usted)?	*What's your name? (formal)*
Me llamo	*My name is ... (literally, I call myself)*
¿Y tú/usted?	*And yours? (inf/formal) (literally, And you?)*

❶ Informal and formal ways of addressing people

Spanish makes a distinction between informal and formal address. The *informal* word for *you* when addressing one person is **tú**, and the formal one is **usted**, shortened in writing to **Vd.** or **Ud.** Generally speaking, **usted** is used for talking to people one doesn't know, especially if there is a difference in age, for example a young person addressing someone much older, or a difference in status such as a person in a subordinate position talking to a superior. **Tú** is used among friends, equals, for example people at work, and generally among younger people, even if they haven't met before. Within the family, the prevalent form is **tú**. Overall, the use of **tú** is very common in Spain today but less so in *Hispanoamérica* (the Spanish-speaking countries of Latin America), where people tend to be more formal, although there are regional differences. Verb forms, like some other grammatical words, change depending on whether you are using *informal* or *formal* address (see examples above).

▶ 2.2 During an excursion, Elena meets José. They are both young, so they use informal language.

Elena   Hola, ¿cómo te llamas?
José   Me llamo José. Y tú, ¿cómo te llamas?
Elena   Me llamo Elena.

2.3 Señor Salas, *Mr Salas*, meets señora Montes, *Mrs Montes*. They use formal language to address each other.

Señor Salas   Buenas tardes. Me llamo Carlos Salas. ¿Cómo se llama usted?
Señora Díaz   Me llamo Julia Montes.

2.4 Say it in Spanish!

a At a party in a Spanish-speaking country someone comes up to you.
  - Hola, ¿cómo te llamas?
  - *Say your name and ask his/her name, using the informal form.*

b Now here is an older person.
  - *Say your name and ask his/her name, using the formal form.*

▶ 3 Perdón, no entiendo

In Part 3 you'll learn some key phrases for seeking clarification and help with your Spanish.

3.1 Listen to the recording and try to imitate the speakers as you hear them.

How do you say it?

Seeking clarification and help

Perdón (or Perdone), no entiendo.	*I'm sorry, I don't understand.*
¿Cómo dice? *or* ¿Cómo?	*Pardon me? (literally How do you say?)*
¿Puede repetir, por favor?	*Can you repeat, please?*
Más despacio, por favor.	*More slowly, please.*
¿Qué significa...?	*What does it mean/does ... mean?*
¿Habla usted inglés?	*Do you speak English?*
Perdone, no hablo muy bien español.	*I'm sorry, I don't speak Spanish very well.*

i An alternative expression for *I'm sorry* is **Lo siento**.

3.2 Say it in Spanish!

a The hotel receptionist mentioned the word *habitación*. Ask what *habitación* means.

b He's speaking too fast. Ask him to speak more slowly.

c You didn't catch what he said again. Apologize and say you don't understand and ask him to repeat.

d A cry for help! Apologize and say you don't speak Spanish very well. Ask whether he speaks English.

▶ 4 ¡Adiós!

In Part 4 you'll learn to say goodbye.

4.1 Look at the drawings in your book and listen to and repeat the expressions you'll hear on the recording.

How do you say it?

Saying goodbye

adiós	*goodbye (formal and inf)*
adiós, buenos días/buenas tardes/noches	*goodbye, have a good morning/afternoon/evening (more formal)*
hasta luego	*see you, bye (formal and inf) (literally, until later) bye,*
chao (chau, in some countries)	*cheerio (inf, especially LAm)*

i In some Latin American countries, **hasta luego** is considered formal. **Adiós** also means *hello*, as a form of greeting when passing bye. Other ways of saying goodbye are **hasta ahora** *see you in a minute* (literally, *until now*) and **hasta la vista** *see you*.

4.2 Say it in Spanish!

a It's Friday evening and you are saying goodbye to your Spanish boss.

b You'll be seeing your Spanish friend later on in the day. Say goodbye to him/her.

c Say goodbye to your Latin American friend.

▶ Check what you have learnt

On a flight home from Spain, Helen meets Enrique. Complete the missing parts of their conversation and then listen to the recording to check whether your answers were correct.

Enrique ¿Cómo se .... usted?

Helen Me .... Helen. Helen Thomas. ¿Y ....?

Enrique Enrique Ramírez.

Helen Perdone, no .... ¿.......... repetir, por favor?

Enrique Enrique Ramírez.

Helen No .... muy bien español. ¿.......... usted inglés?

Enrique No, lo siento.

01

hablo español
I speak Spanish

In this unit you will learn how to:
- say where you are from
- say your nationality
- say what languages you speak

▶ 1 ¿De dónde eres?

At an international conference, Eva meets Pepe. They address each other using the informal form.

1.1 Listen to the dialogue several times and fill in the gaps in the bubbles below without looking at the printed dialogue. A key phrase here is **Soy de ...** *I'm from ...*

> Soy de--- ¿Y tú?
>
> Soy de ---.

Eva ¿De dónde eres?
Pepe Soy de Madrid, ¿y tú?
Eva Soy de Salamanca.

1.2 Now read the dialogue and find the Spanish equivalent for *Where are you from?*

▶ 2 Usted es español, ¿verdad?

Señora Medina meets señor Arenas. The language here is formal, so some of the expressions differ slightly from those in Dialogue 1.

2.1 Listen to the dialogue several times and say whether the following statements are true or false (**verdaderos o falsos**).

a Señor Arenas is Mexican.
b He's from Mexico City.
c Señora Medina is Spanish.
d She's from Puebla.

Señora Medina Usted es español, ¿verdad?

Señor Arenas Sí, soy español, soy de Málaga. ¿De dónde es usted?

Señora Medina Soy mexicana. Soy de Puebla.

2.2 Now read the dialogue and answer the following questions:

a How does señora Medina ask señor Arenas whether he's Spanish?

b How does señor Arenas ask señora Medina where she's from?

Compare his question with that used by Eva in Dialogue 1.

---

usted es ... *you are ... (formal)*

▶ 3 ¿Habla usted inglés?

Señor Arenas is approached by Sarah, who is looking for someone who speaks English.

3.1 Listen to the conversation several times and then answer the questions which follow. The key word here is **hablar**, *to speak*.

a Does señor Arenas speak English?

b What languages does he speak?

Sarah Perdone.

Señor Arenas Sí, ¿dígame?

Sarah ¿Habla usted inglés?

Señor Arenas No, lo siento, no hablo inglés. Sólo hablo español.

3.2 Now read the dialogue and find the Spanish equivalent for:

a Do you speak ...?   **b** I speak ...

Sí, ¿dígame? *Yes, can I help you? (literally, tell me?)*

sólo *only*

---

4 Es de Barcelona

In an e-mail to a friend, Mercedes, from Perú, wrote about Eduardo, whom she met at the conference. What languages does Eduardo speak?

> *... se llama Eduardo y es catalán. Es de Barcelona. Habla catalán, español y un poco de inglés...*

se llama...	*his name is...*	**un poco de**	*some* (literally,
catalán	*from Catalonia*		*a little of*)

How do you say it?

Asking people where they are from and replying

¿De dónde eres (tú)/es (usted)? *Where are you from?*
Soy de... *I'm from...*

Asking someone's nationality and replying

¿Eres español/a? *Are you Spanish?* (inf, m/f)
¿Es usted mexicano/a? *Are you Mexican?* (formal, m/f)

Asking people whether they speak a certain language and replying

¿Hablas/Habla Vd. español? *Do you speak Spanish?* (inf/formal)
Hablo (un poco de) español. *I speak some Spanish.*
No hablo español, hablo inglés. *I don't speak Spanish, I speak English.*

Giving similar information about others

Es... *(nationality)* *He/She is...*
Es de... *(place)* *He/She is from...*
Habla... *(language)* *He/She speaks...*

Grammar

1 Three types of verbs

If you look up verbs, that is words like **ser**, *to be*, **hablar**, *to speak*, in a Spanish dictionary, you'll see that they fall into three main categories according to their endings:

-ar   e.g. **hablar** *to speak*
-er   ser   *to be*
-ir   vivir   *to live*

2 Regular and irregular verbs

The majority of Spanish verbs are 'regular', that is, they change in a fixed way, for example *for person* (e.g. *I, you*) or *for tense* (e.g. *present, past*), but others show some variation, and so are called 'irregular'. In this unit you will learn some of the present tense forms of two important verbs: **hablar**, *to speak*, and **ser**, *to be*. The first one is regular, the second irregular.

	hablar *to speak*		**ser** *to be*	
(yo)	hablo	*I speak*	soy	*I am*
(tú)	hablas	*you speak* (inf.)	eres	*you are* (inf.)
(usted)	habla	*you speak* (form.)	es	*you are* (form.)
(él/ella)	habla	*he/she speaks*	es	*he/she/it is*

Note that the forms for **usted**, *you* (formal), **él**, *he*, and **ella**, *she*, are always identical. These same verb forms are used for **it**, as in 'it is', for which Spanish does not have a specific word, as the verb on its own is sufficient (see 3 below), e.g. **es español**, *it is Spanish*.

3 Yo, tú, él, ella ... *(I, you, he, she ...)*

As the ending of the verb normally indicates the person one is referring to (e.g. *I, you*), words like **yo**, *I*, **tú**, *you* (informal), **él**, *he*, **ella**, *she*, are usually omitted, except for emphasis or contrast.

Soy español.   *I'm Spanish.*
Yo soy mexicano.   *I am a Mexican.*

Usted, *you* (formal) is very often kept, in speaking as well as in writing, for politeness and to avoid ambiguity (see 2 above).

4 Asking questions

As in English, there are different ways of asking questions in Spanish.

- By using the same word order as in a statement.
  ¿Usted es de Madrid?   *Are you from Madrid?*
- By starting your sentence with the verb.
  ¿Habla usted inglés?   *Do you speak English?*
- By placing the word **¿verdad?** or **¿no?** at the end of the statement.
  Usted es español, ¿verdad?/¿no?   *You are Spanish, aren't you?*
- By using a question word.
  ¿Cómo te llamas?   *What's your name?*

Note that all questions in Spanish must carry two question marks, one at the beginning and one at the end of the sentence. Note, too, that all question words, e.g. **¿cómo?**, *how?*, **¿dónde?**, *where?*, carry a written accent.

5 Saying 'no'

To negate something in Spanish simply put the word **no** before the verb.

> **No soy español.**   *I'm not Spanish.*
> **No hablo español.**   *I don't speak Spanish.*

6 Masculine or feminine?

Words for nationality, like other words used for describing people, e.g. **guapo/a**, *good-looking (man/woman)*, have *masculine* and *feminine forms*.

- To form the feminine from a masculine word ending in -o, change the -o to -a.
  Soy británico/(norte)americano/   *I'm British/American/*
    indio.   *Indian* (man)
  Soy británica/(norte)americana/   *I'm British/American/*
    india.   *Indian* (woman)

Most Latin American countries use the word **norteamericano/a**, literally *North American*, instead of **americano/a**. A less common alternative is **estadounidense** (m/f) *of/from the United States* ('de los Estados Unidos')

Some Spanish-speaking countries use the word **hindú** to refer to someone of **Indian** nationality. This word does not change for masculine and feminine (see below).

- To form the feminine from a masculine word ending in a consonant, add -a to the consonant.

Soy español/inglés/alemán.	*I'm Spanish/English/German* (man)
Soy española/inglesa/ alemana.	*I'm Spanish/English/German* (woman)

Note the omission of the written accent in **inglesa** and **alemana** (see Stress and accentuation, pp: xix).

- Words denoting nationality or origin ending in -a, -e, -í, ú remain unchanged.

Soy belga/árabe/paquistaní.   *I'm Belgian/Arab/Pakistani.*

Note that words for nationality are not written with capital letters in Spanish.

7 'México' or 'Méjico'?

Mexicans spell their country's name, *México*, and their nationality, *mexicano/a*, with an *x*, and this is the form adopted in this book. In Spain, you will sometimes find these spelled as *Méjico* and *mejicano*.

▶ Pronunciation

Spanish vowels: 'a', 'e', 'o'

Spanish vowels are different from English vowel sounds, as they are generally short and do not change their quality or length, as do English vowels. Each vowel corresponds to one sound only. References to English below are an approximation to how Spanish should sound.

a, as in 'Salamanca', like the 'a' in 'answer'
e, as in 'Pepe', like the 'e' in 'yet'
o, as in 'Antonio', like the 'o' in 'not'

Listen to your recording and practise these sounds by imitating the speakers.

Se llama Ana, es española, de Granada. Habla español y un poco de francés.

Me llamo Eduardo, soy catalán, de Barcelona. Hablo español y catalán.

Practice

1 Palabra por palabra

How many of the countries listed on the next page can you recognize? Match each country with the corresponding nationality and language.

País		Nacionalidad (m/f)		Idioma
a	Alemania	1	inglés/inglesa	A árabe
b	Francia	2	egipcio/a	B portugués
c	Rusia	3	brasileño/a	C inglés
d	España	4	francés/francesa	D francés
e	Inglaterra	5	ruso/rusa	E alemán
f	Brasil	6	alemán/alemana	F ruso
g	Egipto	7	español/a	G español

▶ 2 ¿Soy española?

Listen to Silvia, Cristóbal and Sofía introducing themselves, and fill in the table below with the nationality, city and language corresponding to each person.

Nombre	Nacionalidad	Ciudad	Idioma(s)
a Silvia			
b Cristóbal			
c Sofía			

3 Me llamo …

How would each of the following people introduce themselves? Follow the models in Activity 2, and look at the **How do you say it?** section and 6 in the **Grammar** section for other nationalities.

a Boris, Moscú.
b Paco, Granada.
c Ingrid, Berlín.
d Marguerite, París.
e Mark, Nueva York.
f Mª Ángeles, Monterrey, México

i María is a very common name in the Spanish-speaking countries, and is frequently used as the first part of a compound name (as in María Ángeles, above). Here María is abbreviated in writing to Mª.

4 Soy de Bogotá

In an e-mail to a correspondent, Ramiro, a student, gave some information about himself. Can you fill in the blanks with the missing verbs?

Querida Patricia:

_____ Ramiro Fernández Salas y _____ colombiano. _____ de Bogotá. Aparte de español, _____ inglés y un poco de francés.

Querido, *dear* (to a man), and **querida**, *dear* (to a woman), are used for close relationships only. Note also that Ramiro, like all Spanish-speaking people, has two surnames (**apellidos**): Fernández Salas. The first surname is his father's, while the second is his mother's. The second surname is used in more formal and in official situations.

5 Ahora tú

You are writing to a Spanish correspondent for the first time. Give similar information to that given by Ramiro in Activity 4.

6 ¿Cómo se llama?

During a visit to a trade fair in Barcelona, a visitor was asked to fill in this form, which is in Spanish and Catalan, the local language. How would you answer someone's questions about him?

a What's the visitor's surname?
b What's his first name?
c What city and country is he from?

Hora de su visita/Hora de la seva visita

☐	☐	☐	☑	☐	☐
Antes de las 8h.	De las 8h.a 11h.	De las 11h.a 14h.	De las 14h. a 17h.	De las 17h. a 20h.	Después de las 20h.
Avant de les 8h.	De les 8h.a 11h.	De les 11h.a 14h.	De les 14h. a 17h.	De les 17h. a 20h.	Després de les 20h.

Fecha de su visita/Data de la seva visita: . . .*23 de julio*. . . . .

Datos personales/Dades personals

Apellido/Cognom . .*Palma*. . . . . .Nombre/Nom .*Guillermo*. . . . .

Dirección/Adreça. *Calle de Linares, 25* . . . .

Ciudad/Ciutat. . *Córdoba* . . . . País/País . . *España* . . . .

Gracias por depositar esta ficha en la urna
Mercès per depositar aquesta fitxa dins l'urna

---

el apellido *surname*	**el nombre** *name*
la ciudad *city*	**el país** *country*

7 Sólo hablo español

During a flight you talk to a Spanish-speaking person. Follow the guidelines below and complete your part of the conversation with him. He's using the polite form, so do likewise.

– *Ask his name.*
– Me llamo Antonio. ¿Y usted?
– *Reply, and ask where he's from.*
– Soy mexicano, de Veracruz. Y usted, ¿de dónde es?
– *Reply, and ask if he speaks English.*
– No, lo siento, sólo hablo español. No hablo nada de inglés.
  Pero usted sí habla español.
– *Say yes, you speak a little Spanish.*

---

no hablo nada de...	*I don't speak any...* (literally, *I don't speak nothing of...*)
pero	*but*

ℹ️ Note the use of **sí**, *yes*, in **Pero usted sí habla español**, *But you do speak Spanish*. This is emphatic.

02

¿cómo está?
how are you?

In this unit you will learn how to:
- introduce yourself and others
- ask people how they are and say how you are
- ask people where they live and say where you live
- ask for and give telephone numbers and e-mail addresses

▶ 1 Mucho gusto

At a fair, people introduce themselves and others and exchange greetings.

1.1 Cristina spots someone she wants to meet. What do you think her question means, and how does she introduce herself? Listen and find out. Note that the language here is formal.

Cristina	Perdone, ¿Es usted el señor Peña?
Señor Peña	Sí, soy yo.
Cristina	Yo soy Cristina Dueñas. Mucho gusto.
Señor Peña	Encantado.

1.2 Look at the vocabulary below, then read the dialogue and play, first Cristina's part, then señor Peña's.

¿Es usted...?	*Are you...?*
Soy yo	*It's me*
encantado/a	*pleased to meet you* (said by a man/woman)
mucho gusto	pleased to meet you (*invariable*)

1.3 How would you say the following in Spanish?

a Are you Mr Santana?
b I am (*your name*). Pleased to meet you.

▶ 2 ¿Cómo está?

Raúl greets someone he knows and introduces his wife to her. The language in this dialogue is formal.

2.1 How does Raúl greet his acquaintance, and how does she reply? Listen and find out.

Raúl	Señora Silva, ¿cómo está?
Señora Silva	Muy bien, gracias. ¿Y usted?
Raúl	Bien, gracias. Le presento a María, mi mujer. Esta es la señora Silva.
Señora Silva	Encantada.
María	Hola, mucho gusto.

2.2 Read the dialogue and find the expressions meaning *Let me introduce you to...*, *This is Mrs...*

> **presentar** *to introduce*
> **mi mujer/marido** *my wife/husband*

▶ 3 Este es Ricardo

Ana introduces her colleague Ricardo to her boyfriend Fernando. The language here is informal.

3.1 Listen to the dialogue and focus attention on the informal equivalents of : **¿Cómo está?**, **¿Y usted?**, and **Le presento a...** What are they?

Ana   Hola, Ricardo. ¿Cómo estás?

Ricardo   Bien, gracias. ¿Y tú?

Ana   Muy bien. Te presento a Fernando, mi novio. Este es Ricardo, un compañero de trabajo.

Ricardo   ¡Hola!

Fernando Hola, ¿qué tal?

Ricardo   ¿Eres argentino?

Fernando Sí, soy argentino, pero vivo en Madrid.

3.2 Read the dialogue a few times, then give the Spanish for:

a Let me introduce you to Luis/Luisa, my husband/wife (**mi marido/mujer**) (inf)

b This is Isabel, a colleague from work.

> **mi novio/a** *my boy/girlfriend*
> **presentar** *to introduce*
> **un/a compañero/a de trabajo** *a colleague from work* (m./f.)
> **vivo** (from **vivir** *to live*) *I live*

i In a formal introduction men and women will normally shake hands and will do so also when saying goodbye. Younger people often dispense with this formality and will simply exchange informal greetings such as **hola** *hello*, or **¿qué tal?** *hi, how are you?*

▶4 ¿Cuál es tu número de teléfono?

Antonio has met Clara and has given her his telephone numbers and email address, and now she gives him hers.

4.1 What's Clara's home number? And her mobile phone? Key words here are **la casa** *house, home,* **el (teléfono) móvil** *mobile phone,* which in Latin America is **el (teléfono) celular.** Numbers from 0 to 20 are on page 28.

Antonio	¿Cuál es tu número de teléfono?
Clara	El teléfono de mi casa es el 981 546 372.
Antonio	Y tu móvil, ¿cuál es?
Clara	Es el 696 00 19 82.
Antonio	¿Tienes correo electrónico?
Clara	Sí, sí tengo. Es claradiaz@hotmail.com

4.2 Read the dialogue and answer the following questions.

a How does Antonio ask Clara what her telephone number is, and how does she reply?

d What phrase does Antonio use to say '*Have you got an e-mail address?*

¿cuál es...?	*what is...?*
el número de teléfono	*telephone number*
tengo/tienes (from **tener**)	*I/you have* (inf.)
arroba	*(@) at*
el punto	*dot*

How do you say it?

Introducing yourself and others

(Yo) soy...	*I am...*
Este/esta es...	*This is...* (man/woman)
Le/te presento a...	*Let me introduce you to...* (formal/inf)
Mucho gusto.	*Pleased to meet you.*
Encantado/a.	*Pleased to meet you* (said by a man/woman).

Asking people how they are and saying how you are

¿Cómo está/s?	*How are you?* (formal/inf)
(Estoy) (muy) bien.	*I'm (very) well/fine.*

Asking people where they live and saying where you live

¿Dónde vive/s?	*Where do you live?* (formal/inf.)
Vivo en...	*I live in...*

Asking and giving telephone numbers and e-mail addresses

¿Cuál es su/tu número de teléfono/correo electrónico?	*What's your telephone number/e-mail (address)?* (formal/inf)
Es el (93 541 26 70).	*It's (93 541 26 70).*
Es juliovera@hotmail.com.	*It's juliovera@hotmail.com.*
¿Tienes correo electrónico?	*Have you got an e-mail address?*
Sí, tengo/No, no tengo.	*Yes, I have/No, I don't have one.*

Grammar

1 Masculine or feminine?

a El, la (*the*)

Nouns are words which denote a person (e.g. **secretaria**, *secretary*), a thing (e.g. **teléfono**, *telephone*) or an abstraction (e.g. **gusto**, *pleasure*). In Spanish, all nouns are either masculine or feminine, and the word for 'the' is **el** for masculine nouns and **la** for feminine nouns. Nouns ending in -o are usually masculine, while nouns ending in -a are normally feminine.

masculine	**el** señor	*the gentleman, Mr*
feminine	**la** señora	*the lady, Mrs*

c The endings of some nouns do not indicate whether they are masculine or feminine, so it is advisable to learn each word with its corresponding article (**el** or **la**).

el nombre	*name*	**la calle**	*street*

2 El señor, la señora/señorita

Note the use of **el** before **señor**, and **la** before **señora/señorita**, in indirect address.

¿Es usted el señor Martínez/la señorita Miranda?

But:

Buenas tardes, señora Vera.

In writing, **señor**, **señora** and **señorita** are often found in abbreviated form, **Sr.**, **Sra.** and **Srta.**, respectively.

3 De (*of*)

Note the use of **de**, *of*, in

el teléfono **de** mi casa/oficina	*my home/office telephone number* (literally, *the telephone of my house/office*)
el teléfono **de** Carmen	*Carmen's telephone number* (literally, *the telephone of Carmen*)

4 Al (*to the*), del (*of the*)

A + el becomes **al**, and de + el becomes **del**.

Te presento **al** señor Lira.	*Let me introduce you to señor Lira.*
El teléfono **del** señor Castro.	*Señor Castro's telephone number.*

5 Un, una (*a*)

The Spanish equivalent of *a*, as in *a colleague*, *a secretary*, is **un** for masculine and **una** for feminine.

un compañero de trabajo	*a male colleague*
una secretaria	*a female secretary*

6 Mi, tu, su... (*my, your, his, her...*)

a The Spanish equivalent of *my, your, his, her, its, their*, is:

mi casa/apartamento	*my house/apartment*
tu piso/oficina	*your flat/office* (inf)

su teléfono/email   *your* (formal), *his, her, their telephone/e-mail.*

These words agree in number (singular or plural) with the thing possessed, for example **mis cosas** *my things* (for plural forms see Unit 3). Note also that **su** *your* can be used to address one or more than one person formally.

b To say *our* use **nuestro**, and to say *your* when addressing more than one person informally, use **vuestro**. These words agree in number (singular or plural) and gender (masculine and feminine) with the thing possessed: **nuestra dirección** *our address*, **nuestros socios** *our partners*, **vuestra empresa** *your company*, **vuestros amigos** *your friends* (see also Unit 3).

Vuestro is not used in Latin America, where **su** is used in both formal and informal address, to address more than one person. A distinction is made, however, between **tu** and **su** (see above) when addressing one person.

7 'Ser' and 'estar' (*to be*)

There are two ways of saying *to be* in Spanish: **ser** and **estar**. Personal information such as where you are from, your nationality and who you are, are expressed with **ser**, e.g. **Soy Cristóbal**, *I'm Cristóbal* (Unit 1).

To ask people how they are and say how you are you need to use **estar**. **Estar** is an irregular verb, and its singular forms are:

(yo)	**estoy**	*I am*
(tú)	**estás**	*you are* (informal)
(usted)	**está**	*you are* (formal)
(él/ella)	**está**	*he/she/it is*

¿**Cómo estás?**   *How are you?*
Estoy bien.   *I'm fine.*

8 Tengo, tienes ... (*I have, you have* ...)

Tener, to have, is an irregular **-er** verb, whose singular forms are:

(yo)	**tengo**	*I have*
(tú)	**tienes**	*you have* (informal)
(usted)	**tiene**	*you have* (formal)
(él/ella)	**tiene**	*he/she/it has*

| ¿Tienes (teléfono) móvil? | *Have you got a mobile phone?* |
| No, no tengo. | *No, I haven't got one.* |

9 *-ir* verbs

The following are the singular present tense forms of **vivir**, *to live*, a regular -**ir** verb.

(yo)	vivo	*I live*
(tú)	vives	*you live* (informal)
(usted)	vive	*you live* (formal)
(él/ella)	vive	*he/she/it lives*

¿Dónde vive/s?	*Where do you live?*
¿En qué barrio/calle vives?	*Which area/street do you live in?*
Vivo en.../la calle...	*I live in.../on...street.*

▶ Pronunciation

Spanish vowels 'i', 'u'

i as in 'oficina', is pronounced like the 'ee' in 'feet'.

u as in 'mucho gusto'. is pronounced like the 'oo' in 'good'.

ñ (n + tilde)

ñ, as in 'señora', is a separate letter of the Spanish alphabet and is pronounced nearly like the 'ni' in 'onion'.

Practise with:

¿Usted es el señor Peña?
Soy Cristina Dueñas, de La Coruña.
Este es Raúl Núñez, de Madrid.
Esta es Alicia Zúñiga, de Logroño.
Mucho gusto.

Practice

1 ¿Ser o estar?

Alfredo meets Marisa, and señor Lira meets señorita Romero. Can you complete the conversations with the correct forms of **ser** and **estar?** The first exchange is informal and the other one formal.

a – Hola, ¿tú _____ Marisa Frías?
   – Sí, _____ yo.
   – Yo _____ Alfredo Ríos, de Sevilla.
   – Hola, ¿cómo _____?
   – Bien, gracias.

b – Buenos días. Usted _____ la señorita Romero, ¿verdad?
   – Sí, soy Mercedes Romero. ¿Usted _____ Alfonso Lira?
   – Sí, sí. ¿Cómo _____ usted?
   – Muy bien. Y usted, ¿cómo _____?
   – Bien, gracias. Mire, esta _____ María, mi mujer.
   – Encantada.

---

mire *look*

---

2 ¿El o la? ¿Un o una?

Fill in the gaps with **el, la, un, una** where necessary.

Sr. Ibarra	Perdone a **a** _____ señora. ¿Usted es **b** _____ señora Santos, **c** _____ secretaria del señor Martínez?
Sra. Santos	Sí, soy yo.
Sr. Ibarra	Yo soy **d** _____ señor Ibarra, de Transibérica.
Sra. Santos	Mucho gusto **e** _____ señor Ibarra.
Sr. Ibarra	Le presento a Carmen, **f** _____ compañera de trabajo. Y este es Alfonso, **g** _____ amigo.
Sra. Santos	Encantada.

3 Una presentación

Señor Barrios is visiting your place of work, and you and your colleague John have been asked to meet him at reception. Follow the guidelines and fill in your part of the conversation, using the formal form.

– *Ask whether he is señor Barrios.*
– Sí, soy yo.
– *Say who you are.*
– Mucho gusto.

– *Say you are pleased to meet him and introduce your colleague to him.*

| una presentación | *an introduction* |

4 Ahora tú

How would you introduce the following people to a friend? Look up the words in the **Vocabulary** and choose as appropriate, using the informal expression **Te presento a ...**

a tu marido/mujer   c tu padre/madre
b tu novio/novia   d tu hermano/hermana

Now introduce each of the following people, using the expression **Este/Esta es ...**, as appropriate.

e Gloria, una compañera de trabajo   g Carlos, un amigo
f Paul, un compañero de clase   h Laura, una vecina

▶ 5 ¿Dónde vive?

Ana, Julio and Silvia are being asked where they live. Listen and complete each sentence with information from the appropriate map below.

a Ana vive en ...
b Julio vive en ...
c Silvia vive en ...

▶ 6 Los números (*numbers*) 0–20

Listen and repeat each number as you hear it.

0	cero	4	cuatro	8	ocho	12	doce	16	dieciséis
1	uno	5	cinco	9	nueve	13	trece	17	diecisiete
2	dos	6	seis	10	diez	14	catorce	18	dieciocho
3	tres	7	siete	11	once	15	quince	19	diecinueve
								20	veinte

Note that **uno** becomes **un** before a masculine noun, e.g. **un amigo**, *a/one friend*.

▶ 7 ¿Qué número desea?

You will hear two conversations in which people request telephone numbers. Listen and write each number as you hear it.

a

**Hotel Sancho
Teléfono ...**

**Sr. Martín Ramos
Teléfono ...**

b

ℹ Telephone numbers in Spanish can be read out in single or double figures. For example, the telephone number 719 2015 can be read out as:

siete-uno-nueve-dos-cero-uno-cinco *or*
siete-diecinueve-veinte-quince.

8 **Ahora tú**

a ¿Dónde vives?
b ¿En qué barrio vives?
c ¿En qué calle?
d ¿Qué número de teléfono tienes?
e ¿Tienes teléfono en tu oficina/trabajo?
f ¿Cuál es el número?

g ¿Tienes extensión?
h ¿Cuál es el número?
i Y el número de tu móvil/celular, ¿cuál es?
j ¿Tienes correo electrónico? ¿Cuál es?

9 Crucigrama

Horizontales

1 ¿Qué número de teléfono _____ usted?
2 ¿(Tú) ———— teléfono en casa?
3 Buenas tardes, señor Bravo, ¿cómo está _____?
4 (Yo) _____ en la Calle de la Rosa.
5 ¿(Tú) _____ Gonzalo Martínez?

Verticales

1 Raquel _____ en Sevilla, en el barrio de Santa Cruz.
2 Te presento a _____ marido.
3 (Yo) no _____ teléfono en casa.
4 Perdone, señora, el teléfono de _____ oficina, ¿cuál es?
5 Y _____ extensión, Mónica, ¿cuál es?

03

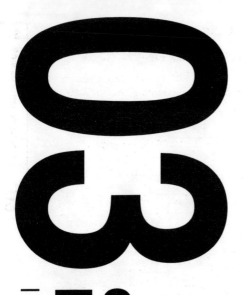

quisiera una habitación
I would like a room

In this unit you will learn how to:
- book into a hotel
- spell your name
- say where something can be done

▶1 ¿Para cuántas personas?

Julio, a hotel receptionist, is attending to some new arrivals.

1.1 Victoria is asking for a room, **una habitación**. Does she want a single or a double room? How many nights does she want it for? Look at the vocabulary below, then listen and find out.

Victoria	Buenas tardes. Quisiera una habitación, por favor.
Recepcionista	¿Para cuántas personas?
Victoria	Para una persona.
Recepcionista	Muy bien. Una habitación individual. ¿Para cuántas noches?
Victoria	Para seis noches.

1.2 Now read the dialogue and then play the parts of a hotel guest and the receptionist, using the following information.

Number of people: dos personas
Type of room: doble
Number of nights: tres

quisiera	*I would like*
¿para cuántas/os...?	*for how many...?* (f/m)

▶2 ¿Tienen habitaciones libres?

Mario and his friend Luis are also trying to get a room.

2.1 What sort of room do they want? What facilities do the rooms have? Look at the vocabulary below, then listen and find out. Note the use of plural verb forms such as **¿tienen...?** *have you got...?*, **son** *you are*, **somos** *we are*, **quisiéramos** *we would like*.

Mario	Por favor, ¿tienen habitaciones libres?
Recepcionista	¿Cuántas personas son?
Mario	Somos dos. Quisiéramos una habitación doble, con dos camas.
Recepcionista	Sí, no hay problema.
Mario	¿Tienen baño las habitaciones?
Recepcionista	Sí, claro, baño, televisión y aire acondicionado.
Mario	¿Está incluido el desayuno?
Recepcionista	No, es sin desayuno. El desayuno es aparte.

2.2 Now read the dialogue and then play the parts of a hotel guest and the receptionist using the following information.

Número de personas: 2
Habitación: doble/cama de matrimonio (*double bed*)
Servicios: baño, teléfono, aire acondicionado, televisión, minibar
¿Desayuno incluido?: sí

libre	*free*	**con**	*with*
la cama	*bed*	**sin**	*without*
hay	*there is*	**el desayuno**	*breakfast*
claro	*certainly*	**aparte**	*separate*

▶ 3 Tenemos una habitación reservada

Pat Johnson and a travelling companion have already booked a room.

3.1 Listen to the dialogue and focus attention on some of the key phrases: **a nombre de...** *in the name of...*, **¿cómo se escribe...?** *How do you spell (it)...?*, **¿dónde se puede cambiar..?** *where can you change...?*.

Pat	Buenas noches. Tenemos una habitación reservada.
Recepcionista	¿A qué nombre?

Pat	A nombre de Pat Johnson.
Recepcionista	¿Cómo se escribe su apellido?
Pat	J-o-h-n-s-o-n. Johnson.
Recepcionista	Muy bien. Sus pasaportes, por favor.
Pat	Aquí tiene.
Recepcionista	Gracias. Tienen la habitación treinta y cinco.
Pat	Quisiéramos cambiar dinero. ¿Dónde se puede cambiar?
Recepcionista	Pueden cambiar aquí mismo.

3.2 Read the dialogue and give the Spanish for

a We have a room booked.
b In what name?
c You have room thirty-five.
d You can change right here.

3.3 Now play Pat's part using and spelling your own name. You'll find the alphabet in Activity 7 on page 40 and also in the recording.

---

reservado/a	*booked*
el nombre	*name*
se escribe (from **escribir** to write)	*it is spelt (written)*
el apellido	*surname*
quisiéramos	*we'd like*
cambiar dinero	*to change money*

How do you say it?

Booking into a hotel

Quisiera una habitación individual/para una persona.	*I'd like a single room/a room for one person.*
Quisiéramos una habitación doble/ para dos personas.	*We'd like a double room/a room for two people.*
¿Tiene/Tienen habitaciones libres?	*Have you got rooms available?*
Tengo/Tenemos una habitación reservada.	*I/We have a room booked.*

Asking someone to spell a name

¿Cómo se escribe su nombre/   *How do you spell your*
apellido?   *name/surname?*

Asking where something can be done and responding

¿Dónde se puede cambiar   *Where can you/one change*
dinero/cenar?   *money/have dinner?*
Pueden cambiar/cenar   *You can change/have dinner*
aquí mismo.   *right here.*

Grammar

1 More than one

Most words form the plural by adding an -s. Nouns ending in a consonant add -es.

una persona   *one person*   cuatro personas *four people*
una habitación   *a room*   dos habitaciones *two rooms*

Note that the written accent on the vowel disappears after adding -es.

2 Los, las (*the*, plural)

The plural of **el** and **la** (*the*, sing.) are **los** and **las**, respectively:

el hotel   *the hotel*   **los** hoteles   *the hotels*
la llave   *the key*   **las** llaves   *the keys*

3 Mis, tus, sus ... (*my, your ...*)

When the object possessed is more than one, **mi, tu, su, nuestro/a**, etc., add an –s. Note that only **nuestro** and **vuestro** change for masculine and feminine. (See Unit 2.)

mi(s)   *my*   **nuestro/a(s)**   *our*
tu(s)   *your* (inf)   **vuestro/a(s)**   *your* (inf)
su(s)   *your* (formal)/*his/her/its* **su(s)**   *your* (formal)
                                                       /their

mis cosas   *my things*
sus pasaportes   *your* (formal), *their passports*
vuestras maletas   *your* (inf) *suitcases*

4 ¿Cuántos/as? *How many?*

¿Cuántos? *how many?* becomes ¿cuántas? before a feminine word: '¿Cuántos euros? (m) ' '*How many euros?*', '¿Cuántas libras (f)?' '*How many pounds?*'.

5 Quisiera, quisiéramos *I'd like, we'd like*

Quisiera and quisiéramos are two special forms of the verb querer *to want*, which are normally used in requests for extra politeness instead of quiero *I want*, queremos *we want*, which may sound a little abrupt (for the full *present tense* forms see Unit 5).

Quisiera el desayuno en mi habitación — *I'd like breakfast in my room.*

Quisiéramos hacer una reserva. — *We'd like to make a reservation.*

6 Poder *can, to be able*

a Stem-changing verbs

A number of Spanish verbs, among them poder, undergo a vowel change in the stem (the infinitive minus –ar, -er or –ir) in certain forms, although their endings remain the same as for regular verbs. Poder changes the –o of the stem pod- into –ue in all persons of the present tense, except the nosotros/as *we* and vosotros/as *you* (informal, plural) forms. Such verbs are known 'technically' as *stem-changing* or *radical-changing verbs*. The symbol > next to a verb has been used to signal a vowel change, for example poder (o>ue). Some verbs change in a different way, for example querer (e>ie) (see Unit 5).

b Present tense forms

The following are the full present tense forms of poder, including the forms for nosotros/as *we* (m/f), vosotros/as *you* (informal, plural, m/f), ellos/ellas *they* (m/f), ustedes *you* (formal, plural). Note that vosotros/as, used to address more than one person in a familiar way, is not used in Latin America, where ustedes and the verb forms that go with it are used in both formal and informal address. This use is not restricted to Latin America, as it is also found in parts of southern Spain.

yo puedo	nosotros/as podemos
tú puedes	vosotros/as podéis
él/ella/Vd. puede	ellos/ellas/Vds. pueden

¿Dónde puedo cambiar dinero?	*Where can I change money?*
No pueden encontrar una habitación.	*They can't find a room.*
¿Qué podemos hacer?	*What can we do?*

7 Ser *to be*, tener *to have*: full present tense forms

In unit 1 you learnt the present tense forms of **ser** for **yo, tú, él, ella** and **usted**. In Unit 2 you learnt the forms for **tener**. In this unit there are further examples of the uses of **ser** and **tener**, which include plural forms.

a Ser

yo soy *I am*	nosotros/as somos *we are*
tú eres *you are*	vosotros/as sois *you are*
él/ella/Vd. es *he/she/it is/you are*	ellos/ellas/Vds. son *they/you are*

¿Es con o sin desayuno?	*Is it with or without breakfast?*
¿Cuántas personas son?	*How many people are you?*
Somos cuatro.	*We're four.*

b Tener

yo tengo *I have*	nosotros/as tenemos *we have*
tú tienes *you have*	vosotros/as tenéis *you have*
él/ella/Vd. tiene *he/she/it has/you have*	ellos/ellas/Vds. tienen *they/you have*

Tengo una reserva a nombre de Ana Godoy.	*I have a reservation in the name of Ana Godoy.*
Tenemos la habitación noventa.	*We have room ninety.*
No tienen televisión por cable.	*They don't have cable TV.*

8 Impersonal sentences

To say *you* or *one*, as in *How do you spell it?*, use **se** followed by the third person of the verb.

¿Cómo se escribe su nombre?	*How do you spell your name?*
¿Dónde se puede aparcar?	*Where can you/one park?*
Aquí no se puede fumar.	*You can't smoke here.*

▶ Pronunciation

The pronunciation of **ll**, as in '**apellido, calle**', varies from region to region, but it is pronounced by most Spanish speakers like the 'y' in 'yatch'. In Argentina and Uruguay it is closer to the 's' in 'pleasure'.

Practise with:

El Hotel del Valle en Valladolid es un hotel de tres estrellas y está en la calle de Mallorca.

¿Cómo te llamas?
Me llamo Estrella.
¿Y cómo te apellidas?
Ulloa. Estrella Ulloa.

Practice

▶ 1 Los números del 21 al 100

Listen and repeat each number as you hear it, and fill in the blanks with the missing ones.

21	veintiuno	26	veintiséis	31	treinta y uno
22	veintidós	27	veintisiete	32	treinta y dos
23	veintitrés	28	veintiocho	36	_____
24	veinticuatro	29	veintinueve	40	cuarenta
25	veinticinco	30	treinta	42	cuarenta y dos

45	_____	64	_____	90	noventa
50	cincuenta	70	setenta	93	_____
53	cincuenta y tres	76	_____	100	cien
59	_____	80	ochenta		
60	sesenta	88	_____		

▶ 2 ¿La habitación del señor Luis García, por favor?

Listen to these brief conversations and fill in the box with the room or office number of each of the people mentioned.

	Nombre	Habitación	Despacho
a	Sr. García		
b	Srta. Sáez		
c	Sres. Silva		

3 Palabra por palabra

Below is a list of some of the facilities you might find in certain hotels. Can you match them with the drawings?

a	la ducha	**d**	el hilo musical
b	el lavabo	**e**	el ascensor
c	la calefacción	**f**	la piscina

4 Say it in Spanish

Play the part of the receptionist and the hotel guest in this dialogue.

Cliente/a	Good evening. We'd like a double room with a bathroom, please.
Recepcionista	For how many nights?
Cliente/a	For five nights. Is breakfast included?
Recepcionista	No, it's without breakfast. Breakfast is separate.
Cliente/a	That's OK. Can you park in the hotel?
Recepcionista	Yes, certainly. Your passports, please. (*Client hands in passports.*) Thank you. You have room seventy-eight.

5 Completa con los verbos

Fill in the blanks in the following sentences with the appropriate form of **tener** *to have* or **ser** *to be*.

a (Yo) .... una habitación reservada.

b ¿ .... (ustedes) una habitación individual?

c Los hoteles aquí .... excelentes.

d (Ellos) .... una reserva para dos noches.

e Carmen .... la habitación 55 y nosotros .... la 82.

f ¿Cuántas personas .... (ustedes)? .... dos, mi mujer y yo.

6 ¿Qué servicios tienen?

Now look at the table below, which lists all the services you can expect to find in the different categories of hotels.

a What services would you find in a 3-star hotel?

b What extra service would you find in a 4-star hotel?

c Where would you find a safe-deposit box? And a fire exit?

Lo que tienen que tener					
	5★	4★	3★	2★	1★
Aire acondicionado	●	●	●(1)	–	–
Teléfono en habitación	●	●	●	●	–
Bar	●	●	●	–	–
Salidas de incendios	●	●	●	●	●
Suites	●	–	–	–	–
Caja fuerte individual	●	●	–	–	–
Superficies mínimas por habitación (en metros cuadrados)					
Doble	17	16	15	14	12
Individual	10	9	8	7	7
(1) En salón, comedor y bar					

▶ **7 El alfabeto**

Listen to the letters of the Spanish alphabet and try saying each as you hear them.

a	a	Ana		**ñ**	eñe	mañana
b	be	Bilbao		**o**	o	Colombia
c	ce	Cuba, gracias		**p**	pe	Perú
d	de	día		**q**	cu	que, quinto
e	e	Elena		**r**	erre, ere	perro, Río, París
f	efe	Francia		**s**	ese	Susana
g	ge	Gloria, Algeciras		**t**	te	Tarragona
h	hache	hasta		**u**	u	Murcia
i	i	Isabel		**v**	uve	Venezuela
j	jota	Juan		**w**	uve doble	Washington
k	ca	kilo		**x**	equis	taxi
l	ele	Londres		**y**	i griega	yo, Paraguay
m	eme	María		**z**	zeta	Cádiz
n	ene	no				

Ch and **ll** were considered separate letters of the alphabet but this is no longer the case. You may still find separate entries for them in some monolingual dictionaries, but most recent bilingual dictionaries treat **ch** within **c** and **ll** within **l**. Many speakers, however, still consider them as separate letters so you should be aware of their names:

ch che Chile
ll elle calle

8 ¿Cómo se escribe?

A group of Spanish speakers arrive at your place of work and you need to spell their surnames to a Spanish person.

a	Aguirre	**d**	Bravo
b	Fernández	**e**	Collado
c	Arredondo	**f**	Julián

9 Ahora tú

¿Cómo se escribe...?: tu nombre, tu apellido, el nombre de tu jefe/a (*boss*), profesor/a (*teacher*), el nombre de tu calle y barrio (*neighbourhood*).

04

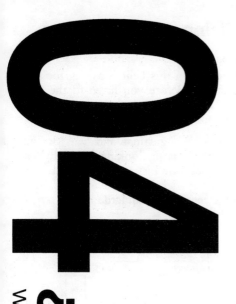

¿dónde está?

where is it?

**In this unit you will learn
how to:**
- ask and say if there is a
  certain place nearby
- ask for and give directions
  (1)
- ask and say how far away a
  place is

▶ 1 ¿Hay una oficina de cambio por aquí?

The main focus of the dialogues in this Unit is asking for and understanding simple directions. Before you listen to the first conversation study the map and the list of places below. How many of them can you recognize?

1.1 Patricia, a tourist, is on *calle* Agustinas and San Martín, facing *calle* Morandé. What places is she looking for, and what phrase does she use in each question? Listen and find out. Key expressions here are **hay** *is/are there?*, *there is/are*, **por aquí** *nearby, near here*, **¿dónde?** *where?*, **a la izquierda** *on the left*, **a la derecha** *on the right*.

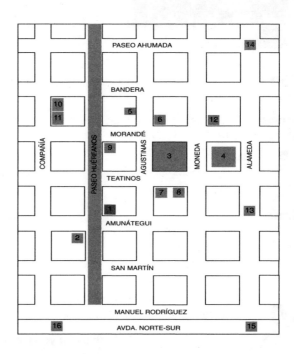

1 una oficina de cambio	7 un hotel
2 un museo	8 una iglesia
3 una plaza	9 un hotel
4 un aparcamiento	10 un banco
5 un restaurante	11 una oficina de turismo
6 un banco	12 (la oficina de) Correos

Patricia	Perdone, ¿hay una oficina de cambio por aquí?
Señor	Hay una en la calle Amunátegui, la primera calle a la izquierda.
Patricia	¿Y dónde hay un hotel?
Señor	Hay uno en la calle Teatinos, la segunda a la derecha, al lado de una iglesia. Hay otro en la calle Morandé, la tercera a la izquierda.
Patricia	Muchas gracias.
Señor	De nada.

1.2 Read the dialogue a few times and then play first Patricia's part, then that of the person giving directions.

1.3 How would you say the following in Spanish? Look up the list of places again if necessary.

a Is there a bank nearby?
b There's one on calle Bandera, the fourth (la cuarta) on the left, next to the tourist office.

primero/a	*first*
segundo/a	*second*
tercero/a	*third*
al lado de	*next to*
otro/a	*another one*
muchas gracias	*thank you very much*
de nada	*you're welcome*

▶ 2 ¿Dónde está?

Patricia is looking for the tourist office now. She's outside the post office, on calle Moneda and Morandé (number 12 on the map).

2.1 Where's the tourist office and how far is it? Listen and find out. Key words and expressions here are **¿dónde está?** *where is it?*, **lejos** *far*, **cerca** *near*, **al final de** *at the end of*.

Patricia Por favor, ¿sabe usted dónde está la oficina de turismo?

Señor Lo siento, no lo sé. No conozco muy bien la ciudad.

(Asking another passer-by)

Patricia Por favor, la oficina de turismo, ¿está muy lejos?

Señora Está cerca. Al final de esta calle, a la derecha, a cinco minutos de aquí.

Patricia Gracias.

Señora No hay de qué.

2.2 Look at the vocabulary below, then read the dialogue and put the following sentences into Spanish. You may need to read the notes on **saber** and **conocer** in the Grammar section.

a Do you know where the cathedral (la catedral) is?

b I'm sorry, I don't know. I don't know Granada very well.

c It is far. At the end of the street, on the left, is the bus stop (la parada del autobús)

no lo sé (from **saber**)	*I don't know*
conozco (from **conocer**)	*I know*
lo siento (from **sentir**, e>ie)	*I'm sorry*
esta	*this* (f)
no hay de qué	*you're welcome*

i In most Spanish towns you will find a tourist information office, **una Oficina de Información y Turismo**, where you can get free plans, **planos**, maps, **mapas**, lists of hotels, **listas de hoteles**, and brochures, **folletos**. To get any of these use phrases like the following: "Por favor, ¿tiene un plano de la ciudad/una lista de hoteles?", "Por favor, quisiera un folleto/un mapa de la región."

▶ 3 ¿Dónde están los servicios?

Víctor is at a trade fair. At the information desk he asks where the toilets are.

3.1 How does he ask where the toilets are? Can you guess what the answer means? Key words here are **los servicios** *toilets*, **el piso** *floor*, **el pasillo** *corridor*, **la escalera** *stairs*.

Víctor	Por favor, ¿dónde están los servicios?
Empleada	Están en el primer piso. Sigue usted todo recto hasta el fondo, luego toma el pasillo de la izquierda y sube la escalera. Los servicios están enfrente del café.
Víctor	Gracias.

3.2 Read the dialogue now and and with the help of the key words above and the vocabulary below translate the answer into English.

sigue (from **seguir**, e>i) **todo recto**	*go straight on*
hasta el fondo	*to the end*
luego	*then*
tomar	*to take*
subir	*to go up*

How do you say it?

Asking and saying if there is a certain place nearby

¿Hay un banco por aquí (cerca)?	*Is there a bank nearby?*
¿Dónde hay un café/una panadería?	*Where's a cafe/baker's?*
Hay uno en la calle.../la primera (calle) a la izquierda /derecha/en la esquina.	*There's one on ... street/the first (street) on the left/right/ at the corner.*

Asking for and giving directions

¿Dónde está el museo?	*Where's the museum?*
Está al final de esta calle/ enfrente de.../al lado de...	*It's at the end of this street/ opposite ... /next to ...*
Sigue (Vd.) todo recto.	*Go straight on.*
Toma/Coge la primera calle.	*Take the first street.*
Sube/Baja por...	*Go up/down ...*

i **Toma** and **coge** *you take* (from **tomar** and **coger** *to take*), both mean the same in the context of directions. The second word is used frequently in Spain but it is a taboo word in some Latin American countries. **Tomar** is a standard word which will be understood everywhere.

Asking how far a place is

¿Está cerca/lejos?	*Is it near/far?*
¿A qué distancia está?	*How far is it?*
Está cerca/lejos/a una hora/ cinco minutos/cien metros de aquí.	*It's near/far/an hour/five minutes/a hundred metres from here.*

Grammar

1 Hay *there is, there are, is there?, are there?*

The single word **hay**, 'there is/are', an impersonal form from **haber**, 'to have' (auxiliary verb used in the Spanish equivalent of sentences such as 'I have gone'), can be followed by a singular or plural word, in statements or in questions.

Hay un supermercado en la esquina.	*There is a supermarket at the corner.*
Hay muchas tiendas cerca.	*There are many shops nearby.*
¿Hay una peluquería por aquí?	*Is there a haidresser's near here?*
¿Hay sitios de interés en la ciudad?	*Are there any places of interest in the city?*

To ask where you can find something you are not sure it exists, use the expression **¿dónde hay ...?**: '¿Dónde hay una gasolinera?' 'Where's a petrol station?'

2 ¿Dónde está/están? *Where is it/are they?*

a To ask and say where a place is use **estar** *to be* (see Unit 2).

¿Dónde está tu casa?	*Where's your house?*
Está detrás de la iglesia.	*It's behind the church.*
¿Dónde están los teléfonos?	*Where are the telephones?*
Están en la planta baja.	*They are on the ground floor.*

Here are some other expressions used to indicate location: al otro lado de... *on the other side of ...* , delante de ... *in front of ...*, entre ... y ... *between ... and ...*, en la segunda planta *or* en el segundo piso *on the second floor,* en la esquina *at the corner*, en la calle (Santa Isabel) esquina a avenida (Duero) *at the corner of (Santa Isabel) street and (Duero) avenue.*

i Note that in Spain the word **el piso** means *floor* or *flat*. An alternative word for *floor* is **la planta**.

b To ask and say how far a place is use **estar** with the preposition **a**.

¿A cuántas horas/cuántos kilómetros está?	*How many hours/kilometres away is it?*
¿A qué distancia está?	*What distance is it from here?*
Está a casi una hora de aquí.	*It's almost an hour from here.*

c To say where *you* or others are you may need other forms of **estar**, including plural forms. Here are the full forms of the *present tense*.

yo estoy	*I am*
tú estás	*you are*
él/ella/Vd. está	*he/she/it is/you are*
nosotros/as estamos	*we are*
vosotros/as estáis	*you are*
ellos/ellas/Vds. están	*they/you are*

¿Dónde estáis ahora?	*Where are you now?*
Estamos en casa de Pepe.	*We are in Pepe's house.*

3 Using the present tense to give directions

There are two main ways of giving directions in Spanish, both equally common: one is with the *present tense*, the other with the *imperative*, a form of the verb which is introduced in unit 23. The two forms are very similar, so being familiar with the present tense, you should be able to understand the other. The examples below correspond to the present tense (**usted** and **tú** forms).

Toma(s) el pasillo de la derecha.	*You take the corridor on the right.*
Sube(s)/Baja(s) la escalera.	*You go up/down the stairs.*
Gira(s) a la izquierda.	*You turn left*

4 Otro, otros *another, others*

Otro agrees in number (sing or pl) and gender (m or f) with the noun it refers to: otro mercado *another market*, otra farmacia *another chemist's*, otras tiendas *other shops*.

Otro can replace a noun when this is understood: 'Hay una frutería en la esquina y otra a la vuelta de la esquina', '*There's a fruit shop at the corner and another one round the corner*'.

5 Saber, conocer *to know*

There are two ways of saying *to know* in Spanish: **saber** and **conocer**. The first refers to *knowledge of a fact* and *ability to do something*. The other indicates *acquaintance with something, a person or a place*. Both are irregular in the first person singular of the present tense, but regular in all other persons: **sé, sabes, sabe** ...etc; **conozco, conoces, conoce** ... etc.

No sé dónde está.	*I don't know where it is.*
No sabe nadar.	*He/she doesn't know how to swim.*
Conozco muy bien el barrio.	*I know the area very well.*

6 Ordinal numbers

Ordinal numbers agree in gender (m or f) and number (sing or pl) with the noun they refer to.

Here are ordinal numbers from *first* to *tenth*: **primero/a, segundo/a, tercero/a, cuarto/a, quinto/a, sexto/a, séptimo/a, octavo/a, noveno/a, décimo/a.**

las primeras dos calles	*the first two streets*
el segundo semáforo	*the second traffic light*

Primero and **tercero** become **primer** and **tercer** before a singular masculine noun: el primer/tercer piso *the first/third floor*.

▶ Pronunciation

c, before a, o, u, as in 'casa, conozco, Cuba', is pronounced like the 'c' in 'coast'.

c, before e, i, as in 'cerca, cinco', is pronounced like the 'th' in 'thin'.

z, as in plaza, izquierda, is also pronounced like the 'th' in 'thin'.

Practise with:

¿Conoce usted la ciudad? No, no la conozco.

¿Hay una oficina de cambio por aquí cerca? Hay una en la plaza de Cádiz, a la izquierda, entre la oficina de turismo y la estación de metro.

Latin American pronunciation

c, before e, i, as in cerca, cinco, is pronounced like the 's' in 'sale'.
z, as in plaza, izquierda, is also pronounced like the 's' in 'sale'.

Practice

1 ¿Hay o está?
Fill in the gaps in these conversations with **hay** and **está(n)**, as appropriate.

a ¿Dónde _____ una panadería, por favor?
   La más cercana es la Modelo, a dos calles de aquí.
b Perdone, ¿la Telefónica _____ muy lejos?
   A unos cinco minutos en coche.
c Oiga, perdone, ¿ _____ una lavandería por aquí cerca?
   Sí, en la calle de Zamora, la tercera a la izquierda.
d Perdone, ¿sabe dónde _____ el mercado central?
   Lo siento, no lo sé. No conozco bien este barrio.
e Los teléfonos, por favor, ¿dónde _____?
   En la planta baja.
f ¿Dónde _____ un camping, por favor?
   En la Avenida del Mar, la segunda a la derecha.

el/la más cercano/a	*the nearest one*
oiga	*excuse me* (literally, *listen*)
la lavandería	*launderette*

2 Ahora tú

You are spending a few days in a Spanish city and you need to find your way around. How would you ask if there is one of the following nearby?

a	un restaurante	c	una tienda de ropa
b	una librería	d	una tienda de comestibles

And how would you ask where the following places are?

e	la estación de autobuses	g	la biblioteca
f	la iglesia	h	la Plaza Mayor

---

una librería   *bookshop*   **la biblioteca**   *library*

---

3 ¿Saber o conocer?

Martín is trying to find a **hostal** (less expensive family-run hotel). Fill in the gaps in the conversation with **saber** or **conocer**, as appropriate, using the informal form.

Martín   Perdona, ¿_____ (tú) dónde hay un hostal por aquí?

Chica   No (lo) _____. No _____ este barrio. _____ un hostal, pero está un poco lejos de aquí, en la calle de Los Olivos. ¿_____ (tú) la calle de Los Olivos?

Martín   No soy de aquí. No _____ la ciudad.

4 Entre el banco y la papelería

You are working in a Spanish-speaking country and have been asked to look after some visitors who don't know your area. Study the map opposite and answer their questions, using expressions from the following. First, look at the example.

al lado (de)	detrás (de)
a la derecha/izquierda	delante (de)
al final (de)	entre
enfrente (de)	en la esquina

Ejemplo: ¿Hay un restaurante por aquí?

Hay dos, uno enfrente y otro cerca de la parada de autobuses, entre el banco y la papelería.

a   ¿Hay un aparcamiento por aquí cerca?
b   ¿Dónde hay un banco?
c   ¿Dónde está Correos?
d   ¿Dónde hay un quiosco de periódicos?
e   La parada de autobuses, ¿dónde está?
f   ¿Dónde hay una agencia de viajes?

g ¿Hay una papelería por aquí?

h La Plaza de la Luz, ¿dónde está?

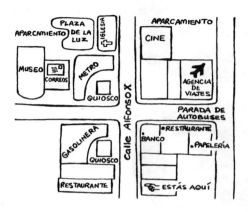

▶ 5 ¿Dónde están?

Where is each of the following? Listen and make a note of the directions and translate them into English.

a la avenida del Mar

b la playa

c Correos

d los teléfonos

6 Ahora tú

a ¿En qué calle está tu casa? ¿Y en qué barrio está?

b ¿Hay una parada de autobús o estación (de metro) cerca de tu casa? ¿A qué distancia está?

c ¿Qué tiendas hay en tu barrio?

d ¿Qué sitios importantes hay?

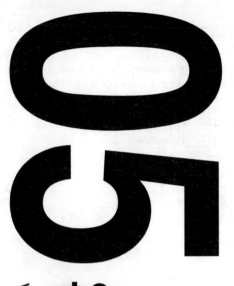

05

¿qué van a tomar?

what are you going to have?

In this unit you will learn how to:

- ask people what they would like to eat or drink
- ask and say what's on the menu
- order food and drinks

▶ 1 Queremos el menú del día

Ángeles and her boyfriend Javier are having lunch in a restaurant. How many of the words in the menu can you guess? Look up the rest of the vocabulary before you listen to the conversations which follow.

RESTAURANTE SANTA MARIA
Menú del día

Sopa
Gazpacho
Ensalada mixta
Guisantes con jamón

*****

Paella
Merluza a la plancha con ensalada
Pollo con patatas
Cordero asado

*****

Pan, vino, helado, flan, fruta

1.1 Listen to the dialogue several times and, as you do, answer the following questions:

a What is Ángeles having for lunch?
b What is Javier having?
c What is Ángeles having to drink?
d What does Javier want to drink?

Camarero	Hola, buenas tardes. ¿Qué van a tomar?
Ángeles	Queremos el menú del día. Para mí, gazpacho de primero, y de segundo quiero merluza a la plancha con ensalada.
Camarero	¿Y para usted?
Javier	Yo, guisantes con jamón, y de segundo pollo con patatas fritas.

Camarero	¿Y para beber?
Ángeles	Agua mineral sin gas, para mí.
Javier	Yo quiero vino tinto.

1.2 Now read the dialogue and find the Spanish equivalent of *We want the day's menu, For me ... , And for you?. As a first/second course.* Then read the dialogue again a few times and, once you are familiar with it, try playing each one of the parts. Use the menu on page 53 and the vocabulary below.

el gazpacho	cold soup made from tomatoes, peppers, cucumber, etc.
¿qué van a tomar?	what are you going to have? (formal, pl)
patatas/papas (LAm) **fritas**	chips, crisps
beber	to drink
el agua (mineral)	(mineral) water

▶2 ¿Me trae otra agua mineral?

Javier calls the waiter to order something else.

2.1 What is each person ordering? Listen and find out.

Javier	Por favor, ¿nos trae un poco más de pan?
Ángeles	¿Y me trae otra agua mineral, por favor?
Camarero	Ahora mismo.
(Ángeles and Javier order a dessert)	
Ángeles	¿Qué tienen de postre?
Camarero	Hay flan, helados y fruta.
Ángeles	Un helado de chocolate, para mí.
Javier	Yo quiero un flan y un café.

2.2 Now read the dialogue and note the following two key phrases ¿Me trae ...? *Will you bring me ..?* (formal), ¿Nos trae ...? *Will you bring us...?* (formal). Use them to say the following in Spanish and then try playing each one of the parts, varying what you order.

a Will you bring **us** some more wine?
b Will you bring **me** another coffee?
c Will you bring **us** the bill? (**la cuenta**)

traer	*to bring*
el postre	*dessert*
el helado de (chocolate)	*(a chocolate) ice cream*
un poco más de	*some more* (literally, *a little more of*)
el flan	*creme caramel*
ahora mismo	*right away*

▶ 3 En el bar

Silvia and her friends Paco and Gloria are having a snack in a bar.

3.1 Listen and find out who is having each of the following.

a a portion or plate of mushrooms
b black coffee
c white wine
d a beer
e a cheese sandwich
f crisps

Camarero	Hola, ¿qué van a tomar?
Paco	¿Qué quieres tú, Silvia?
Silvia	Quiero un café solo y un bocadillo de queso.
Paco	¿Y para ti, Gloria?
Gloria	Un vino blanco y patatas fritas.
Paco	Para mí, una cerveza y una ración de champiñones.

3.2 Match each phrase on the left with an appropriate word on the right and use them to write a dialogue similar to the one above.

a un bocadillo de ...	**1**	calamares
b una ración de ...	**2**	naranja
c un zumo de ...	**3**	jamón serrano/de York

el jamón serrano/de York	*cured/cooked ham*
el zumo/jugo (LAm)	*juice*
el calamar	*squid*
la naranja	*orange*

i Eating habits have changed substantially in Spain and in large Latin American cities in the last few years. Many working people no longer enjoy the traditional leisurely lunch, **la comida o almuerzo**, at home during the week, opting instead for **el menú del día** in a restaurant near their office, or for a quick meal, **una comida rápida**, in a fast-food place. Many restaurants serve **el menú del día**, known as **la comida corrida** in Mexico, at reasonable prices, with **vino** or an alternative drink, **una bebida**, normally included in it. In smaller towns, though, people still go home for lunch, and at weekends the majority have the traditional family lunch.

How do you say it?

Asking people what they would like to eat or drink

¿Qué van/va(s) a tomar/ beber?

What are you going to have/ drink?

¿Qué quieren/quiere(s) tomar/comer/beber?

What do you want to have/ eat/drink?

¿Y para beber?

And to drink?

Asking and saying what's on the menu

¿Qué tiene/hay (de segundo/ de postre)?

What do you have/is there (as a second course/for dessert)?

¿Qué tiene/hay para (beber/ comer)?

What do you have/is there to (drink/eat)?

Tengo/Tenemos/Hay (helados de fresa ...)

I/We have/There's (strawberry ice cream ...)

Ordering food and drinks

(Yo) quiero .../Yo, ... /Para mí, ... (una ensalada, un bocadillo, un agua mineral con/sin gas, un café solo/ con leche, un té).

I want .../For me ... (a salad, a sandwich, a fizzy/still mineral water, a black/white coffee, tea).

Grammar

1 Para *for*, con *with*, sin *without* ...: prepositions

Words like **para, con, sin, de, a**, etc. are called *prepositions*. As in English, Spanish prepositions can have several uses and different meanings, and they don't always translate in the same way in English, as you can see from the examples below.

Para mí, una sopa.	*Soup for me.*
¿Y **para** beber?	*And to drink?*
con/sin gas	*with/without gas*
con leche/limón	*with milk/lemon*
de primero/segundo	*as a first/second course*
un helado **de** vainilla/un bocadillo **de** queso	*a vanilla ice cream/a cheese sandwich*
un poco más **de** pan/agua	*some more bread/water*
de postre	*for dessert*
pescado/carne **a** la plancha	*grilled fish/meat*

2 Para mí, para ti, para usted... *For me, for you ...*

In phrases such as *for me, for you, without him,* etc. words like *me, you, him* are called pronouns. In Spanish, as in English, prepositions are often followed by a pronoun. The forms of these pronouns are **mí** (for **yo**), **ti** (for **tú**) and subject pronouns for the rest of the persons, that is **él, ella, Vd., nosotros/as, vosotros/as, ellos, ellas, Vds.** Note the written accent on **mí**, to distinguish this from **mi** *my.*

Una cerveza para mí, una Coca-Cola para ella y otra para él.	*A beer for me, a coke for her and another one for him.*
¿Y para ti/usted?	*And for you?*

A special case is the use of **con** *with,* which in combination with **mí** and **ti** gives **conmigo** *with me* and **contigo** *with you.*

3 Making requests

Polite requests such as *Will you bring me/us some coffee?, Will you give me/us the bill?,* are often expressed in Spanish with the *present tense* preceded by **me** *me* or **nos** *us.*

¿Me trae un cortado/un té con limón?	*Will you bring me a coffee with a dash of milk/a lemon tea?*
¿Nos trae un vaso/una botella de vino tinto?	*Will you bring us a glass/bottle of red wine?*
¿Me pasa la sal y la pimienta/el azúcar?	*Will you pass me the salt and pepper/the sugar?*
¿Nos da la cuenta?	*Will you give us the bill?*

The verbs above are all in the formal **usted**. To make them informal, simply add –s: ¿Me pasas el aceite y el vinagre? *Will you pass the oil and vinegar?* In the spoken language, requests of this kind are usually expressed with a slighly rising intonation to make them more polite and to differentiate them from an order or command.

4 Querer (e>ie) *to want*: full present tense forms

Querer, like a number of other verbs, changes **e** into **ie** in the present tense, except in the **nosotros/as** and **vosotros/as** forms (see *stem-changing* or *radical-changing* verbs, Unit 3). Here are the full present tense forms.

yo quiero	*I want*
tú quieres	*you want*
él/ella/Vd. quiere	*he/she/ wants/you want*
nosotros/as queremos	*we want*
vosotros/as queréis	*you want*
ellos/ellas/Vds. quieren	*they/you want*

Quiero la carta, por favor.	*I want the menu, please.*
¿Qué quieres tomar (tú)?	*What do you want to have?*

Note that **querer** also means *to love*: 'Te quiero mucho' *'I love you very much'*.

Tener, *to have*, also belongs to this category of verbs, except that **tener** is irregular in the first person singular: **tengo** *I have*, **tienes** *you have* (inf), **tiene** *he/she/it has, you have* (formal), etc.

4 Same word, different meaning!

Just as in English, Spanish words related to food and meals can have different meanings in some regions. The standard words for the main meals are **el desayuno** *breakfast*, **el almuerzo** or **la comida** *lunch* and **la cena** for the *evening meal*. But **el almuerzo** is a mid-morning snack in some places (for example Barcelona and Mexico City), while **la comida** refers to the evening meal in some Latin American countries. In Spain, **un sandwich** is a sandwich made from a tin loaf, and **un bocadillo** is one made with French bread. A number of Latin American countries use the word **sandwich**, without making a distinction between the two types of bread.

▶ Pronunciation

j, as in 'Javier, jamón, ajo' is pronounced like a strong 'h', or like the Scottish 'ch' in 'loch'.

g, before **e**, **i**, as in 'Ángeles, general, Gibraltar', is pronounced like Spanish **j** (see above).

g, before **a**, **o**, **u**, as in 'gas, Diego, segundo', is pronounced like the 'g' in 'government'. The same pronunciation occurs before **r** and **n**, for example 'gracias, ignorante'.

g, in the combination **gue** and **gui**, as in 'Guernica, guisante', is also pronounced like the 'g' in 'government'. Here the **u** remains silent.

Practice with:

Para Javier, un bocadillo de jamón y un agua mineral con gas. Para Ángeles, un gazpacho, y de segundo pollo con guisantes y judías verdes. ¿Y para ti, Juan?

Practice

1 Una comida

Raquel and her friend Francisca are having lunch in a restaurant. Fill in the gaps in the dialogue with one of these words: **a, con, de, sin, para**.

Camarero	¿Qué van a tomar?
Raquel	..... mí, sopa ..... verduras ..... primero, y ..... segundo quiero cordero asado ..... arroz.
Camarero	¿Y ..... usted?
Francisca	Yo, una ensalada ..... lechuga ..... tomates, y ..... segundo quiero pescado ..... la plancha ..... puré.
Camarero	¿Y ..... beber?
Francisca	Dos aguas minerales y una botella ..... vino tinto.
Camarero	¿Quieren agua ..... gas o ..... gas?
Francisca	Una ..... gas y la otra ..... gas.

la lechuga	*lettuce*	**el tomate**	*tomato*

▶ 2 ¿Tú o usted?

You are going to hear some people asking for things. Which of the requests are informal and which formal? Classify them accordingly, using **tú** for informal and **usted** for formal.

a _____   c _____   e _____
b _____   d _____   f _____

la servilleta	*napkin*

3 Un almuerzo informal

On a visit to Spain you and your friend Pepe go out for lunch. Use the guidelines in English to fill in yours and Pepe's part of this dialogue with the waitress.

Camarera ¿Qué van a tomar?

Tú *We want the day's menu, please.*

Camarera Aquí tienen.

Pepe *I want a mixed salad as a first course, and as a second course I want a paella.*

Tú *For me, soup, and as a second course I want roast lamb with mashed potatoes.*

Camarera ¿Y para beber?

Tú *Red wine for me, please. And for you Pepe? What do you want to drink?*

Pepe *I want a glass of white wine.*

Tú *Will you also bring us a bottle of still mineral water?*

Camarera Ahora mismo.

(Ordering dessert)

Tú *What do you have for dessert?*

Camarera Tenemos melón, fresas con nata y arroz con leche.

Pepe *I want strawberries with cream.*

Tú *Rice pudding for me. And will you bring us two coffees and the bill, please?*

las fresas con nata/ crema	(LAm) *strawberries with cream*
el arroz con leche	*rice pudding* (literally, *rice with milk*)

▶ 4 En un bar

What snacks do they serve in this Spanish bar? First, study the words in the menu board below, then listen to Ramón, Sofía and Clara placing their order. What is each one having? Fill in the table below with each order.

BAR LAS GAVIOTAS	
<u>Tapas</u>	<u>Bocadillos</u>
champiñones	jamón
gambas	queso
calamares	chorizo
tortilla de patatas	salchichón

	Para comer	Para beber
Sofía		
Clara		
Ramón		

5 Palabra por palabra

Here are some common words related to food and eating. Look them up and list them under the appropriate headings below.

cuchillo	lechugas	uvas	merluza	cerdo
piñas	pollo	manzanas	cordero	tenedor
atún	cuchara	ajos	cebollas	plato

Pescado, Carne, Verdura, Fruta, Utensilio

Can you add other words to each list?

6 ¡Que aproveche!/¡Buen provecho! (LAm) *Bon appetit!*

The following passage describes the main meals in Spain and Latin America. How do eating habits compare with those in your country? Read and find out and say whether the following statements are true or false (**verdaderos o falsos**).

a En España se toma un desayuno muy abundante.

b En México se toma un desayuno ligero.

c La comida principal en España y Latinoamérica es el almuerzo o la comida.

d El primer plato normalmente lleva pescado o carne.

En España, el desayuno es una comida ligera, que consiste normalmente en café y tostadas, pero en algunos países latinoamericanos – México por ejemplo – el desayuno es generalmente abundante. Aparte de café, un desayuno mexicano puede incluir fruta, huevos, y algún plato típico de la región.

La comida o el almuerzo es la comida principal, se toma entre la una y las tres y consiste normalmente en dos platos, postre y café. El plato principal o segundo plato generalmente lleva carne o pescado. A la

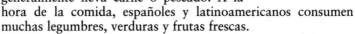

hora de la comida, españoles y latinoamericanos consumen muchas legumbres, verduras y frutas frescas.

La cena se toma entre las nueve y las diez y es normalmente una comida ligera.

se toma	*people take, it is taken*
ligero/a	*light*
la comida	*meal, lunch*
llevar (here)	*to contain*
el plato	*dish (also plate)*
el huevo	*egg*
la legumbre	*pulse*

06

¿a qué hora llega?

what time does it arrive?

In this unit you will learn how to:
- ask and tell the time
- get travel information
- buy tickets

▶1 ¿Qué hora es?

1.1 Listen to some people asking and telling the time and, as you do, look at the clock faces only and repeat each question and answer after the speakers several times. Note the two alternative questions.

¿Qué hora es? (*What time is it?*) / ¿Tiene hora? (*Have you got the time?*)

a Es la una   **b** Son las cuatro y diez   **c** Son las seis y cuarto

d Son las siete y media   **e** Son las diez   **f** Son las doce
menos cinco   menos cuarto

1.2 Listen again several times while you read the phrases under each clock and say them aloud until you feel confident that you have learned them. Then look at the clock faces only, and practise asking and saying the time. You can then practise in a similar way with other times.

▶2 Quería hacer una reserva

A tourist is making enquiries about rail travel to Seville.

2.1 Listen to the conversation several times and, as you do, answer the questions which follow. Key words and phrases in this dialogue are **sale** (from **salir**) *it leaves*, **llega a ...** (from **llegar**) *it arrives in ...*, **¿a qué hora ...?** *at what time ...?*. Note also the use of the 24-hour clock, with 1.00 p.m., for instance, becoming **las trece horas,** and fractions of a time like 6.45 p.m. expressed as **las dieciocho cuarenta y cinco.**

a What time are the trains to Seville?

b Does the tourist get a single ticket, **un billete de ida**, or a return ticket, **un billete de ida y vuelta**?

c Is he travelling in tourist, business (**clase preferente**) or club class?

Turista	Buenos días, quería hacer una reserva para Sevilla, para el domingo.
Empleada	Pues, hay un tren que sale a las nueve y cuarto de la mañana, otro a las once y media, y por la tarde hay uno a las catorce treinta, otro a las dieciséis quince ...
Turista	El tren de las dieciséis quince, ¿a qué hora llega a Sevilla?
Empleada	A las dieciocho cuarenta y cinco. ¿Quiere un billete de ida o de ida y vuelta?
Turista	De ida.
Empleada	¿En clase turista, preferente o club?
Turista	¿Cuánto cuesta la clase preferente?
Empleada	Ciento veinticinco euros con cuarenta.
Turista	Bueno, deme clase preferente.

2.2 Read the dialogue several times and play, first the part of the traveller, then that of the ticket clerk. Once you feel confident with it, put the following sentences into Spanish. *(For the days of the week see Grammar, para 2.)*

a I'd like to make a reservation for Barcelona, for Saturday.

b There's a train which leaves at 13.45, another one at 15.15 and another one at 17.20.

c The 15.15 train, what time does it arrive in Barcelona?

d I want a return ticket.

e How much is the tourist class?

f A hundred and thirty five euros.

quería	*I'd like* (literally *I wanted*)
... que sale	*which leaves ...*
(11:30) de la mañana	*(11.30) in the morning*
por la tarde	*in the afternoon*
bueno	(here) *well then*
deme	*give me* (formal)

▶ 3 ¿A qué hora hay autobuses?

Here's a traveller – **un/a viajero/a** – wanting to go from Málaga to Ronda on a bus.

3.1 Listen to the dialogue a few times and, as you do, answer the following questions.

a How frequent are the buses from Málaga to Ronda.
b How long does it take to get to Ronda.
c What time is the next bus and what time does it arrive in Ronda.
d Does the traveller get a single or a return ticket?

Viajera	Por favor, ¿a qué hora hay autobuses para Ronda?
Empleado	Cada hora. El próximo sale dentro de media hora, a las nueve y cinco.
Viajera	¿Cuánto tarda el viaje?
Empleado	Una hora y media. Llega a Ronda a las once menos veinticinco.
Viajera	Deme un billete de ida y vuelta, por favor.
Empleado	Aquí tiene.
Viajera	¿Cuánto es?
Empleado	Son veintidós euros.

El próximo autobús sale
dentro de media hora

3.2 Now read the dialogue and find the phrases which mean the following.

a every hour
b the next one leaves ...
c How long does the journey take?
d How much is it?

el autobús	*bus*	**tardar**	*to take* (time)
dentro de	*within*	**el viaje**	*journey*

How do you say it?

Asking and telling the time

¿Qué hora es?/¿Tiene hora?	*What time is it?/Have you got the time?*
(Es) la una/una y diez.	*(It's) one o'clock/ten past one.*
(Son) las once menos cuarto/veinte.	*(It's) a quarter/twenty to eleven.*
(Son) las dos y cuarto/y media.	*(It's) a quarter/half past two*
(Son) las cinco de la mañana /tarde.	*(It's) five o'clock in the morning/afternoon.*

Getting travel information

¿A qué hora sale el tren/ autobús para (Bilbao)?	*What time does the train/bus for (Bilbao) leave?*
Sale a las 2:00/dentro de una hora/media hora/ cinco minutos.	*It leaves at 2.00/in an hour/half an hour/five minutes.*
¿A qué hora llega a (Madrid)?	*What time does it arrive in (Madrid)?*
Llega a (Madrid) a las 7:30.	*It arrives in (Madrid) at 7.30.*

Buying tickets

Quería/Quisiera/Quiero dos billetes/boletos (LAm) para ...	*I'd like/want two tickets for ...*
un billete/boleto de ida/ida y vuelta	*a single/return ticket*
¿Cuánto cuesta/es?	*How much does it cost/is it?*
Son treinta euros con veinte (céntimos).	*It's thirty euros twenty (cents).*

Grammar

1 La hora *the time*

To tell the time use **ser** *to be*: **es** for 'midday', 'midnight' and 'one o'clock' and **son** for all other times. Note that Spanish uses **la** (sing) or **las** (pl) *the* before the actual time.

Es mediodía/medianoche/ la una en punto.	*It's midday/midnight/one o'clock sharp.*
Son las tres menos cuarto.	*It's a quarter to three.*

Some Latin American countries use expressions like **es un cuarto para (las dos)** *it's a quarter to (two)*, **son diez para (las seis)** *it's ten to (six)*, instead of **son (las dos) menos cuarto, son (las seis) menos diez.**

2 Los días de la semana *days of the week*

lunes	martes	miércoles	jueves	viernes	sábado	domingo
Monday	*Tuesday*	*Wednesday*	*Thursday*	*Friday*	*Saturday*	*Sunday*

Days are masculine in Spanish and are normally written with a small letter. They are preceded by **el** (sing) or **los** (pl) in phrases like the following.

el lunes	*on Monday*
para el martes	*for Tuesday*
los sábados	*on Saturdays*
todos los jueves	*every Thursday*

3 a, con, de, para, por: more prepositions

a

¿**A** qué hora llega **a** Madrid?	*At what time does it arrive in Madrid?*
A las dos y tres minutos.	*At three minutes past three.*

con

diez euros **con** cincuenta	*ten euros fifty*

de

Sale **de** Valencia a las cuatro **de** la tarde.	*It leaves Valencia at four in the afternoon.*
el tren **de** las seis	*the six o'clock train*
dentro **de** una hora	*within an hour*
un billete **de** ida/ida y vuelta	*a single/return ticket*

para

un billete **para** Zaragoza	*a ticket for/to Zaragoza*
para las nueve/hoy/el lunes	*for nine o'clock/today/Monday*

mañana/el domingo **por** la mañana/tarde/noche	*tomorrow/on Sunday morning/ afternoon/evening*

4 Que *that, which, who*

To say 'that' or 'which' as in *There is a bus which/that leaves Barcelona at midday*, use the word **que**: Hay un autobús **que** sale de Barcelona al mediodía.

Que can also be used for people: La persona **que** está allí es mi marido *The person who is there is my husband*.

5 Quería *I'd like*

An alternative to **quisiera** *I'd like* is **quería**, literally *I wanted*. The **nosotros/as** form is **queríamos** *we'd like*, literally *we wanted*. These two forms correspond to the *imperfect tense*, a tense which will be covered in Units 17 and 18.

6 ¿Cuánto cuesta/vale? *How much does it cost?*, ¿Cuánto es? *How much is it?*

To ask how much something costs you can use **costar** (o>ue) *to cost*, **cuesta** if you are enquiring about one thing only, and **cuestan** if there is more than one: '¿Cuánto **cuesta** el viaje/**cuestan** los billetes?' '*How much does the journey cost/do the tickets cost?* **Valer** *to cost* is used in a similar way : ¿Cuánto **vale/n**? '*How much does it/do they cost?*'. When you are ready to pay for a service or something you bought use ¿Cuánto **es**? *How much is it?*

▶ Pronunciation

q occurs only in the combination **que** and **qui**, and is pronounced like [ke] and [ki].

Practise with:

¿A qué hora sale el avión para Quito?
Quiero un billete para el tren que sale a las quince treinta.
Queremos cambiar quinientos euros.

Practice

1 La hora en el mundo

You need to make some international phone calls from Chile, where you have been sent by your company. How would you ask the operator what the time is in the following cities, and how would she/he reply? Look at the table below and ask and answer using the twelve-hour clock and expressions like **de la mañana/de la tarde**.

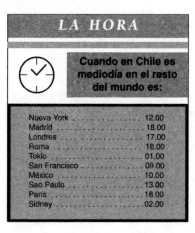

LA HORA	
	Cuando en Chile es mediodía en el resto del mundo es:
Nueva York	12.00
Madrid	18.00
Londres	17.00
Roma	18.00
Tokio	01.00
San Francisco	09.00
México	10.00
Sao Paulo	13.00
París	18.00
Sidney	02.00

a Madrid
b Londres
c Tokio
d San Francisco
e Sao Paulo
f Nueva York

2 De Sevilla a Málaga

You are now in Spain with a travelling companion and you want to take a train from Sevilla to Málaga. Check the time-table and answer your partner's questions using the 12-hour clock.

ORIGEN				
SEVILLA STA. JUSTA	7,50	12,20	17,30	18,40
La Salud	–	12,28	–	–
Dos Hermanas	8,01	12,35	17,41	18,51
Utrera (Ll.)	8,13	12,47	17,53	19,03
Utrera (S)	8,15	12,50	17,55	19,05
El Arahal	–	13,07	–	–
Marchena	8,39	13,18	18,19	19,29
Osuna	9,05	13,45	18,44	19,55
Pedrera	9,34	14,12	19,08	–
La Roda Andalucía	9,47	14,26	19,21	20,36
Fuente Piedra	–	14,37	–	–
Bobadilla (Ll.)	10,05	14,46	19,42	21,00
Bobadilla (S)	10,09	15,04	–	21,01
MALAGA (LL)	10,58	16,17	–	22,03

a ¿A qué hora hay trenes para Málaga?
b ¿A qué hora llegan a Málaga?

▶ 3 Un recado

María Luisa is being sent by her company overseas and her travel agent leaves *a message*, **un recado**, on her answerphone with details of her flight. Can you fill in the box below with the appropriate information?

Destino	Salida	Llegada	Presentación en aeropuerto
- - - - -	- - - - -	- - - - -	- - - - -

la salida *departure*	**la llegada** *arrival*

▶ 4 Números

Listen, tick the numbers that you hear, and then try learning them all.

100	cien	800	ochocientos
101	ciento uno	900	novecientos
200	doscientos	1 000	mil
299	doscientos noventa y nueve	2 000	dos mil
300	trescientos	3 500	tres mil quinientos
400	cuatrocientos	10 000	diez mil
500	quinientos	100 000	cien mil
600	seiscientos	1 000 000	un millón
700	setecientos	2 000 000	dos millones

Note that **-cientos** becomes **-cientas** before a feminine plural noun.

| doscientos euros | *two hundred euros* |
| doscientas libras | *two hundred pounds* |

The plural of **millón** is **millones,** and the word loses the accent.

Years are read in the following way:

1985	mil novecientos ochenta y cinco
1999	mil novecientos noventa y nueve
2007	dos mil siete

5 Un programa de vacaciones

You have seen the following holiday advertisement in a Spanish paper and you phone a Spanish friend to tell him/her about it. How would you read the prices?

EUROPA

AMSTERDAM, 3 días
Hotel 2*   desde **240 €**

MALTA, 3 días
Hotel 3*   desde **328 €**

CAPITALES DE RUSIA, 7 días
Hotel 4*   desde **900 €**

AFRICA

TWENDE (KENIA), 10 días
Hotel 4*   desde **1.477 €**

ASIA

BANGKOK-BALI, 10 días
Hotel 5*   desde **933 €**

INDIA, 8 días
Hotel 4/5*   desde **1.206 €**

CHINA MILENARIA + GUILIN, 15 días
Hoteles 5*   desde **1.693 €**

---

6 El vuelo dura una hora

While on business in Bogotá, Colombia, you decide to spend a weekend in the colonial town of Cartagena de Indias. Follow the guidelines and fill in your part of the conversation with the travel agent. Key words here are **el vuelo** *flight,* **el/la siguiente** *the next one,* **la vuelta** *return,* **último/a** *last.*

Tú	*Good morning. I'd like to make a reservation for Cartagena for Friday morning. What time are there flights?*
Empleada	Hay un vuelo a las ocho y cuarto, pero está completo. El siguiente es a las once y media.
Tú	*What time does it arrive in Cartagena?*
Empleada	A las doce treinta. ¿Para cuándo quiere la vuelta?
Tú	*For Sunday night. What time does the last flight leave Cartagena?*
Empleada	A las veintiuna quince.
Tú	*How much does the return ticket cost?*
Empleada	Doscientos cuarenta dólares.
Tú	*It's all right. Give me return ticket, please.*

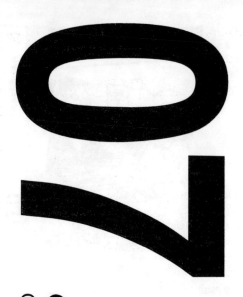

07

¿qué desea?

can I help you?

In this unit you will learn how to:
- buy food in a market
- buy groceries
- find out what things cost

▶1 ¿Cuánto cuestan?

Lola is doing her shopping in a Spanish market.

1.1 First, look at the list of fruit and vegetables below. How many of them can you guess? Look up the words you don't know.

Frutas

el albaricoque/damasco (LAm.)
la fresa/frutilla (Perú, Chile, Arg)
el limón
la manzana
el melocotón/durazno (LAm.)
el melón
la naranja
la piña/ananá (Arg)
el plátano/banana (Perú, Arg)
la uva

Verduras

el ajo	el pepino
la cebolla	el perejil
la coliflor	el pimiento (verde/rojo)
la lechuga	el tomate/jitomate (Méx)
la patata/papa (LAm.)	la zanahoria

1.2 Now listen to the dialogue several times. Can you say what and how much Lola is buying?

Vendedor	Buenos días. ¿Qué quería?
Lola	¿Me da un kilo de plátanos?
Vendedor	¿Algo más?
Lola	¿Cuánto cuestan estas naranjas?
Vendedor	Un euro con noventa el kilo.
Lola	¿Me pone un kilo y medio?
Vendedor	¿Alguna cosa más?
Lola	¿A cómo están estos tomates?
Vendedor	A dos euros veinte el kilo.
Lola	Póngame dos kilos ... ¡ah!, y me da una lechuga y dos kilos de patatas.
Vendedor	¿Quiere algo más?
Lola	No, nada más. ¿Cuánto es todo?
Vendedor	Son doce euros con noventa.

1.3 Now read the dialogue and find the expressions meaning

a What would you like?
b How much are these ...?
c Anything else?
d How much is it all?

i Note the use of **poner** to put when asking for things that normally need to be weighed (to be put on a scale): ¿Me pone ...? Will you give me ...? (literally, To me you put...), Póngame ... Give me ... (literally, Put me ...). In the same context you may also hear the expression ¿Qué le pongo? What shall I give you? (literally, What to you I put?)

dar	to give	**medio**	half
estos/estas	these (m/f)	**nada más**	nothing else

▶ 2 ¿Me da un cuarto de kilo?

Listen to Lola buying some groceries now.

2.1 What is Lola buying and how much?

Dependiente	Hola, buenas tardes. ¿Qué desea?
Lola	¿Me da un cuarto de kilo de ese queso?
Dependiente	¿Qué más?
Lola	Póngame ciento cincuenta gramos de aquel jamón ..., y medio kilo de esas aceitunas.
Dependiente	¿Algo más?
Lola	Un paquete de mantequilla ... una lata de atún ... una barra de pan ... y media docena de huevos. ¡Ah!, tiene mermelada de naranja?
Dependiente	No, no tengo. ¿Alguna cosa más?
Lola	¿Cuánto vale este aceite de oliva?
Dependiente	Cuatro euros con noventa y cinco la botella de un litro.
Lola	Deme una.
Dependiente	¿Desea algo más?
Lola	Eso es todo. ¿Cuánto es?
Dependiente	Son veintidós euros con cuarenta.

2.2 You ask a Spanish friend to do some shopping for you. Write a shopping list in Spanish using expressions from the dialogue and the words in brackets.

a   two hundred grams of cured ham (**jamón serrano**)
b   one kilo of sugar (**azúcar**)
c   one packet of chocolate buiscuits (**galletas de chocolate**)
d   one tin of salmon (**salmón**)
e   a quarter of **chorizo** (*a spicy hard sausage*)
f   one loaf of wholemeal bread (**pan integral**)

¿qué desea?	*can I help you?* (literally, *what do you wish?*)
este/ese	*this/that* (m)
esas	*those* (f)
aquel	*that* (m)
las aceitunas/olivas	*olives*
la mantequilla	*butter*
una lata	*a tin*
una barra	*a loaf*
media docena de ...	*half a dozen ...*
la mermelada	*jam/marmalade*
¿cuánto vale?	*how much does it cost?*
eso es todo	*that's all*

How do you say it?

Buying food in a market

¿Qué quería/desea?	*What would you like?*
¿Qué le pongo?	*What shall I give you?*
Quería/Quiero un kilo de ...	*I'd like/want a kilo of ...*
¿Me da medio kilo de ...?	*Will you give me half a kilo of...?*
¿Me pone un cuarto de kilo de ...?	*Will you give me a quarter kilo of ...?*
Póngame un kilo y medio.	*Give me one and a half kilos.*
¿Algo más/Alguna cosa más?	*Anything else?*
¿Qué más?	*What else?*
Nada más.	*Nothing else.*
Eso es todo.	*That's all.*

Buying groceries

Quería/Quiero ...	*I'd like/want ...*
¿Me da...?/Deme...	*Will you give me?/Give me ...*
una docena de ...	*a dozen ...*
doscientos gramos de ...	*two hundred grams of ...*
un paquete de ...	*a packet of ...*
una lata/botella de...	*a tin/bottle of ...*
una barra de ...	*a loaf of ...*

Finding out what things cost

¿Cuánto cuesta/vale?	*How much is it?*
¿Cuánto cuesta/vale este/ esta...?	*How much is this ...?* (m/f)
¿Cuánto cuestan/valen estos/estas...?	*How much are these ...?*
¿A cómo/cuánto está/están?	*How much is it/are they?*

Grammar

1 ¿A cómo/cuánto está(n)? *How much is it/ are they?*

When prices change from day to day, as may be the case with fruit and vegetables in a market (or foreign currency), you can use this construction with **estar**.

¿A cómo (*or* cuánto) está el perejil?	*How much is the parsley?*
¿A cómo (*or* cuánto) están los tomates?	*How much are the tomatoes?*
Está/Están a (dos euros).	*It is/They are (two) euros.*

2 Este, ese, aquel *this, that*: demonstratives

a Words like **este** *this*, **ese**, **aquel** *that,* are known as *demonstratives* and they take different forms depending on whether the word they refer to is masculine or feminine, singular or plural. To refer to something which is more distant or far from you, Spanish uses **aquel**, which also translates *that* in English, but which is much less common than the other two forms.

Masculine/feminine singular	Masculine/feminine plural
este melón *this melon*	estos melones *these melons*
esta lechuga *this lettuce*	estas lechugas *these lettuces*
ese pepino *that cucumber*	esos pepinos *those cucumbers*
esa naranja *that orange*	esas naranjas *those oranges*
aquel limón *that lemon*	aquellos limones *those lemons*
aquella manzana *that apple*	aquellas manzanas *those apples*

b These words can also stand in place of a noun which is understood, in which case they are sometimes written with an accent: **éste, ésta, ésos,** etc. This written accent is now optional, so in this book we have used them without it.

Quiero este/esa.   *I want this/that one.*

c Other useful words to learn in this context are the invariable forms **esto** *this,* **eso** *that* and **aquello** *that,* which are *neuter,* that is, they are neither masculine nor feminine.

Eso es todo.   *That's all.*
Perdone, ¿qué es esto?   *Excuse me, what's this?*
Quiero esto/eso.   *I want this/that.*

The last sentence will be useful if you want something but are not sure of the Spanish word for it.

▶ Pronunciation

Spanish does not make a distinction between **b** and **v**. The 'b' in 'barra' and the 'v' in 'vino' are pronounced in the same way, nearly like an English 'b', as in 'big'. More frequently, in other positions, as between vowels, for example 'uva', 'cebolla', they sound softer.

Practise with:

Buenos días, ¿qué desea?

Quería un kilo y medio de albaricoques ..., un kilo de uvas ..., dos cebollas ..., un pimiento verde ..., una docena de huevos ..., una barra de pan blanco ..., y una botella de vino blanco también, por favor.

Practice

1 Una lista de compras

You and a Spanish-speaking friend are spending a few days in a small town. It is your turn to buy some food today and you need to prepare a shopping list. Complete each of the phrases which follow with the name of the appropriate product opposite.

> 1 un kilo de ...
> 2 una lata de ...
> 3 una barra de ...
> 4 medio litro de ...
> 5 media docena de ...
> 6 una botella de ...

2 Ahora tú

You are in a Spanish market doing some shopping. Follow the guidelines below, and fill in your part of the conversation with the stallholder.

Dependiente/a	Tú
¿Qué le pongo?	*Say you wanted one and a half kilos of tomatoes.*
¿Qué más?	*Ask how much the strawberries are.*
Tres euros el kilo.	*Ask him/her to give you one kilo.*
¿Algo más?	*Ask if he/she has green peppers.*
Sí, ¿cuántos quiere?	*Say you want four.*
¿Quiere algo más?	*Yes, you want some parsley too.*
¿Qué más?	*That's all, thank you.*

3 Palabra por palabra

Each row below contains a word which is unrelated to the rest. Can you spot it? Some of the words will be new to you and you may need to look them up.

a queso, chorizo, aceitunas, plato, jamón, atún

b harina, botella, arroz, azúcar, aceite, sal.

c ajo, judías verdes, espinaca, lata, guisantes, puerros.

▶ 4 ¿Cuánto es?

A customer has done some shopping and is ready to pay. How much is the customer paying for each of the items below and what is the total? Listen and find out. Note the use of the word **céntimo** *cent*, normally used when the amount falls below one euro, as in 'sesenta céntimos', 0.60 €. Amounts which exceed one euro, for example 1.60 €, are usually expressed as 'un euro con sesenta' or 'un euro sesenta'.

a fresas
b manzanas
c naranjas
d uvas
e melón
f ajos

5 ¿Este o esta?

a Use este, esta, estos, estas, esto, as appropriate.

i ¿Cómo se llama ..... en español?

ii ¿Cuánto cuestan ..... galletas de chocolate?

iii Quería dos botellas de ..... vino.

iv ¿Cuánto vale ..... cerveza?

v ¿Me pone un kilo de ..... limones?

b Use **ese, esa, esos, esas, eso,** as appropriate

i ¿A cómo están _____ patatas?

ii Por favor, ¿me da una botella de _____ aceite de oliva?

iii Perdone, ¿qué es _____

iv Póngame medio kilo de _____ melocotones.

v ¿Cuánto vale _____ mermelada de naranja?

i The text which follows, which has no follow-up questions, is in Spanish, and it tells you a little about shopping habits among Spanish and Latin American people. Try to get the gist of what the passage says with the help of the key words below and your dictionary. As you read, focus attention on where people prefer to buy their food, and on opening and closing times for shops.

De compras *Shopping*

En España y en Latinoamérica la mayoría de la gente compra los alimentos en pequeñas **tiendas de alimentación** o **de comestibles,** *food shops,* y mercados. Esta costumbre es mucho más evidente en pueblos y ciudades pequeñas donde no hay supermercados. Pero aun en ciudades grandes, como Barcelona, Madrid, Valencia, donde hay muchos supermercados, la gente prefiere el contacto directo con **el/la dependiente/a,** *shop assistant,* o **el/la tendero/a,** *shopkeeper.*

Las tiendas normalmente abren entre 9:00 y 10:00 de la mañana, cierran al mediodía y abren nuevamente a las 3:00 o 4:00 de la tarde. En ciudades grandes muchas tiendas, especialmente **los grandes almacenes,** *department stores,* están abiertas todo el día.

comprar	*to buy*
los alimentos	*food*
aun	*even*
la costumbre	*custom*
el pueblo	*small town, village*
cerrar (e>ie)	*to close*
abrir	*to open*
están abiertos/as	*they are open* (m/f)

08

de compras

shopping

In this unit you will learn how to:

- buy clothes
- talk about size and colour

▶ 1 ¿Puedo probármela?

A customer is buying clothes for herself.

1.1 Match the words and the items below, then listen to the conversation several times and say what clothes the customer is buying. Key words here are **la talla** *size*, **el color** *colour*, **probarse** *to try on*.

1 una chaqueta	4 un jersey/suéter (LAm)
2 unos calcetines	5 unos pantalones
3 unos zapatos	6 una camisa

a.   b.   c.

d.   e.   f.

Clienta	Por favor, quisiera ver esa chaqueta.
Dependienta	¿Qué talla tiene?
Clienta	La cuarenta.
Dependienta	¿De qué color la quiere?
Clienta	La prefiero en rojo.
Dependienta	Aquí tiene una en rojo.
Clienta	¿Puedo probármela?
Dependienta	Sí, claro, el probador está al fondo.

(The customer comes back)

Dependienta	¿Qué tal le queda?
Clienta	Me queda un poco grande. ¿Tiene una más pequeña?
Dependienta	Sí, aquí tiene una de la talla treinta y ocho.
Clienta	(*Size 38 fits her well*) Sí, esta me queda bien. Me la llevo.
Dependienta	¿Alguna otra cosa?
Clienta	Sí, quiero un jersey negro.

1.2 Look at the vocabulary below, then read the dialogue and try finding the phrases which mean the following. Note that they all refer to *the jacket* – **la chaqueta** – which is feminine.

a What colour do you want it?
b I prefer it in red
c It's too big for me (literally, *it fits me big*)
d Have you got a smaller one?
e This fits (me) well.
f I'll take it.

ver	*to see*	**quedar**	*to fit*
en rojo	*in red*	**el probador**	*fitting-room*
pequeño/a	*small*	**llevar**	*to take*
prefiero (from **preferir** e>ie) *I prefer*			

▶ 2 ¿De qué color?

Another customer, this time a man, is buying clothes for himself.

2.1 What is he buying?

Cliente	Por favor, ¿tiene estos pantalones en la talla cuarenta y seis?
Dependiente	¿De qué color los quiere?
Cliente	Grises.
Dependiente	Un momento, por favor ... Sì, aquí tiene unos en gris.
Cliente	¿Puedo probármelos?
Dependiente	Sí, claro, el probador está al fondo, a la derecha.
(*The customer comes back*) ¿Cómo le quedan?	
Cliente	Me quedan muy bien. Me los llevo.
Dependiente	¿Desea algo más?
Cliente	Sí, quiero una camisa blanca, talla mediana.

2.2 Read the dialogue and answer these questions.

a What size clothes does the customer wear?
b Where's the fitting-room?
c What phrase does he use to say 'May I try them on?'
d What phrase does the shop assistant use to say 'How do they fit?'
e How does the customer express the following: 'They fit very well. I'll take them'.

gris *grey*	**blanco/a** *white*

How do you say it?

Buying clothes

Quiero/Quisiera/Quería ver ... esa chaqueta/esos vaqueros.	*I want/would like to see ... that jacket/those jeans.*
Quiero/Quisiera/Quería unos zapatos/unas sandalias.	*I want/would like some shoes/sandals.*
¿Tiene esta camisa/este jersey en la talla ...?	*Have you got this shirt/sweater in size ...?*
¿Puedo probármelo/la(s)?	*May I try it/them on? (m/f)*
¿Quiere probárselo/la(s)?	*Would you like to try it/them on?*

Talking about size and colour

¿Qué talla (tiene)?	*What size (are you)?*
¿De qué talla?	*In what size?*
(La talla) cuarenta/pequeña (S)/mediana (M)/grande (L).	*(Size) forty/small/medium/large.*
¿Cómo/Qué tal le queda(n)?	*How does it/do they fit?*
Me queda(n) (muy) bien.	*It fits/They fit (me) (very) well.*
Me queda(n) grande(s).	*It is/They are too big for me.*
¿Tiene uno/a(s) más pequeño/a(s)?	*Have you got a/some smaller one(s)?*
¿De que color lo/la(s) quiere?	*What colour do you want it/them? (m/f)*
Lo/La(s) quiero/prefiero en rojo/azul/blanco.	*I want/prefer it/them in red/blue/white.*
Quiero una camisa blanca/un jersey negro.	*I want a white shirt/black sweater.*

Grammar

1 Lo, los *it, them*

To say 'it' or 'them' as in '*I'll take it/them*', use **lo** for masculine and **la** for feminine. In the plural use **los** or **las**.

¿En qué color quiere el sombrero/la blusa?	*In what colour do you want the hat/blouse?*
Lo/La prefiero en negro	*I prefer it in black.*
¿Y los pantalones/las medias?	*And the trousers/stockings?*
Los/Las quiero en azul.	*I want them in blue.*

Position

These words, known 'technically' as *direct object pronouns* (see 9 of Grammar Summary), normally come before the verb, translating literally as '*It/Them I prefer/want ...etc.*'. But in sentences with a main verb followed by an infinitive, they may be placed before the main verb (as above) or may be added to the infinitive, becoming one word with it. A sentence such as '*I want to take it*' may then be expressed as 'Lo/la quiero llevar' or 'Quiero llevarlo/la'.

(For a definition of *direct object* see **object** in the Glossary of grammatical terms and sections 9.1 and 9.2 of the Grammar Summary.)

2 Me, te/le, nos ... *me, you, us ...*

You are already familiar with the use of **me** and **nos** in phrases such as **me/nos trae ...** *will you bring me/us?* (Unit 5), **me da ...** *will you give me ...?* (Unit 7), **deme ...** *give me ...* (Unit 6). In this unit there are further examples of the use of **me** in a construction with **quedar** *to fit*, in which **me** stands for *me* and for *me*. As with **lo(s)** and **la(s)** above, its position is normally before the verb.

Me quedan muy bien.	*They fit (me) very well.*
No **me** queda bien.	*It doesn't fit (me) well.*
Me queda grande.	*It's too big for me.*

The corresponding form for **tú** is **te**, and for **él/ella/Vd.** is **le**.

¿Qué tal **te/le** queda?	*How does it fit you/him/her?*
Te/Le queda corto.	*It's too short for you/him/her.*

La chaqueta **te/le** queda estupendamente.	*That jacket looks great on you /him/her.*

For **nosotros/as, vosotros/as, ellos/ellas/Vds.** use **nos, os, les,** respectively.

¿**Nos** enseña esos cinturones?	*Will you show us those belts?*
Os quedan muy bien.	*They fit (you) very well*
¿**Les** enseño otros?	*Shall I show you others?*

Me, te, le, nos, os, les are known as *indirect object pronouns* and you can find more information on them in Unit 9, and in sections 9.1 and 9.2 of the Grammar Summary. For a definition of *indirect object* see **object** on page 288 of the Glossary of grammatical terms.

3 ¿Puedo probármelo? *May I try it on?*, **Me lo llevo** *I'll take it*

Me, like **te,** has other uses and meanings which do not correspond to those in **2** above. Sentences such as ¿**Puedo probármelo?** and **Me lo llevo** can be learned as set phrases at this stage, but if you are interested in their grammar you can refer to the notes on *reflexive pronouns* in Unit 12.

4 Los colores *colours*

negro	*black*	**azul**	*blue*
blanco	*white*	**verde**	*green*
rojo	*red*	**malva**	*mauve*
amarillo	*yellow*	**naranja**	*orange*
gris	*grey*	**rosa**	*pink*
marrón	*brown*	**violeta**	*violet*

The following alternatives may be heard in some Latin American countries: **café** *brown*, **rosado** *pink*.

Some simple rules

a Colours are masculine in Spanish: 'El negro te queda bien', '*Black suits you*'.

b Colours ending in –o change for feminine and plural: 'unas blusas blancas', '*some white blouses*'.

c Colours ending in a consonant or –e change for plural but not for masculine and feminine: 'los jerseys/las camisas azules', *'the blue sweaters/shirts'*, 'las faldas/los pantalones verdes', *'the green skirts/trousers'*.

d Colours ending in –a, some of which correspond to names of things, are usually invariable: 'los sombreros naranja/violeta', 'the orange/violet hats'.

e Like other words which describe things, *colours* normally follow the noun they describe (see 5 below) : 'unas bragas negras', *'some black panties',* 'unos calzoncillos blancos', *'some white underpants'.*

5 Describing things: *adjectives*

a Position and agreement

Words which describe things, for example **grande** *big*, **largo** *long*, are called *adjectives*, and they normally come after the noun that they describe (see also **4 e** above). In Spanish, adjectives agree in gender (m/f) and number (sing/pl) with the word being described (see special rules for *colours* above): 'un abrigo largo', *'a long coat'*, 'una camiseta pequeña', *'a small T shirt'*, 'unos pantalones cortos', *'short trousers'*.

b Más + adjective

To say that you would like something *bigger, cheaper*, etc. place the word **más** before the adjective: '¿Busco unos calcetines más grandes?', *'I'm looking for some bigger socks?'*, '¿Tiene un vestido más barato? Este es muy caro, *'Have you got a cheaper dress? This is too expensive'.* (For more information on **más + adjective** see Unit 10.)

Practice

 1 Quería ver ...

Here is a brief exchange between a customer and a shop assistant. Listen to the dialogue a few times before you read it, then look at the words in the box and make up similar conversations, making all necessary changes. Try doing this without looking at the dialogue.

Clienta	Por favor, quería ver esas botas negras.
Dependienta	¿Estas?
Clienta	Sí, esas. ¿Puedo probármelas?
Dependienta	Sí, por supuesto. (*Customer tries them on*). ¿Qué tal le quedan?
Clienta	Me quedan grandes.

Artículo	Color	Característica
a botas	negro	grande
b zapatos	marrón	pequeño
c camiseta	amarillo	ancho
d vestido	gris	largo

por supuesto	*certainly, of course*
estrecho/a	*tight*
ancho/a	*loose, loose-fitting*

2 Find the opposite

Complete each sentence with the construction **más +** adjective, using proper *agreement* between the adjective and the word this refers to. Choose from **pequeño, corto, ancho, barato, grande, largo.**

a Esta falda me queda larga. ¿Tiene una .....?
b Estas sandalias son muy caras. ¿Tiene unas.....?
c Esta blusa me queda grande. ¿Tiene una .....?
d Estos vaqueros me quedan cortos. ¿Tiene unos .....?
e Estos calcetines me quedan estrechos. ¿Tiene unos .....?
f Esta camisa es demasiado pequeña. ¿Tiene una .....?

3 Ahora tú

You are buying some clothes and shoes for yourself. Use the guidelines below to reply to each question or statement.

a Esos zapatos son muy buenos. (*Ask whether you can try them on.*)
b Ese cinturón marrón le queda muy bien. (*Say you'll take it*).
c ¿Qué tal le quedan las zapatillas? (*Say they fit well. You'll take them.*)

d Estos guantes negros son preciosos. *(Say you'll take them.)*

e La camisa azul es muy bonita. *(Ask whether you can try it on.)*

f ¿Qué tal le queda el jersey verde? *(Say it doesn't fit well. You won't take it.)*

| las zapatillas | *trainers* | bonito/a | *nice, pretty* |
| los guantes | *gloves* | precioso/a | *beautiful* |

▶ 4 De compras

Carmen is buying some shoes for herself. Listen and answer the questions below. Note that the word for *size* when referring to shoes is **el número**, literally *number*.

a What size shoes does she wear?

b What colour shoes does she prefer?

c What colours is she offered?

d Which colour does she choose?

e How do the shoes fit?

| ¿cuál/cuáles? | *which one/ones?* |
| pues, ... entonces | *well, ... then* |

este jersey es demasiado grande

09

queríamos alquilar un coche

we would like to hire a car

In this unit you will learn how to:

- change money
- hire a car
- request a service on the phone

▶ 1 En el banco

Ester is on holiday in Spain. Today she is changing some money at a bureau de change.

1.1 What currency is Ester changing and how much? What is the rate of exchange for that currency? Listen and find out.

Ester   Por favor, quisiera cambiar doscientos cincuenta dólares a euros. ¿A cuánto está el cambio? Tengo cheques de viaje.

Empleado   Está a setenta y nueve céntimos. ¿Me permite su pasaporte, por favor?

Ester   Aquí tiene.

Empleado   Muy bien, puede firmarlos. ¿Qué dirección tiene en Madrid?

Ester   Calle Salvador Nº 26, 2º, 4ª.

cambiar	*to change*
el cheque de viaje	*traveller's cheque*
el cambio	*exchange rate*
firmar	*to sign*

1.2 Can you make sense of the following conversation which takes place in a South American country? Place the sentences in the right sequence and you'll get a dialogue on the same subject with some alternative expressions. The 'peso' is the currency in a number of Latin American countries, but the rate for the dollar is not the same in all countries.

– Está a 540 pesos por dólar. ¿Cuánto quería cambiar?
– ¿Cuál es su dirección aquí?
– Tengo billetes. ¿A cómo está el cambio?
– Muy bien. ¿Tiene su pasaporte?
– Calle del Ángel, 842.

- ¿Tiene cheques de viaje o billetes?
- Sí, aquí tiene.
- Quería cambiar dólares a pesos.
- Cien dólares.
- ¿Qué desea?

ℹ️ Direcciones *Addresses*

Addresses in Spanish do not follow the same pattern as in English. What makes them different? Read and find out.

Observa esta dirección: **Salvador nº 26, 2º, 4ª. Salvador** corresponde a la calle (*street*), **26** indica el número de la casa o edificio (*house or building number*), **2º** corresponde al piso o planta (*floor*), y **4ª**, 'cuarta', indica la puerta (*the door or flat number*). En **avenida del Mar nº 150, 5º** ('quinto'), **B**, 'B' indica la puerta B. En **calle Rosas nº40, 6º** ('sexto'), **derecha**, 'derecha' indica la puerta derecha. De manera similar, 'izquierda' indica la puerta izquierda. En cartas, las direcciones se utilizan normalmente en forma abreviada: C/ = calle; Avda. = avenida (*avenue*); Pº = paseo (*walk, avenue*); dcha. = derecha; izq. o izda. = izquierda.

▶ 2 Alquilando un coche

Pablo and a friend are hiring a car.

2.1 First, look at the key words below, then listen to the dialogue several times and, as you do, say whether the following statements are true or false (**verdaderos o falsos**). Key words here are **alquilar** *to hire*, **el alquiler** *hire charge*, **el coche** *car*, **recomendar** (e>ie) *to recommend*.

a Pablo y su amigo quieren un coche para una semana.
b Quieren un coche grande.
c El seguro (*insurance*) obligatorio está incluido.
d Los impuestos (*taxes*) están incluidos.

2.2 Listen again a few times and fill in the gap in the following table with the car rate.

		KMS. ILIMITADOS		
Grupo	Modelo Model	1–2 Días Por día/ Per day	3–6 Días Por día/ Per day	7+ Días Por día/ Per day
A	Ford Fiesta 1.1 Renault Clio		16 €	13 €
C	R. 19RL/Megane 1.4 A/C – Radio	25 €	19 €	15 €
D	Ford Escort 1.6 A/C – Radio	30 €	23 €	17 €
F	Seat Toledo 1.8 A/C – Radio	72 €	51 €	45 €
P	Renault Espace A/C 7 Pax. – Radio	92 €	79 €	67 €

Pablo   Buenas tardes. Queríamos alquilar un coche para el fin de semana. Un coche mediano. ¿Qué nos recomienda?

Empleado   Pues, les recomiendo el Ford Fiesta.

Pablo   ¿Cuánto es el alquiler?

Empleado   Para uno o dos días son diecinueve euros por día. El seguro obligatorio está incluido, pero los impuestos no. Es un buen coche. Se lo recomiendo.

Pablo   De acuerdo. ¿Podemos pagar con tarjeta?

Empleado   Sí, claro.

2.3 Read the dialogue and find the Spanish for

a What do you recommend (to us)?
b I recommend (to you) ... (formal, pl)
c I recommend it (to you). (formal)
d Can we pay ...?

2.4 Look at the car rental information now and use it to make up similar dialogues. Use words and phrases like **pequeño**, **grande**, **económico**, **una semana**, **cinco días**, etc.

el fin de semana	*weekend*
mediano/a	*medium size*
buen	*good* (before a m, sing noun)
de acuerdo	*fine, all right*
pagar	*to pay*
la tarjeta (de crédito)	*(credit) card*

▶ 3 Quería un taxi

Sara phones for a taxi.

3.1 Where does she want to go, and when does she want it for? Listen and find out.

Empleado	Radio taxi, ¿dígame?
Sara	Hola, buenas tardes. Quería un taxi para ir al aeropuerto, por favor.
Empleado	¿Para qué hora lo quiere?
Sara	¿Me lo puede enviar ahora mismo?
Empleado	Muy bien. ¿Me dice su nombre y dirección, por favor?
Sara	Sara Moreno, calle Mistral 45, 3°, B.
Empleado	¿Su teléfono?
Sara	93 512 34 42.
Empleado	Pues, se lo envío en seguida.
Sara	Vale, gracias.
Empleado	A usted.

3.2 It's 10 a.m. now and you want a taxi for 11.00 o'clock to go to *Estación de Atocha* (one of the main stations in Madrid). You are staying at calle de Los Cerezos 62, 5°, izquierda. Your phone number there is 93 412 30 88. Read the dialogue and then use the information to write a similar conversation between you and the cab company attendant.

enviar	*to send*
me dice (from **decir**)...	*will you tell me ...?*
en seguida	*straightaway*
(gracias) a usted	*thank you*

How do you say it?

Changing money

Quería cambiar (dólares) a (euros).	*I'd like to change (dollars) into (euros).*
¿A cuánto/cómo está el cambio?	*What's the rate of exchange?*

Hiring a car

Quería/Queríamos alquilar un coche/carro *or* auto. (LAm)	*I/We would like to hire a car.*
para una semana/tres días/el fin de semana	*for a week/three days/the weekend.*
¿Cuánto es/cuesta el alquiler?	*How much is the rental?*
¿Está incluido el seguro/IVA?	*Is insurance/vat included?*
¿Va con gasolina o gasóleo?	*Does it run on petrol or diesel?*

Requesting a service on the phone

Quería un taxi/hacer un pedido/encargar algo para cenar.	*I'd like a taxi/to place an order/to order something for dinner.*
¿Para qué hora lo quiere?	*What time do you want it for?*
¿Me lo puede enviar ahora mismo/a las 9:00?	*Can you send it (to me) right now/at nine?*
¿Qué dirección tiene?/¿Cuál es su dirección?	*What's your address?*
Me dice su nombre/dirección/ (número de) teléfono/ (número de) habitación.	*Will you tell me your name/ address/telephone number/ room number?*

Grammar

1 Me, te, le ...: *indirect object pronouns*

In Unit 8 you learned to use words such as **me** and **le/s** in phrases such as '¿Cómo le quedan?', '*How do they fit (you)?*', 'Me quedan bien', '*They fit (me) well*'. This unit brings in further examples of their use, which also include **nos**.

¿**Me** permite (from **permitir** *to* allow) su pasaporte?	*Will you let me have your passport?* (literally, *Allow me your passport.*)
¿**Me** dice su nombre?	*Will you tell me your name ...?*
¿**Me** lo puede enviar ...?	*Can you send it (to me ...)?*
¿Qué **nos** recomienda?	*What do you recommend (to us)?*
Les recomiendo el Ford Fiesta.	*I recommend (to you) the Ford Fiesta.*

As explained in Unit 8, **me, te, le**, etc. are part of a set of words known 'technically' as *indirect object pronouns*, the full set being:

singular	plural
me *(to/for) me*	**nos** *(to/for) us*
te *(to/for) you* (informal)	**os** *(to/for) you* (informal)
le *(to/for) you/him/her/it*	**les** *(to/for) you/them*

Here are some further examples of their use:

¿Puede recomendar**nos**/ sugerir**nos** un hotel/ restaurante? (*or* ¿**Nos** puede recomendar/ sugerir ...?)	*Can you recommend/suggest a hotel/restaurant?*
¿Qué **nos** sugiere?	*What do you suggest?*
Les sugiero el hotel/ restaurante Don Sancho.	*I suggest the hotel/restaurant Don Sancho.*

2 Order of object pronouns

In a sentence with two object pronouns, one *indirect,* for example **me**, and the other *direct,* for example **lo** (see Unit 8), the indirect object pronoun must come first. The following examples illustrate this point:

¿**Me** puede enviar el taxi ahora mismo? — *Can you send me the taxi right now?*

¿**Lo** puede enviar ahora mismo? — *Can you send it right now?*

¿**Me lo** puede enviar ahora mismo? *or* — *Can you send it to me right now?*

¿Puede enviár**melo** ...?

3 Se in place of le, les

Le and **les** become **se** before **lo, la, los, las,** as shown in the examples below.

Le/Les recomiendo esta excursión. — *I recommend this excursion (to you).*

La recomiendo. — *I recommend it.*

Se la recomiendo. — *I recommend it (to you).*

¿**Le/Les** envío un taxi ahora? — *Shall I send a taxi for you now?*

¿**Lo** envío ahora? — *Shall I send it now?*

¿**Se lo** envío ahora? — *Shall I send it to you now?*

Practice

▶ 1 Cambiando dinero

You'll hear three people changing money into euros. What's the rate for each currency and how much money is each person changing?

Moneda	Cambio	Cantidad
1 libras		
2 francos suizos		
3 coronas suecas		

| **la moneda** | *currency* | **la corona sueca** | *Swedish crown* |
| **la cantidad** | *amount* | **la libra (esterlina)** | *pound* |

2 Cambio

You are at a bureau de change in Mexico, **una casa de cambio,** changing some money into *pesos*. Fill in the gaps in the conversation between you and the employee. You are staying at *Calle Vergara 640, 6°, C.*

Tú	.... dólares a pesos.
	¿..........?
Empleado	¿.......... billetes?
Tú	No, tengo cheques ....
Empleado	.... once pesos por dólar.
	¿Cuánto quiere ....?
Tú	*Say you'd like to change two hundred dollars.*
Empleado	Muy bien.
Tú	Y el cambio .... la libra,
	¿..........?
Empleado	La libra .... veintiún pesos.
Tú	*Say you'd like to change a hundred and eighty pounds.*
Empleado	¿.......... dirección .... en México?
Tú	....

CAMBIO

| **la casa de cambio** | *bureau de change* (LAm) (in Spain, **una oficina de cambio**) |
| **el billete** | *banknote* |

i La **moneda oficial**, *official currency*, de México es *el peso*. El peso es también la moneda oficial en Argentina, Chile, Colombia, Cuba, República Dominicana y Uruguay. Otras monedas latinoamericanas son: *el boliviano* en Bolivia, *el colón* en Costa Rica, *el dólar* en Ecuador, *el colón y el dólar* en El Salvador, *el quetzal* en

Guatemala, *la lempira* en Honduras, *el córdoba* en Nicaragua, *el balboa y el dólar* en Panamá, *el guaraní* en Paraguay, *el nuevo sol* en Perú, y *el bolívar* en Venezuela.

3 Con cheque

Fill in the gaps in this conversation with one of the following pronouns: **lo, me, le**.

Clienta	Quería alquilar un coche pequeño. ¿Cuál _____ recomienda Vd.?
Empleado	_____ recomiendo este. Es pequeño y económico. ¿Para cuándo _____ quiere Vd.?
Clienta	Quisiera llevar_____ mañana a ser posible. ¿Puedo pagar el alquiler con cheque?
Empleado	Sí, puede pagar_____ con cheque, con tarjeta de crédito o en efectivo.

cuándo	*when*	**en efectivo**	*cash*
a ser posible	*if possible*		

4 Ahora tú

You and a travelling companion want to hire a car. What questions would you ask to get the following replies? Some of the questions allow more than one alternative.

a ¿Un coche económico? Les recomiendo este.
b El alquiler cuesta treinta euros por día.
c Sí, el seguro obligatorio está incluido.
d No, los impuestos no están incluidos.
e Va con gasolina.
f Sí, claro, pueden pagar con tarjeta de crédito.
g Sí, por supuesto, lo pueden llevar ahora mismo.

5 ¿Cómo se dice?

It is your last day at your holiday hotel and you phone reception to request certain things for you and your partner. Use the **nosotros** form for verbs and pronouns.

a We'd like breakfast in the room, please. We are in room 12.
b Can you send it to us right now? We want one tea and one coffee, a pineapple juice and an orange juice, and wholemeal bread, please.
c Can you send us an English newspaper?

d We'd also like a taxi to go to the airport.

e The plane leaves at 12.30. We want it for half past ten.

f (You are ready to leave and you want the bill) Will you give us the bill, please? We'd like to pay with a credit card.

---

el periódico *newspaper*	**dar** *to give*

---

6 Crucigrama

Horizontales

1 Puede pagar con cheque o en _____ .

2 Queremos _____ un coche.

3 (Yo) _____ llevarlo mañana.

4 ¿Puedo pagar con _____ de crédito?

5 El seguro y los impuestos no están _____ .

6 Va con _____.

7 Le _____ este coche. Es estupendo.

Verticales

1 ¿Cuánto cuesta el _____ de este coche?

2 ¿A _____ está el cambio del dólar?

3 ¿Puede _____ los cheques, por favor?

4 Quería _____ cien euros.

5 ¿Tiene cheques o _____?

6 ¿Puedo pagar con cheques de _____?

7 ¿Hay una _____ de cambio por aquí? (L.Am.)

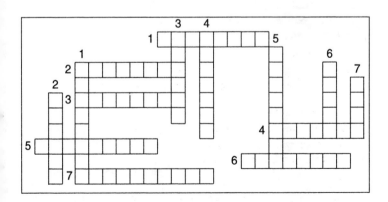

10

¿cuántos años tienes?

how old are you?

In this unit you will learn how to:
- talk about yourself and your family
- describe places
- make comparisons

▶ 1 Tengo dos hijos

Pablo and her new colleague María talk about themselves and their families.

1.1 Listen to the conversation several times and say whether the statements which follow are true or false (**verdaderos o falsos**). Note the use of **tener** *to have*, to talk about someone's age.

a María has an eight year old daughter and a six year old son.
b Pablo is single.
c He lives with his family.
d He has two younger brothers.

Pablo	Estás casada, ¿verdad?
María	Sí, estoy casada. Tengo dos hijos. El mayor, Gonzalo, tiene ocho años y la menor, Laura, tiene seis. Tú estás soltero, ¿no?
Pablo	Sí, vivo con mis padres y mis hermanos.
María	Eres muy joven. ¿Cuántos años tienes?
Pablo	Tengo veintidós años.
María	¿Cuántos hermanos tienes?
Pablo	Tengo dos, un hermano y una hermana. Yo soy el más pequeño.

1.2 Now read the dialogue and say how the following is expressed:

a You're married, aren't you?   **c** I'm twenty two years old.
b You are single, aren't you?   **d** the eldest/the youngest

los hijos	*children*
los padres	*parents*
los hermanos	*brothers and sisters*
joven	*young*
el/la hermano/a	*brother/sister*
el/la más pequeño/a	*the youngest*

▶2 ¿Qué tal tu nuevo piso?

Pablo and María describe their homes and neighbourhoods.

2.1 Here are some words you may need when talking about the place where you live and your neighbourhood. How many of them can you recognize? Check their meaning before you listen to the dialogue and answer the questions below: **el baño, el barrio, la calefacción, la cocina, la habitación, el piso, el salón.** Note also the following expressions: **¿Qué tal ...?** *What is ...like?*, **más ... que** *more ... than*, **tan ... como** *as ... as.*

a How does María describe her flat?
b How does she describe the area where she lives?
c How does Pablo describe his own flat?

Pablo   ¿Qué tal tu nuevo piso?

María   No está mal. Tiene cuatro habitaciones, un gran salón, cocina equipada, dos baños y mucho sol.

Pablo   Es bastante grande. ¿Y qué tal el barrio?

María   Es muy bueno y es más tranquilo que el centro.

Pablo   Mi barrio es bastante ruidoso y el piso no es tan grande como el tuyo, pero es muy cómodo. Tiene tres habitaciones, un salón, una cocina grande, calefacción individual...

2.2 Read the dialogue and say which of the flats advertised below fits in: **a** María's description; **b** Pablo's description.

**GENOVA
V. MONTSERRAT**

Luminoso, sol, 3 hab.
salón, gran cocina,
baño nuevo, calef.
indiv. buenos
acabados.
210.000 €

**GRACIA
T. VIDALET**

Todo reformado, alto,
mucho sol, gran
salón, 4 hab. cocina
equip. y 2 baños.
270.000 €

**RONDA SAN
ANTONIO**

2 hab. salón, cocina
y aseo.
140.000 €

**COLLBLANCH
JTO METRO**

Muy tranquilo, sol, 3
hab. gran salón, coc. y
baño completo.
170.500 €

nuevo/a	new
el/la tuyo/a	yours (inf)
ruidoso/a	noisy
buenos acabados	high finish
equipado/a	fitted
reformado/a	converted
el aseo	toilet
jto. (junto a)	next to

i **La casa, el piso, el apartamento.** Peninsular Spanish uses three main words to describe a dwelling: **la casa** house or home, **el piso** flat or apartment, and **el apartamento**, used to name a smaller flat or apartment, such as holiday apartments. The word for a flat or apartment in Latin America is **el departamento**, or **el apartamento** in some regions. **La habitación** means room, but it is also used to designate a bedroom: 'esta es mi habitación', 'this is my bedroom'. A more specific word for bedroom is **el dormitorio**: 'un piso de dos dormitorios', 'a two-bedroom flat'.

How do you say it?

Talking about yourself and your family

a Marital status:

| ¿Estás/Está Vd. soltero(a) o casado(a)? | Are you single or married? |
| Estoy soltero(a)/casado(a)/ divorciado(a)/separado(a). | I'm single/married/divorced/ separated. |

b Family:

¿Tienes/Tiene Vd. hijos/ hermanos?	Have you got children/ brothers and sisters?
¿Cuántos hijos/hermanos tienes /tiene Vd.?	How many children/brothers and sisters do you have?
Tengo un(a) hijo(a)/un(a) hermano(a).	I have one son/daughter/one brother/sister.

c Age:

| ¿Cuántos años tienes/tiene Vd.? | How old are you? |
| ¿Qué edad tienes/tiene Vd.? | What age are you? |

Tengo veintidós (años).	*I'm twenty-two (years old).*
Él/Ella tiene ocho años.	*He/She is eight years old.*

d Describing places

Es un piso muy/bastante grande/bueno/cómodo.	*It's a very/quite a large/good/ comfortable flat.*
Tiene dos habitaciones/baños.	*It has two rooms/bathrooms.*

e Making comparisons

Es más tranquilo/caro que el centro.	*It's quieter/more expensive than the centre.*
No es tan grande/pequeño como el tuyo/el de María.	*It's not as large/small as yours/María's.*

Grammar

1 Expressing marital status: *estar* and *ser*

Marital status, **el estado civil,** is normally expressed with **estar,** which signals a *state*. But to define someone as being a single, married or divorced person, use **ser**. Words denoting marital status change for gender (m/f) and number (sing/pl).

Está casada con Víctor.	*She's married to Victor.*
Todavía **está** soltero.	*He's still single.*
Están divorciados.	*They're divorced.*
Es una mujer casada/un hombre casado.	*She's a married woman/He's a married man.*

2 Expressing age

Age, **la edad,** is expressed with **tener,** but to define someone as being young, old, etc., use **ser**.

Tengo cuarenta años.	*I'm forty years old.*
¿Cuántos años/Qué edad **tiene** tu padre/madre?	*How old/What age is your father/mother?*
Es una persona muy joven/ mayor.	*He/She's a very young/old person.*

3 Words for relatives

The masculine plural form of words referring to people such as **el padre** *father*, **el hijo** *son*, **el hermano** *brother*, can refer to members of both sexes: **los padres** *parents*, **los hijos** *children*, **los hermanos** *brothers and sisters*. Likewise with **el tío** *uncle*, **el primo** *cousin*, **el nieto** *grandson*, **el suegro** *father-in-law*. Note that **los parientes** means *relatives*.

4 Describing

a To describe something or someone in terms of its or his/her characteristics, use **ser**.

Es un barrio excelente.	*It's an excellent area.*
Son pisos caros.	*They are expensive flats.*
Eres muy joven.	*You are very young.*

b To describe something or someone in terms of a state or condition at a certain point in time, use **estar**.

La casa **está** limpia/tranquila.	*The house looks clean/is quiet (now).*
María **está** contenta con su piso.	*María is happy with her flat.*

5 Making comparisons

a To say that something is *smaller*, *more expensive*, etc. than something else, or that someone is *prettier, more intelligent*, etc. than someone else, use **más ... (que)**

Madrid es más pequeño que Londres.	*Madrid is smaller than London.*
Este barrio es más caro.	*This area is more expensive.*
Rebeca es más guapa que Elsa.	*Rebeca is prettier than Elsa.*
Eva es más inteligente.	*Eva is more intelligent.*

Más is not needed with irregular forms:

Este hotel es mejor/peor.	*This hotel is better/worse.*
Cristina es mayor/menor que yo.	*Cristina is older/younger than I.*

Más joven *younger* is also correct when reference is to adults.

Mayor can also be used to refer to size:

Buenos Aires es más grande/ mayor que Santiago.	*Buenos Aires is bigger than Santiago.*

b To say that something is *the cheapest, the most comfortable*, etc., or that someone is *the nicest, the most efficient*, etc. , use **el/la/los/las más** + adjective.

Este hostal es el más barato/ cómodo.	*This boarding house is the cheapest/most comfortable.*
Sara es la más simpática/ eficiente.	*Sara is the nicest/most efficient.*

Más is not needed with irregular forms:

Mi apartamento es el mejor/ peor.	*My apartment is the best/worst.*
Elvira es la mayor/menor de todas.	*Elvira is the oldest/youngest of all.*

Mayor can also refer to size:

México es el mayor país de habla hispana.

or

Es el más grande de los países de habla hispana.	*Mexico is the largest Spanish speaking country.*

c To say that something or someone is *as interesting as, as quiet as* something or someone else, use **tan ... como**.

Nueva York es tan interesante como Londres.	*New York is as interesting as London.*
Delia es tan tranquila como su hermana.	*Delia is as quiet as her sister.*

◖ Pronunciation

rr, as in 'barrio, perro', is strongly rolled.
r, after n, l, and s, for example 'Enrique, alrededor (*around*), Israel', and at the beginning of a word, for example 'Ronda, rosa', is also strongly rolled, and is pronounced like **rr**.
r, between vowels, as in 'caro, pero', is much softer and closer to the English 'r' in 'very'.

Practise with:

Enrique y Rosa viven en un barrio muy caro de Tarragona.
Sara vive en Gerona.
Ramón y Carmen tienen un apartamento en Sanlúcar de Barrameda.

Practice

1 Mi familia y yo

In his first letter to a correspondent Ricardo wrote about himself and his family. Can you fill in the gaps with the missing words?

Querida Pat:

¡Hola! Como esta es mi primera carta, quiero contarte algo sobre mí y mi familia. Me (a) _____ Ricardo Gutiérrez, (b) _____ veintiún años, (c) _____ soltero, y (d) _____ con mi madre, mis tres hermanos y mi abuela. Mis (e) _____ están divorciados. Yo soy el (f) _____ de los cuatro hermanos. El segundo se (g) _____ Javier y (h) _____ diecinueve años, después viene Carmen, (i) _____ tiene dieciséis, y la (j) _____ es mi hermana Isabel, que va a cumplir catorce.

contar (o>ue)	*to tell*	**después**	*then*
sobre	*about*	**venir**	*to come*
la abuela	*grandmother*	**va a cumplir**	*she's going to be*

2 Ricardo y su familia

How would you tell someone else about Ricardo? Begin like this: *Se llama Ricardo Gutiérrez …*

3 Me llamo Luisa …

Look at this family tree. How would Luisa write about herself and her family?

LUISA, 45

PEDRO, 47

TERESA, 23

RAQUEL, 20

FELIPE, 17

4 Estoy casado

You'll hear two people, Rodrigo and Rosa, giving information about themselves and their families. Listen and answer these questions:

a ¿Cuántos años tiene Rodrigo?
b ¿Cuántos hijos tiene?
c ¿Cuántos años tiene el mayor? ¿Y la menor?
d ¿Cuántos años tiene su mujer?
e ¿Cuántos años tiene Rosa?
f ¿Cuál es su estado civil?
g ¿Con quién vive?

el/la ingeniero/a	*engineer*	**el/la abogado/a**	*lawyer*
mi mujer	*my wife*	**¿con quién?**	*with whom?*

5 Ahora tú

¿Cómo te llamas? ¿Cuántos años tienes? ¿Estás casado(a) o soltero(a)? ¿Cómo se llama tu marido/mujer? ¿Cuántos años tiene? ¿Tienes hijos/hermanos? ¿Cómo se llaman? ¿Cuántos años tienen?

6 Un nuevo piso

Elena has moved into a new flat and, in an e-mail, she describes it to her friend Roberto. Read this extract from her letter and then answer the questions which follow.

Hola Roberto:

¡No te imaginas lo contenta que estoy! Tengo un nuevo piso. Es estupendo, mucho mejor que el anterior y más barato. Tiene dos dormitorios y un salón bastante grande, con mucha luz. Es exterior y da a una pequeña plaza. El barrio es muy tranquilo y la calle donde vivo no tiene mucho tráfico. Además, tiene calefacción y aparcamiento, pero no tiene terraza. ¡Una lástima! Pero está muy cerca del metro. Tienes que venir. Es muy fácil llegar aquí ...

a ¿Cuántos dormitorios tiene el piso de Elena?
b ¿Qué tal es?
c ¿Cómo es el barrio?
d ¿Qué servicios tiene?

¡No te imaginas lo contenta....!	*You can't imagine how happy...!*
la luz	*light*
exterior	*facing the street*
dar a	*to give onto*
además	*besides*
¡qué lástima!	*what a pity!*

7 ¿Cuál es el mejor?

You've been posted to a Spanish-speaking country and are looking for a place to live. You've made notes about two flats you've seen, rating them from 0 to 5, with 5 being the most convenient for you. Write sentences comparing the two flats, using the words in brackets. The first one has been done for you.

	calle Lorca	avenida Salvador
precio	1	3
tamaño	5	3
situación	2	5
comodidad	4	4
seguridad	2	0
tranquilidad	3	3

a (barato) El piso de la avenida
   Salvador es *más barato que*
   el (piso) de la calle Lorca.
b (grande)
c (céntrico)

d (cómodo)
e (seguro)
f (tranquilo)

el precio *price*		**la comodidad** *comfort*	
el tamaño *size*		**la tranquilidad** *peace*	

8 Ahora tú

Can you describe the place where you live and your neighbourhood? Use the letter in Activity 6 as a model.

11

¿a qué te dedicas?

what do you do?

In this unit you will learn how to:

- say what you do for a living
- say what hours and days you work
- say how long you have been doing something (1)

▶ 1 ¿Qué haces?

A group of people attending a conference talk about each other's occupations.

1.1 Listen to Elena and Álvaro first. Can you say what they do? Two key phrases here are **¿A qué te dedicas?** and **¿Qué haces?**, *What do you do for a living?*

Elena	¿A qué te dedicas, Álvaro?
Álvaro	Soy estudiante.
Elena	¿Qué estudias?
Álvaro	Estudio historia. Y tú, ¿qué haces?
Elena	Soy enfermera. Trabajo en un hospital.
Álvaro	¿Cuánto tiempo hace que trabajas allí?
Elena	Trabajo allí desde hace dos años.

Soy enfermera, trabajo en un hospital

1.2 Now listen to Cristóbal, Cristina and Ángeles tell Rafael what they do. Who is: **a** a journalist? **b** a teacher? **c** an out of work actress?

Rafael	¿Qué haces tú, Cristóbal?
Cristóbal	Soy profesor. Doy clases de inglés en un colegio.
Rafael	Y tú, Cristina, ¿a qué te dedicas?
Cristina	Yo soy periodista, pero estoy jubilada.
Rafael	¿Y tú, Ángeles?
Ángeles	Soy actriz, pero estoy sin trabajo.

1.3 Now read the dialogues and identify the phrases which mean the following:

a What are you studying?
b I work in a hospital.
c How long have you been working there?
d I teach English.
e I'm retired.
f I'm out of work.

el/la estudiante	*student*
desde hace dos años	*for two years*
el colegio	*school*
la actriz/el actor	*actress/actor*

▶2 ¿Qué horario tienes?

Hernán, a computer expert, **un técnico en informática,** and Sol, a translator, **una traductora,** talk about their working hours.

2.1 Listen and answer the following questions:

a What hours does Hernán work?
b How many weeks' holiday does he have?
c Where does Sol work?

Sol   ¿Qué horario de trabajo tienes?
Hernán   Trabajo de ocho y media a una, y de dos y media a seis y media de la tarde, de lunes a viernes. Los sábados no trabajo.
Sol   ¿Cuántas semanas de vacaciones tienes al año?
Hernán   Tengo tres semanas. Y tu horario, ¿cuál es?
Sol   No tengo horario fijo. Soy traductora y trabajo en casa. Pero trabajo muchas horas.

2.2 Use the following information about Isabel, a librarian, and Hugo, a shop-assistant, to write a similar dialogue.

Isabel, bibliotecaria:	9:00-17:00, lunes a viernes 10:00-14:00, sábados un mes de vacaciones
Hugo, dependiente:	9:00- 14:00/16:00-19:00, lunes a sábado

el horario (de trabajo)	*working hours, time table*
de ... a	*from ... to*
las vacaciones	*holidays*
al año	*a/per year*
el horario fijo	*fixed working hours*

How do you say it?

Saying what you do for a living

¿A qué te dedicas/se dedica Vd.?	*What do you do for a living?*
¿Qué haces/hace Vd.?	*What do you do?*
Soy ingeniero(a)/ secretario(a)/estudiante.	*I'm an engineer/a secretary/ student.*
Trabajo en una fábrica/para una empresa.	*I work in a factory/for a company.*
Estudio lenguas/español/arte.	*I'm studying languages/ Spanish/art.*
Estoy sin trabajo/en paro.	*I'm out of work/unemployed.*
Estoy jubilado(a).	*I'm retired.*

Soy estudiante. Estudio español

Saying what hours and days you work and what holidays you have

a The hours and days you work:

¿Qué horario (de trabajo) tienes/tiene Vd.?	*What are your working hours/is your timetable?*
¿Cuál es tu/su horario?	*What's your timetable?*
Trabajo de 9:00 a 5:00, de lunes a viernes.	*I work from 9.00 to 5.00, from Monday to Friday.*
No trabajo los sábados/Los sábados no trabajo.	*I don't work on Saturdays.*
Tengo clases de 9:00 a 1:00.	*I have classes from 9.00 to 1.00.*

b Your holidays:

¿Cuántas semanas de vacaciones tienes/tiene Vd.?	*How many weeks' holidays do you have?*
Tengo tres semanas/un mes.	*I have three weeks/a month.*

Saying how long you have been doing something

¿Cuánto tiempo hace que trabaja(s)/vive(s) aquí?	*How long have you been working/living here?*
Trabajo/Vivo aquí desde hace un año. *Or*	*I've been working/living here for a year.*
Hace un año que trabajo/ vivo aquí.	

Grammar

1 Omission of 'a', with professions and occupations

To say what your job is you need the verb **ser** *to be*, followed directly by the occupation or profession. The Spanish for 'a', as in 'a plumber', is not used in this context.

Soy fontanero/plomero (L.Am.).	*I'm a plumber.*
Soy pintor/a.	*I'm a painter.*
Soy fotógrafo/a.	*I'm a photographer.*

2 'Hace' with a time phrase and the present tense

To ask someone how long he or she has been doing something, use the following construction: **¿Cuánto tiempo hace que** + *present tense?*

¿Cuánto tiempo hace que estudias/estudia Vd. español?	*How long have you been studying Spanish?*

To reply use either of the following constructions: **Hace** + *time phrase* + **que** + *present tense*, or *Present tense* + **desde hace** + *time phrase*.

Hace seis meses que estudio español. *Or*	*I've been studying Spanish for six months.*
Estudio español desde hace seis meses.	

These constructions, which help to establish a link between the present and the past, can refer not just to an action, as above, but also to a state.

¿Cuánto tiempo hace que estás/está Vd. en España?	*How long have you been in Spain?*
Hace diez años que estoy en España. *Or*	*I've been in Spain for ten years.*
Estoy en España desde hace diez años.	

In short replies use phrases like the following:

hace una semana/un mes/año	*for a week/month/year*
desde hace mucho tiempo	*for a very long time*

3 More prepositions: a, de, desde, en, para, sin

¿A qué te dedicas?	*What do you do for a living?*
dedicarse a	literally, *to devote oneself to*
al año/mes/día, a la semana	*per year/month/day, per week*
de 8:00 a 1:00	*from 8.00 to 1.00*
dar clases de inglés	*to teach English*
una semana de vacaciones	*a week's holiday*
desde hace un siglo	*for a century*
trabajo en una tienda/en casa	*I work in a shop/at home*
trabajo para una empresa	*I work for a company*
estar sin trabajo	*to be without a job or work*

▶ Pronunciation

h, as in 'hace', is silent.
ch, as in 'ocho', is pronounced like the 'ch' in 'chair'.

Practise with:

Hace ocho años que Charo trabaja en Chile. Héctor trabaja desde las ocho de la mañana hasta las nueve de la noche.

Practice

1 Palabra por palabra

Can you match each occupation with the most likely activity?

a	Soy médico/a.	1	Doy clases en un colegio.
b	Soy azafata.	2	Tengo una industria.
c	Soy conductor/a.	3	Escribo artículos para una revista.
d	Soy profesor/a.	4	Trabajo en un hospital.
e	Soy dependiente/a.	5	Hago muebles.
f	Soy cartero/a.	6	Conduzco camiones.
g	Soy periodista	7	Reparto cartas.
h	Soy abogado/a.	8	Vendo ropa en una tienda.
i	Soy carpintero/a.	9	Trabajo en una línea aérea.
j	Soy empresario/a.	10	Trabajo en un tribunal.

escribo (from **escribir**)	*I write*
hago (from **hacer**)	*I make*
conduzco (from **conducir**)	*I drive*
reparto (from **repartir**)	*I deliver*

2 ¿A qué se dedica?

What might the following people say with regard to their work?
Match the drawings with the sentences below.

1 Soy muy rico y no necesito trabajar.
2 Tengo ochenta años y estoy jubilada.
3 Soy ama de casa.
4 No tengo trabajo.

▶ 3 ¿Qué hace Alfonso?

Alfonso talks about his occupation. Listen and answer the questions below.

a ¿Qué hace Alfonso?
b ¿Cuánto tiempo hace que trabaja allí?
c ¿Cuáles son los horarios de trabajo?
d ¿Qué turno prefiere?
e ¿Cuántos días de vacaciones tiene?

el turno (de la mañana)	*(morning) shift*
¿es igual?	*is it the same?*
porque	*because*
durante	*during*

4 Busco trabajo

Look at these advertisements placed by people offering their services. Who wants to do the following work? Give their names.

a receptionist or secretary
b company psychologist
c childminder
d waiter
e teacher and translator
f shop assistant

• Profesor de ESO, con título de inglés a nivel Proficiency, da clases particulares y traduce artículos. *Eugenio*, Tel. 91 543 02 91, Madrid.

• Busco trabajo cuidando niños por las mañanas. Llamar a partir de las 21 horas. *María Ángeles*, Tel. 91 942 30 56, Madrid.

• Tengo 20 años y busco trabajo sólo por las mañanas o por las tardes como recepcionista, secretaria o puesto similar. *Mónica*, Tel. 93 208 45 83, Barcelona.

• Licenciada en psicología en la especialidad industrial busca trabajo como psicóloga preferentemente en una empresa, en cualquier ciudad de España. *Victoria*, Tel. 986 85 27 93, Pontevedra.

• Tengo 17 años y estudio segundo de bachillerato. Quisiera trabajar por las mañanas. Tengo experiencia como dependienta. *Adela*, Tel. 93 782 16 74, Barcelona.

• Camarero, 23 años, quiere trabajar en hotel o restaurante. *Juan Carlos*, Tel. 94 672 95 54, Vizcaya.

ESO (Enseñanza Secundaria Obligatoria)	compulsory secondary education
el título	degree
particular	private
cuidar	to look after
licenciado/a	graduate
cualquier	any
segundo de bachillerato	second year of secondary education

5 Ahora tú

Can you write an advertisement offering your services or expertise? Use as a model the advertisements in Activity 4. Here are some key phrases:

Busco trabajo en/como ...	*I'm looking for work in/as...*
(Estudiante) busca trabajo en/como...	*(Student) seeks employment in /as...*
Quiero/Quisiera trabajar en/como ...	*I want/would like to work in/as...*
(Persona de habla inglesa) quiere/quisiera trabajar en/como...	*(English-speaking person) wants/would like to work in/as...*

6 ¿Cuánto tiempo hace?

Your friend Paul has just introduced you to Carmen, who is studying English in your country and is living in your area. How would you ask her how long she has been doing each of the following, and how would she reply? Use the phrases below.

actividad	*período de tiempo*
a estar aquí	dos meses y medio
b estudiar inglés	dos meses
c vivir en este barrio	tres semanas
d conocer a Paul	un año y medio

7 Ahora tú

Answer the questions below using real or imaginary information.

a ¿A qué te dedicas?, ¿Dónde trabajas?, ¿Cuánto tiempo hace que trabajas allí?, ¿Cuál es tu horario de trabajo?, ¿Cuántas vacaciones tienes al año?

b ¿Qué estudias?, ¿Dónde?, ¿Cuánto tiempo hace que estudias español?, ¿Qué horario de clase tienes?

i El empleo en España

The following passage gives an insight into employment in Spain. As you read the text, focus attention on the questions below. Try to get the gist of what the text says rather than translate it word for word. There are no answers in the Key to the Activities for this text, as it is an exercise in developing understanding of a longer piece of writing rather than a test in itself.

Soy periodista. Hace un año que trabajo en un periódico

a Where do most Spanish people work?

b Where do most women work?

c In what areas do most immigrants work?

Del total de españoles con trabajo, la mayor parte trabaja en el *sector servicios*. El segundo lugar lo ocupa el *sector industrial*. El tercero lo ocupa el *sector agrícola*, y el cuarto lugar la *construcción*. Las mujeres trabajan preferentemente en el sector servicios, y en menor número en la agricultura y la industria. En la construcción, la mayoría de los trabajadores son hombres.

En España hay un gran número de trabajadores extranjeros, especialmente árabes, africanos, hispanoamericanos y también de Europa del Este, de países tales como Rumanía, Bulgaria. Estos inmigrantes trabajan preferentemente en los servicios, la agricultura, la construcción y en labores domésticas.

el empleo	*employment*
los trabajadores (extranjeros)	*(foreign) workers*
los hombres	*men*
las mujeres	*women*

12

me levanto a las siete

I get up at seven

In this unit you will learn
how to:

- talk about things you do
  regularly
- say how often you do certain
  things

▶ 1 ¿A qué hora te levantas?

Joaquín, an office clerk, **un administrativo**, tells Amaya about his daily routine.

1.1 Listen to the dialogue and, as you do, complete the sentences below. Key verbs here are **levantarse** *to get up*, **empezar** (e>ie) *to start*, **tardar** *to take* (time), **ir** *to go*, **almorzar** (o>ue) *to have lunch*, **salir** *to leave*, **volver** (o>ue) *to come back*, **acostarse** (o>ue) *to go to bed*.

a Joaquín se levanta a las .....
b Empieza a trabajar a las .....
c Tarda casi ..... en llegar a .....
d Va al trabajo en ..... y a veces en .....
e Almuerza en ..... cerca de .....
f Sale del trabajo a las .....y vuelve a casa sobre las .....
g Nunca se acuesta antes de las ..... u .....

Amaya ¿A qué hora te levantas?
Joaquín Normalmente me levanto a las siete. Empiezo a trabajar a las nueve, pero tardo casi una hora en llegar a la oficina.
Amaya ¿Cómo vas al trabajo?
Joaquín Voy en autobús, y a veces en el coche.
Amaya ¿Y dónde almuerzas?
Joaquín Almuerzo en un restaurante cerca de la oficina.
Amaya ¿A qué hora sales del trabajo?
Joaquín Salgo a las cinco y vuelvo a casa sobre las seis.
Amaya ¿Te acuestas muy tarde?
Joaquín Nunca me acuesto antes de las once u once y media.

1.2 Now read the dialogue and list the forms corresponding to each of the verbs in **1.1** above, for example 'levantarse' - 'me levanto', te levantas.

1.3 How would you express the following in Spanish? Read the dialogue again if necessary before you reply.

a I get up at a quarter past seven.
b I start work at half past nine.
c I go to work by train.
d I have lunch in the office.
e I never leave the office before half past five.

casi	*almost*	**nunca**	*never*
a veces	*sometimes*	**antes**	*before*
el trabajo	*work*	**u**	*or* (before 'o')
sobre	*about*		

▶ 2 ¿Qué haces los fines de semana?

Joaquín and Amaya tell each other what they do at the weekends.

2.1 Which of the activities below are mentioned by them? Listen and tick them as they come up. Note that Joaquín uses mostly the 'yo' '*I* ' form of the verb, whose present tense ending is normally -o while Amaya uses the 'nosotros/as' '*we*' form, ending in -**mos**.

Joaquín...
a se levanta tarde ☐
b escucha música ☐
c lee novelas ☐
d ve televisión ☐
e visita a sus padres ☐
f lee su correo ☐
g va al gimnasio ☐
h almuerza fuera ☐

Amaya y Ramiro...
i hacen la limpieza ☐
j hacen la compra ☐
k van a la piscina ☐
l preparan el almuerzo ☐
m echan una siesta ☐
n salen con los chicos ☐
ñ van al cine ☐
o invitan a sus padres ☐

Amaya ¿Qué haces los fines de semana?

Joaquín Pues, suelo levantarme tarde, escucho música, leo el periódico, veo la televisión, leo mi correo ... Los sábados por la tarde voy siempre al gimnasio y por la noche suelo salir con mi novia. A veces cenamos fuera o vamos al cine o a bailar. Y vosotros, ¿qué hacéis?

Amaya Los sábados por la mañana Ramiro y yo hacemos la limpieza y la compra, luego preparamos el almuerzo y por la tarde salimos con los chicos. Por la noche vemos alguna película en la televisión. Los domingos generalmente vamos a casa de mis padres.

2.2 Read the dialogue several times and then, without looking at the text, try listing as many of the activities as you can remember, using the 'yo' or the 'nosotros/as' form, as appropriate. Which of them do you normally do?

suelo... (from **soler**)	*I usually ...*
el periódico	*newspaper*
el correo (electrónico)	*e-mail*
siempre	*always*
la novia/el novio	*girl/boyfriend*
los chicos	*children*
alguno/a	*some, a*

How do you say it?

Talking about things you do regularly

a Asking people what time they do certain things:

¿A qué hora te levantas/se levanta Vd.?	*What time do you get up?*
¿A qué hora te acuestas/ se acuesta Vd.?	*What time do you go to bed?*
¿A qué hora empiezas/ empieza Vd. a trabajar?	*What time do you start work?*
¿A qué hora sales/sale Vd.?	*What time do you leave?*

b Saying what time you do certain things:

Me levanto/me acuesto a las 9:00.	*I get up/go to bed at 9.00.*
Empiezo a trabajar/Salgo del trabajo a las 8:00.	*I start/leave work at 8.00.*

c Asking people what they normally do:

¿Qué haces/hace Vd. (normalmente) los sábados/ fines de semana/en las vacaciones?	*What do you (normally) do on Saturdays/at the weekends/on your holidays?*

d Saying what you do and how often:

Voy siempre/normalmente al gimnasio.	*I always/normally go to the gym.*
A veces cenamos fuera.	*Sometimes we have dinner out.*
Nunca me acuesto antes de las 11:00.	*I never go to bed before 11.00.*
Suelo salir con mi novia.	*I usually go out with my girlfriend.*

Grammar

1 Talking about things you do regularly:
the present tense

a To talk about things you do regularly, you use the *present tense*. Below is the present tense of three regular verbs: **hablar** *to speak*, **comer** *to eat*, **escribir** *to write*.

	-ar verbs	**-er** verbs	**-ir** verbs
yo	hablo	como	escribo
tú	hablas	comes	escribes
él, ella, Vd.	habla	come	escribe
nosotros/as	hablamos	comemos	escribimos
vosotros/as	habláis	coméis	escribís
ellos/ellas/Vds.	hablan	comen	escriben

A veces hablo por teléfono con mis amigos.	*Sometimes I speak to my friends on the phone.*
Siempre comemos en casa.	*We always eat at home.*
Nunca escribo cartas.	*I never write letters.*

b Soler + infinitive

You can also talk about actions you do regularly by using the present tense of **soler** (o>ue) *to usually (do something)*, followed by an *infinitive* (the dictionary form of the verb).

Suelo conocer gente por Internet.	*I usually meet people through Internet.*
Suelen desayunar muy temprano.	*They usually have breakfast very early.*
Solemos ir al cine.	*We usually go to the cinema.*

2 Stem-changing verbs

In Units 3 and 5 you learned that some Spanish verbs, known as *stem-changing verbs*, undergo a vowel change in the stem (the verb minus the –**ar**, -**er**, -**ir**), in all forms of the present tense, except the **nosotros** and **vosotros** forms, but that their endings remain the same as for regular verbs. Examples of these were **querer** *to want* (Unit 5), in which the –**e** of the stem changes into –**ie** (e.g. **quiero** *I want*), and **poder** *to be able to, can* (Unit 3), in which the –**o** changes into –**ue** (e.g. **puedo** *I can*). In this unit you find **empezar** (e>ie) *to begin*, **almorzar** (o>ue) *to have lunch*, **volver** (o>ue) *to come back*, **acostarse** (o>ue) *to go to bed*, **soler** (o>ue) *to usually (do something)*, but there are many others. A few verbs change in a different way, for example **jugar** *to play*, in which the –**u** of the stem changes into **ue**, as in **juego** *I play*. Here are the full forms for **empezar**, **volver** and **jugar**:

e > ie	o > ue	u > ue
empiezo	vuelvo	juego
empiezas	vuelves	juegas
empieza	vuelve	juega
empezamos	volvemos	jugamos
empezáis	volvéis	jugáis
empiezan	vuelven	juegan

Empiezo muy temprano/ pronto por la mañana.	*I start very early in the morning.*
Vuelven a casa a almorzar.	*They come back home for lunch.*
Los sábados juego al fúbol.	*On Saturdays I play football.*

3 Irregular verbs

a In the present tense, some verbs are irregular only in the *first person singular*. **Salir** *to leave*, **ver** *to see*, **hacer** *to do, make*, belong in this category.

Salgo del trabajo a las seis.	*I leave/finish work at six.*
Por la noche **veo** televisión.	*In the evening I watch television*
Los lunes **hago** yoga.	*On Mondays I do yoga.*

b Ir *to go* is completely irregular.

Singular		Plural	
voy	*I go*	vamos	*we go*
vas	*you go* (inf)	vais	*you go* (inf)
va	*you go* (formal) *he, she, it goes*	van	*you go* (formal) *they go*

(See also **irse**, *to leave*, in **4c** below).

4 Me, te, se, nos, os, se: *reflexive pronouns*

a Definition

Levantarse *to get up*, like a number of other verbs, carries the particle **se**, literally *onself* , attached to it, and forms like *I get up, you get up*, carry the Spanish equivalent of words like *myself, yourself*, etc. : **me** (for **yo**), **te** (for **tú**), **se** (for **él, ella, Vd.**), **nos** (for **nosotros/as**), **os** (for **vosotros/as**) and **se** (for **ellos, ellas, Vds.**). These words, which are known as *reflexive pronouns*, refer back to the subject of the sentence, so in a number of verbs a difference in meaning may be established through their use.

Yo levanto (algo).	*I raise/lift* (something).
Yo me levanto.	*I get up.* (literally, *I myself get up*)

(See also Unit 8, paragraph 2 of Grammar).

b Usage

Usage does not always correspond to that of English. There are many verbs which function as reflexive in Spanish, but which are used without a reflexive pronoun in English, among them **acostarse** *to go to bed*, **irse** *to leave*, **llamarse** *to be called*,

sentarse *to sit down*. But note **divertirse** *to enjoy oneself*, **dedicarse a** *to devote oneself to*, in which the reflexive is made explicit in English.

c Forms

The endings of these verbs are the same as for regular verbs, and only the addition of **me, te, se,** etc., makes them different. Here's an example:

	levantarse *to get up*
yo	me levanto
tú	te levantas
él, ella, Vd.	se levanta
nosotros/as	nos levantamos
vosotros/as	os levantáis
ellos, ellas, Vds.	se levantan

Me levanto a las 7:00 y me acuesto a las 11:30.	*I get up at 7.00 and I go to bed at 11.30.*
¿A qué hora te vas al trabajo/a la universidad?	*What time do you leave for work/the university?*
Me voy a las 8:00.	*I leave at 8.00.*

d Position

Reflexive pronouns normally precede the verb, but when a main verb is followed by another form of the verb such as an infinitive, the pronoun can either precede the main verb or be attached to the infinitive:

No quiere acostarse. *Or* No **se** quiere acostar.	*He/she doesn't want to go to bed.*

▶ Pronunciation

y, as in 'yo' is pronounced like the 'y' in 'yes', but in some regions, notably Argentina and Uruguay, it is stronger and nearly like the 's' in 'pleasure'. In many areas too, 'y' is pronounced like the 'll' in 'calle'. 'Y', *'and'*, is pronounced like the 'e' in 'be'.

Practice with:

yo, yoga, yogur, desayuno, mayo
Yo desayuno en un bar de la calle Dos de mayo.
Yolanda hace yoga.

Practice

1 Palabra por palabra

Below are some key verbs related to daily activities. Look them up and classify them into the following categories:

a personal hygiene **b** personal appearance **c** getting dressed

1 ponerse la ropa	4 peinarse	7 afeitarse
2 bañarse	5 vestirse	8 lavarse
3 maquillarse	6 ducharse	9 lavarse los dientes

Note that **vestirse** is a stem-changing verb, with **e** changing into **i**, e.g. me **visto**. **Ponerse** is irregular in the first person singular of the present tense, me **pongo**.

2 La rutina de Ramiro

Ramiro is a very methodical man. Every morning he follows exactly the same routine. How would Ramiro tell someone what he does? Use the pictures to write a description. One of them has been done for you.

Me levanto a las seis.

3 Mi fin de semana

▶ Listen to Ana saying what she normally does at the weekends, and answer the questions below:

a What does Ana do after she gets up on Saturdays?
b What does she do after lunch?
c What does she do on Saturday night?
d What does she normally do on Sunday mornings?

las tostadas	toast	**la exposición**	exhibition
el cine	cinema	**el campo**	country
el teatro	theatre	**pasar**	to spend (time)
el concierto	concert	**algo ligero**	something light

4 ¿A qué hora ...?

How would you ask your new friend Antonio the following? Use an appropriate question word from the following:

¿dónde?, ¿a qué hora ...?, ¿qué?, ¿cómo?

a What time do you get up?
b How do you go to work?
c What time do you start work?
d Where do you have lunch?
e What time do you leave work?
f What do you do in the evening?

5 Ahora tú

Write a brief passage describing some of the things you do on a normal day or at the weekend, including times where appropriate. Use as models the dialogues and the Activities in the **Practice** section, including the listening comprehension transcript for Activity 3.

6 Un día en la vida de Plácido Domingo

Plácido Domingo, the famous Spanish tenor, talks to a journalist about some of his habits. As you read the interview, try answering the following questions. The key words below will help you to understand.

a What is his day like before a performance?
b What sort of meal does he have before a performance?
c How many hours does he normally sleep at night? And when
   he has a performace?
d Where does he normally spend his holidays?

¿Cómo es un día de Plácido Domingo antes de una función?

Completamente tranquilo, no acepto ningún compromiso, no hago
absolutamente nada. Me quedo en casa, repaso, estudio, leo ...

¿Alguna dieta especial?

Como una comida muy ligera, un poquito de pollo o un poco de
ternera y algo de sopa.

¿Cuántas horas duerme por la noche?

En días normales duermo ocho horas. El día de la función duermo
hasta once horas.

¿Dónde pasa sus vacaciones Plácido Domingo?

Depende, en la playa la mayoría de las veces.

la función	*performance*
el compromiso	*engagement*
me quedo (from **quedarse**)	*I stay*
repasar	*to rehearse, review*
una comida ligera	*a light meal*
un poquito	*a little bit*
la ternera	*veal*
duerme (from **dormir**)	*you sleep*
hasta	here, *up to*

i The following article looks at reading habits among Spanish
people. Think of reading habits in your own country before you
read the text.

What percentage of Spaniards never read? What are the most
popular newspapers and magazines? Do reading habits differ
between men and women? Read and find out.

Los españoles leen poco

En España, con alrededor de cuarenta millones de habitantes, casi la mitad de los españoles mayores de 18 años no lee nunca, y el 63 por ciento no compra libros. Lo que más se lee son los periódicos deportivos y las revistas del corazón, la más popular de ellas *¡Hola!*. De los periódicos serios, el más vendido es *El País*, con 400.000 ejemplares al día.

los españoles leen poco

Sólo doce millones de españoles leen periódicos, dieciocho millones leen revistas, treinta millones de personas ven televisión y sólo dos millones van al cine.

El hombre lee el doble de periódicos que la mujer; la mujer lee más revistas semanales. El hombre prefiere escuchar radio, pero hombres y mujeres ven por igual la televisión.

alrededor de	*around*
la mitad	*half*
leer	*to read*
el periódico deportivo	*sports paper*
la revista (del corazón)	(*true romance*) *magazine*
el más vendido	*the one that sells most*
por igual	*equally*

13

me gusta

I like it

In this unit you will learn how to:
- express intentions
- say what you want to do
- express liking and dislike

▶ 1 ¿Qué vas a hacer esta noche?

Miguel, Nieves and Eduardo talk about their plans for tonight, **esta noche,** and about some of the things they like.

1.1 What is each person going to do? First, look at the key words and phrases on page 139, then listen to the dialogue several times and match the names with the drawings, inserting the appropriate numbers in the boxes next to each name.

Nieves ☐   Miguel ☐   Eduardo ☐

Miguel	¿Qué vas a hacer esta noche, Nieves?
Nieves	Voy a ir al cine con David.
Miguel	Te gusta el cine, ¿no?
Nieves	Sí, me gusta mucho. ¿Quieres venir conmigo?
Miguel	No, gracias, voy a salir con Raquel. Vamos a ir a una discoteca. A Raquel le encanta bailar y a mí también.
Nieves	Y tú Eduardo, ¿vas a salir?
Eduardo	No, estoy muy cansado. Voy a ver el tenis en la televisión.

1.2 Now read the dialogue and say how the following is expressed:

a I'm going (to go) to the cinema.
b Are you going out?
c Do you like cinema?
d I like it very much.
e Raquel loves dancing.

voy a + infinitive	*I'm going to + -ing*
gustar	*to like*
encantar	*to love* (something/doing something)
querer + infinitive	*to want* + infinitive
venir (e>ie)	*to come*
conmigo	*with me*
estar cansado/a	*to be tired*

▶ 2 Me gusta ir de camping

Nieves and Eduardo talk about the things they like to do on their holidays

2.1 First, look at some of the things people like to do on their holidays. Can you match the pictures to the sentences below?

Me gusta

1 ir de camping/acampar   4 dormir hasta muy tarde
2 viajar al extranjero   5 nadar
3 montar en bicicleta   6 tomar el sol

2.2 Which of the activities above does Eduardo like to do on his holidays? Which does Nieves like to do? Listen and find out.

Nieves	¿Qué haces en tus vacaciones, Eduardo?
Eduardo	Me gusta ir de camping, montar en bicicleta, viajar al extranjero... En mis próximas vacaciones quiero ir a Nueva York.
Nieves	Me gusta mucho Nueva York, pero viajar en avión no me gusta nada.
Eduardo	A mí tampoco. Y tú, ¿qué piensas hacer este verano?
Nieves	David y yo vamos a pasar diez días en Ibiza. Nos encanta la playa, tomar el sol, nadar y dormir hasta muy tarde.

2.3 Now read the dialogue and answer the following questions:

a Where does Eduardo want to go on his next holiday?
b How does Nieves feel about that place?
c What is it they both dislike?
d What are Nieves's and David's plans for this summer?

próximo/a	*next*
no me gusta nada	*I don't like it at all*
tampoco	*neither/not...either*
pensar (e>ie)	*to think*
este verano	*this summer*

How do you say it?

Expressing intentions

¿Qué va(s) a hacer?

What are you going to do? (formal/inf)

¿Qué piensa(s) hacer?

What are you planning to do?

Voy a salir/ver el tenis.

I'm going (to go) out/ watch tennis.

Vamos a pasar/estar una semana allí.

We're going to spend a week there/be there for a week.

Saying what you want to do

Quiero/queremos viajar/ir a los Estados Unidos.

I want/we want to travel/go to the United States.

To ask someone what he or she wants to do or whether he or she wants to do something, you can say:

¿Qué quiere(s) hacer?	*What do you want to do?* (formal/inf)
¿Quiere(s) venir conmigo?	*Do you want to come with me?*

Expressing liking and dislike

¿Te gusta/gustan?	*Do you like it/them?* (inf)
¿Le gusta/gustan?	*Do you (formal)/Does he/she/it like it/them?*
Me gusta/gustan (mucho).	*I like it/them (very much).*
Me gusta el teatro/chatear.	*I like theatre/to chat (Internet)*
No me gusta/gustan (nada).	*I don't like it/them (at all).*
Me encanta/encantan.	*I love it/them.*

Grammar

1 Expressing intentions

To express intentions you can use:

a *Present tense* of **ir** (*to go*) + **a** + infinitive (the form of the verb ending in **–ar, -er, -ir**). For the present tense of **ir** see Unit 12.

¿Qué vas/vais a hacer?	*What are you going to do?*
Voy a hacer la compra.	*I'm going to do the shopping.*
Vamos a acostarnos.	*We're going (to go) to bed.*

b **Pensar** *(to think, be planning to,* e>ie*)* + infinitive

¿Qué piensa hacer Vd.?	*What are you planning to do (thinking of doing)?*
Pienso salir.	*I'm planning to go out (thinking of going out).*

2 Saying what you want to do

To say what you want or do not want to do and to ask someone what he/she wants to do, use **querer** (*to want,* e>ie).

Quiero estudiar español.	*I want to study Spanish.*
Queremos vivir en América del Sur.	*We want to live in South America.*

3 Expressing liking and dislike:

Gustar *to like,* **encantar, fascinar** *to like very much, to love*

a To say you like or do not like something use **gustar,** which literally means *'is pleasing'.* The person who does the liking – the person who is *being pleased -* goes before **gustar.** So you literally say *'to me, to you'* etc. *'is pleasing':* **Me gusta el sol** *I like the sun* (literally, *To me is pleasing the sun* or *The sun pleases me*), **Me gustar nadar** *I like swimming* (literally, *To me is pleasing to swim* or *To swim pleases me),* or simply **Me gusta** *I like it* (literally, *To me it is pleasing*). If what you like is *plural,* use **gustan: Me gustan** *I like them* (literally, *To me they are pleasing*), and to say that you do *not* like something, simply place **no** before **me, te, le, nos,** etc.: **No nos gustan** *We don't like them.*

You'll find a list of the words for 'to me', 'to you', etc., (technically, *indirect object pronouns*) in Unit 8 and in 9.1 of **Grammar summary.**

b To express stronger liking use **encantar,** or **fascinar** for even stronger liking: **Me encanta/fascina la comida española** *I love Spanish food,* **Le encantan/fascinan las teleseries** *He/she loves TV series.*

c For emphasis or to express contrast between your likes and someone else's, use **'a'** followed by one of the following words: **mí** (for **yo**), **ti** (for **tú**), **usted, él, ella, nosotros/as, vosotros/as, ellos, ellas: A mí me gusta el jazz** *I like jazz,* **¿A ti te gusta?** *Do you like it?,* **A él/ella no le gusta nada** *He she doesn't like it at all.*

d **'A'** must also be used before a person's name when you want to make clear who does the liking: **A Isabel le gustan los perros, pero a Carlos no** *Isabel likes dogs but Carlos doesn't.*

e You also need to use **'a'** in short questions and replies: (**A mi madre le encantan los gatos** *My mother loves cats*) **¿Y a ti?** *And what about you?,* **A mí también** *So do I,* **A él no, y a ella tampoco** *He doesn't, and she doesn't either.*

▶ Pronunciation

'd' is pronounced approximately like English 'd' in 'day' after 'l', 'n', and at the beginning of a word, when this is preceded by a pause: 'falda', 'andar', 'deporte'. In other positions 'd' is pronounced nearly like the 'th' in 'that': 'verde', 'Adela'. There are, however, regional differences: in Andalusia and certain parts of Latin America, for example, in informal language, 'd' in final position, as in 'Madrid' and between vowels, as in 'pescado', is pronounced very softly or not at all.

Practise with:

A David le gusta andar y hacer deportes todos los días, sobre todo nadar.

Adela va a pasar diez días en Andalucía.

Eduardo está cansado y va a quedarse en casa para ver un dvd.

Practice

1 Un email

Angela, who is studying Spanish, is sending an e-mail to her friend Mario. Can you help her with some of the verbs? Put the infinitives in brackets in the appropriate form, using pronouns where necessary.

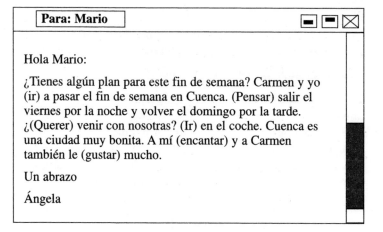

> **Para: Mario**   ▬ ▬ ☒
>
> Hola Mario:
>
> ¿Tienes algún plan para este fin de semana? Carmen y yo (ir) a pasar el fin de semana en Cuenca. (Pensar) salir el viernes por la noche y volver el domingo por la tarde. ¿(Querer) venir con nosotras? (Ir) en el coche. Cuenca es una ciudad muy bonita. A mí (encantar) y a Carmen también le (gustar) mucho.
>
> Un abrazo
>
> Ángela

2 Ahora tú

Send an e-mail to your Spanish friend saying what you are planning to do at the weekend and invite him/her to join you.

3 De vacaciones

Your friend Rocío is going on holiday. How would you ask her about her travel plans? Use question words from the following: ¿(a)dónde?, ¿cuándo?, ¿cuánto tiempo?, ¿qué?, ¿con quién?

a Ask where she's going to go this summer.
b ... who she's going with.
c ... how long she's going to stay.
d ... where she's going to stay.
e ... what she likes to do on her holidays.
f ... whether she likes swimming.
g ... when she's coming back.

alojarse to stay at	**¿(a)dónde?** where (to)?

4 ¿Qué te gusta hacer?

A group of people where asked what they like to do in their spare time, 'el tiempo libre'. Look at their answers, which are placed in order of preference below, and then fill in your own preferences next to each of the following phrases:

Me encanta .....   (No) **me gusta nada**...
Me gusta .....   **Detesto** ...

¿Qué te gusta hacer en tu tiempo libre?

1	ver TV/cable/dvd	7	viajar
2	hacer deportes	8	andar
3	escuchar música	9	ir al cine
4	realizar tareas domésticas	10	trabajar/estudiar
5	salir con amigos/ir a fiestas	11	ir al teatro/a conciertos
6	leer	12	asistir a cursos

andar	to walk
asistir a cursos	to attend courses

▶ 5 Me encanta cocinar

Lola talked to a magazine about her likes and interests. Complete the text with the correct form of the verbs in brackets, then listen to the recording.

a mí me encanta planchar

A mí (gustar) estar con mi familia, mis amigos y mis dos perros. (Encantar) cocinar y arreglar la casa, pero (detestar) planchar. (Fascinar) la lectura, especialmente la novela y la poesía, y también (gustar) la fotografía y la pintura. Los fines de semana (gustar) desayunar en la cama, levantarme tarde y salir de compras con Pedro, mi marido. En las vacaciones, a Pedro y a mí (gustar) ir a la playa. A él y a mí (encantar) nadar y tomar el sol. A Pedro también (gustar) el campo, pero a mí no (gustar) nada.

cocinar	*to cook*	**la lectura**	*reading*
arreglar	*to tidy up*	**la poesía**	*poetry*

6 Pasatiempos

Four people looking for correspondents wrote to a magazine and listed their hobbies. Look up the new words in your dictionary and then answer the questions below.

> **Elvira Gutiérrez, 25 años, secretaria**
>
> Calle Juárez, 6, Jalisco, México
> **Pasatiempos:** Me gusta bailar, ver películas de terror, leer revistas, salir con amigos, jugar al baloncesto.

David Escobar, 37 años, psicólogo

Calle Lorca, 12, 4º, 3ª, Burgos, España

Pasatiempos: Me interesa conocer gente por internet, escribir cuentos, ir al teatro y conciertos, escuchar música clásica, hacer atletismo, ver programas deportivos en la tele.

Cristina López, 18 años, estudiante

Paseo del Mar, 452, Valparaíso, Chile

Pasatiempos: Me encanta tocar la guitarra y cantar, dibujar, ver tele, cocinar, ir a discotecas, enviar mails a mis amigos, chatear en el computador, jugar con videojuegos y salir en mi bici.

Daniel Miranda, 28 años, futbolista

Calle de la Luz, 86, 5º, B, Málaga, España

Pasatiempos: Me gusta jugar al fútbol, hacer footing, pescar, ver películas de acción y de guerra, viajar al extranjero, jugar en el ordenador, bajarme música de Internet.

Which of the people above likes to do each of the following?

a draw
b play basketball
c watch war films
d sing

e watch horror films
f write short stories
g travel abroad
h watch sports programmes

hacer footing	*to jog, to go jogging*
chatear	*to chat* (computer)
el ordenador	*computer* (Spain)
la computadora/el computador	*computer* (LAm)
el videojuego	*video game*
la bici (short for **bicicleta**)	*bike*
bajar(se)	*to download*

7 Ahora tú

Write about your own interests using the advertisements above as a model. Note the use of **me interesa** *I'm interested in*, from **interesar** *to be interested in*, a verb which functions like **gustar**.

i What would you say is the main leisure activity in your country? What do you think Spanish and Latin american people like to do? Read and find out.

A los españoles y latinoamericanos les encanta ver televisión. Cada español ve unas tres horas y treinta minutos de televisión al día. Los programas más populares son los "del corazón" y la telerrealidad, y también las películas y teleseries o " culebrones" y, por supuesto, los deportivos. Entre los deportes, lejos el más popular es el fútbol, aunque en los últimos años se aprecia un mayor interés por otros deportes, especialmente el tenis.

la telerrealidad	*Big Brother type of programmes*
los programas del corazón	*entertainment TV programmes which tend to focus on people's private lives*
los culebrones	*soap operas usually from Latin America*

Nos encanta esquiar ·

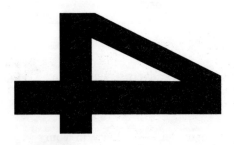

14

¿dígame?

hello?

In this unit you will learn how to:
- ask to speak to someone on the phone
- take and leave messages
- make appointments on the phone
- say what you or others are doing

▶ 1 ¿Quiere dejarle algún recado?

Carlos, from London, is trying to reach señor Bravo at a Spanish firm.

1.1 Why can't señor Bravo answer the phone? Listen and choose the right activity from the drawings below.

1. **2.** **3.**

Secretaria	Agrohispana, ¿dígame?
Carlos	Buenos días. ¿Está el señor Bravo, por favor?
Secretaria	¿De parte de quién?
Carlos	De Carlos Miranda.
Secretaria	Un momentito, por favor... ¿Señor Miranda?, el señor Bravo no puede ponerse en este momento. Está hablando por otra línea. ¿Quiere dejarle algún recado?
Carlos	Por favor, dígale que voy a llamar más tarde. Necesito hablar con él.
Secretaria	Muy bien, le daré su recado.

1.2 Now read the dialogue and try learning those expressions which are proper to the use of the phone. Listen to the dialogue again a few times and then put the sentences in the following dialogue in the right order.

- No, no está en este momento.
- De José Luis.
- Sí, ¿diga?
- No, luego la llamo.
- ¿Está María?
- ¿Quieres dejarle algún recado?
- ¿De parte de quién?

¿de parte de quién?	*who's calling?*
no puede ponerse	*he/she can't answer/come to the phone*
¿quiere dejarle algún recado?	*would you like to leave him/her a message?*
dígale que ...	*tell him/her that... (formal)*
le daré su recado	*I'll give him/her your message*
luego	*later*

▶ 2 En seguida le pongo

Luis phones his friend Gloria at work.

2.1 Listen to the conversation several times and, as you do so, make a note of the expressions used to say each of the following:

a I'd like to speak to ...
b This is not her extension.
c It's (extension) 368.
d Can you put me through to ...?

Voz 1 Ibertur, ¿dígame?

Luis Quisiera hablar con Gloria Araya, por favor.

Voz 1 Se ha equivocado. Su extensión no es esta. Es la tres, sesenta y ocho.

No cuelgue, por favor. En seguida le pongo.

Luis Gracias.

Voz 1 ¡Oiga!, está comunicando. No se retire.

Voz 2 Sí, ¿diga?

Luis ¿Me puede poner con Gloria Araya, por favor?

Voz 2 Sí, ahora mismo se pone.

2.2 Study the expressions in the box below before you listen to the dialogue again and read it a few times. Then try playing each one of the parts.

se ha equivocado	*you've got the wrong number*
no cuelgue	*don't hang up*
en seguida le pongo	*I'll put you through right away*
¡oiga!	*hello?*
está comunicando	*it's engaged*
no se retire	*hold the line!*
ahora mismo se pone	*he/she'll be with you right away*

i Expressions such as **no cuelgue**, *don't hang up*, **no se retire**, *hold the line!* (both of which are *commands*, covered in Units 23 and 24), like some other expressions used on the phone, are *set phrases*, and you can learn them as such, without the need to go into their grammar at this stage.

▶ 3 Hora con el doctor

Mónica is trying to make an appointment with her doctor.

3.1 Listen and answer the following questions.

a When does she want her appointment for?
b Which day is she offered instead?
c What times is she offered?
d Which time suits her?

Recepcionista	Consulta, ¿dígame?
Mónica	Quisiera pedir hora con el doctor para mañana.
Recepcionista	Lo siento, pero no hay hora disponible hasta el jueves, a las nueve y media, o por la tarde a las cuatro y cuarto.
Mónica	A las nueve y media me va bien.
Recepcionista	¿Su nombre, por favor?
Mónica	Mónica Urrutia.

3.2 How would you express the following in Spanish?

a I'd like to ask for an appointment with the dentist (**el/la dentista**) for Monday.

b There's no appointment available until Wednesday at 10.20 or in the afternoon at 2.45.

c A quarter to three suits me well.

---

no hay hora disponible	*there's no appointment available*
me va bien	*it suits me*

---

i The general word for 'appointment' in Spanish is **la cita**, which also means 'date':

Tengo una cita con el/la gerente a las 9:30, *I have an appointment with the manager at 9.30.* The word **la hora** is used for appointments with doctors, dentists, hairdressers, etc.: **Tengo hora con el/la doctor/a a las 5:15,** *I have an appointment with the doctor at 5.15.* To request an appointment you can say: **Quisiera pedir (una) cita para mañana/las 11:00,** *I'd like to make/ask for an appointment for tomorrow/11.00,* or **Quería pedir hora con.../para el lunes,** *I'd like to make/ask for an appointment with.../for Monday.* And when you arrive for your appointment you may be asked **¿Tiene usted cita/hora?,** *Do you have an appointment?*

How do you say it?

Asking to speak to someone on the phone and replying

¿Dígame?/¿Diga?/¿Sí?	*Hello?* (especially Spain)
¿Está María/la señora Díaz?	*Is María/Mrs Díaz in?*
Quisiera hablar con Juan/el señor Ríos.	*I'd like to speak to Juan/Mr Ríos.*
¿Me puede poner con Carmen?	*Can you put me through to Carmen?*
¡Al habla!/Soy yo.	*Speaking.*
¿De parte de quién?	*Who's speaking?*
De Cristóbal.	*Cristobal.*
¿Quién lo(le)/la llama?	*Who's calling him/her?*
Soy Dolores.	*I'm Dolores.*

José/la señorita Peña no está.	*José/Miss Peña is not in.*
En seguida le pongo.	*I'll put you through right away.*
No puede ponerse.	*He/she can't come to the phone.*
Ahora (mismo) se pone.	*He/she will be with you right away.*
Se ha equivocado (de número).	*You've got the wrong number.*

Taking and leaving messages

¿Quiere dejar(le) algún recado?	*Would you like to leave (him/her) a message?*
Por favor dígale/dile que ...	*Please tell him/her that...* (form/inf)

Making appointments on the phone

Quisiera pedir hora con el doctor (para ...)	*I'd like to ask for an appointment with the doctor (for ...)*
Quería pedir/solicitar una cita/entrevista con la señora Salas.	*I'd like to ask for/request an appointment/interview with Mrs Salas.*

Saying what you or others are doing

Está hablando por otra línea.	*He/she is speaking on another line.*
Estoy/Está atendiendo a un cliente.	*I am/He/she is looking after a client.*

i The following passage tells you how to make certain types of calls in Spain.

Para llamar por teléfono fuera de España tienes que **marcar,** *to dial*, el 00 y luego el **prefijo,** *code*, del país al que quieres llamar, el prefijo de la ciudad, y después el número al que quieres llamar. Por ejemplo, para llamar a Londres marcas 00-44 (Reino Unido) + 20 (Londres) + número que deseas. Para hacer **una llamada personal,** *a personal call*, o **una llamada de cobro revertido,** *a transferred charge call*, tienes que llamar a la **operadora** o al **operador,** *operator*, y decir: **"Quiero hacer una llamada...",** *'I want to make a ... call'*.

Grammar

1 Saying what you are doing

To express ideas such as 'He is speaking', 'She is working', which refer to actions taking place at the moment of speaking, Spanish uses **estar** *to be*, followed by the equivalent of *–ing*, as in 'speaking', 'working', which is known as *gerund*. This is formed by adding **–ando** to the stem of **–ar** verbs, and **–iendo** to that of **–er** and **–ir** verbs: habl**ar** - habl**ando**, hac**er** – hac**iendo**, escrib**ir** – escrib**iendo**

¿Qué está haciendo tu hermano?	*What is your brother doing?*
Está llamando a un amigo.	*He's calling a friend.*
¿Qué estás haciendo?	*What are you doing?*
Estoy escribiendo un mail.	*I'm writing an e-mail.*

Note the use of the same construction in

Está comunicando.	*It's engaged.* (literally, *It's communicating*)

2 Poner *to put through*, ponerse al teléfono *to come to the phone*

In Unit 7 you learned to use **poner** in the context of shopping. As the English verb 'to put', **poner** has a number of other meanings, for example 'to put through':

¿Me puede poner con Enrique?	*Can you put me through to Enrique?*
¿Me pones con tu madre, por favor?	*Will you put me through to your mother, please?*
En seguida le/te pongo	*I'll put you through right away.* (formal/inf)

Ponerse (**al teléfono**), 'to come to the phone' (literally 'to put yourself to the phone'), is another useful expression to learn in this context. The phrase 'al teléfono' is normally left out.

Ahora se pone.	*He/she will be with you right now.*

3 Latin American usage on the phone

Latin American usage on the phone is not much different from that of Peninsular Spanish, but there are a few expressions which are different or more proper to the area.

Hello?	'¿Aló?' (especially South America), '¿bueno?' (Mexico), '¿hola?' (Argentina, Uruguay)
Speaking	'Con él/ella (habla)', 'con él mismo/ella misma', 'habla Marta'
You've got the wrong number	'Está equivocado/a' or simply 'equivocado'
It's engaged	Está ocupado.

Practice

1 Una conversación telefónica

Ricardo phoned his friend Leonor but she wasn't at home. How would you fill the gaps in this conversation between Ricardo and the speaker at the other end of the line?

- ¿Dígame?
- ¿..........?
- No, Leonor está en la universidad. ¿..........?
- Soy Ricardo.
- ¿..........?
- Sí, por favor. Dígale que me llame al número 580 2133, que necesito hablar urgentemente con ella.
- Muy bien.

▶ 2 ¿Qué está haciendo?

Listen to Raquel phoning her friend Lorenzo at home.

a What is Lorenzo doing? Choose the right picture below.
b What message does Raquel leave for him?

> **la entrada**   *ticket*

3 ¿Me puede poner con la señora Smith?

A Spanish-speaking person phones your place of work and asks to speak to one of your colleagues. Follow the guidelines in English and fill in your part of the conversation.

– *Hello?*
– ¿Me puede poner con la señora Smith, por favor?
– *Mrs Smith can't come to the phone at the moment. She's having lunch with a client. Who's calling?*
– Soy Andrés Calle, de Málaga.
– *Would you like to leave her a message?*
– Por favor, dígale que la voy a llamar dentro de una hora.
– *Very well, Mr Calle. I'll give her your message.*
– Perdone, el señor Roberts, ¿está en su despacho hoy?
– *Yes, Mr Roberts is in. Please hold the line! He'll be with you right away.*

4 Un momento, por favor

While waiting to be served at a travel agency you hear the receptionist talk to different people on the phone. Complete her sentences with the proper form of the verbs in brackets.

a Hola Ana, soy Camila. Mira, ¿me (*poner*) con Miguel, por favor? La gerente (*necesitar*) hablar con él.

b ¿El señor Ortíz? Lo siento, el señor Ortíz está (*atender*) a una clienta en este momento. ¿(*Querer*) usted dejarle algún recado?

c ¿La señora Martínez? Muy bien, un momentito, por favor. Ahora (*ponerse*).

d Por favor, no (*retirarse*). En seguida (yo) le (*poner*) con ella.

e Un momento, por favor. No (*colgar*).

f ¿Quiere usted esperar un momento, por favor? La extensión del señor González está (*comunicar*).

▶ **5 Una entrevista**

Sandra, a graphic designer, has seen the job advertisements, 'los anuncios', below and she telephones to ask for an interview. How does she express the following? Listen and find out.

Diseñadora Gráfica

Súper despierta y con la mejor disposición.

Necesita
Agencia de Publicidad
Llamar por entrevista al
fono: 246 08 17

DISEÑADOR GRÁFICO

Ambiente Macintosh, 3 años
Conocimientos:
Page Maker 7.0,
Freehand, Photoshop,
Disponibilidad inmediata.
Solicitar entrevista:
Lunes 14 ☎ 555.00.68
Depto. Publicidad

a I'm phoning about the advertisement for the post of graphic designer.

b I'd like to ask for an interview.

c Yes, half past nine suits me well.

llamar por	*to call about*
el anuncio	*advertisement*
el puesto	*post, job*
solicitar	*to request, ask for*

15

¿cuándo naciste?

when were you born?

In this unit you will learn how to:
- ask and give biographical information
- say how long ago something happened
- say how long you have been doing something (1)

▶ 1 ¿Cuándo llegaste?

Raúl and Gloria work in a hotel in Madrid. In the first dialogue Gloria asks Raúl about some important events in his life.

1.1 Here's the English for Gloria's questions. What are Raúl's answers? Listen and find out.

a When did you arrive in Madrid?
b How long ago did you meet Clara?
c When did you (two) get married?

Gloria	¿Cuándo llegaste a Madrid?
Raúl	Llegué en diciembre de 1997.
Gloria	¿Cuánto tiempo hace que conociste a Clara?
Raúl	La conocí hace un año y medio.
Gloria	¿Y cuándo os casasteis?
Raúl	Nos casamos en octubre del año pasado.

Nos casamos el año pasado

1.2 Read the dialogue now and then play, first Gloria's part, then Raúl's until you feel confident with the new language.

conocer	(here) *to meet* (for the first time)
hace	(here) *ago*
casarse	*to get married*
el año pasado	*last year*

▶ 2 Trabajé en Sevilla

Raúl asks Gloria about her life before she came to work in Madrid.

2.1 How long has Gloria been working in the hotel, and where did she live and work before? Listen and find out.

Raúl	¿Cuánto tiempo llevas trabajando aquí?
Gloria	Llevo tres años en este hotel.
Raúl	¿Dónde trabajaste antes?
Gloria	Trabajé dos años en Sevilla, en un hotel más pequeño.
Raúl	¿Viviste mucho tiempo en Sevilla?
Gloria	Sí, viví allí casi cinco años. Estudié en Sevilla.

2.2 Read the dialogue now, study the vocabulary and related grammar notes and then give the Spanish for

a I've been five years in Spain.
b I worked in Salamanca for two years.
c I studied Spanish there.

¿Cuánto tiempo llevas ...?	*How long have you been ...?*
¿Dónde trabajaste?	*Where did you work?*
¿Viviste mucho tiempo en...?	*Did you live a long time in...?*

▶ 3 ¿Dónde naciste?

Raúl is getting a little more personal and he asks Gloria some more questions about her life.

3.1 Where and when was Gloria born? Listen and find out.

Raúl   ¿Dónde naciste?

Gloria   Nací en Santander.

Raúl   ¿Cuándo naciste?

Gloria   Nací el 15 de marzo de 1983. ¿Y tú?

Raúl   Yo nací el 4 de abril del setenta y nueve, y Clara nació en octubre de 1981. Soy un año y medio mayor que ella.

3.2 Now read the dialogue, study the vocabulary and complete the following sentences with information about yourself.

a Nací en ...
b Nací el ...

¿cuándo?	*when*	**nacer**	*to be born*

How do you say it?

Asking and giving biographical information

¿Dónde/cuándo naciste/ nació Vd.?	*Where/when were you born?*
Nací en Toledo/1965/el 20 de enero de 1980.	*I was born in Toledo/ 1965/on 20th January 1980.*

Él/ella nació en el (año) 2001.	*He/she was born in (the year) 2001.*
¿Dónde estudiaste/estudió Vd.?	*Where did you study?*
Estudié en ...	*I studied in ...*
¿Dónde trabajaste/trabajó Vd. (antes)?	*Where did you work (before)?*
Trabajé en .../como ...	*I worked in .../as ...*

Asking and saying how long ago something happened

¿Cuánto tiempo hace que lo or le/la conociste/ conoció Vd.?	*How long ago did you meet him/her?*
Lo or le/la conocí hace un año/el año pasado.	*I met him/her a year ago/last year.*

Asking and saying how long someone has been doing something

¿Cuánto tiempo llevas/lleva Vd. trabajando/ viviendo aquí?	*How long have you been working/living here?*
Llevo un año (trabajando/ viviendo) aquí.	*I've been (working/living) here for a year.*

llevo diez años
jugando al tenis

Grammar

1 Meses y fechas (*Months and dates*)

Months, like the days of the week, are not written with capital letters in Spanish.

enero	*January*	mayo	*May*	se(p)tiembre	*September*
febrero	*February*	junio	*June*	octubre	*October*
marzo	*March*	julio	*July*	noviembre	*November*
abril	*April*	agosto	*August*	diciembre	*December*

To say 'in', as 'in January', use en: **en enero**.

To say 'on', as 'on 20th March', use el: **el 20 de marzo**.

Before the year, use de: **el 18 de julio de 2007**.

2 Saying what you did or what happened: *the preterite tense*

To say what you did at some specific point in the past, as in *She finished last year,* you need the simple past, which is known as *preterite tense*: **Terminó el año pasado**. There are two sets of endings for the preterite tense, one for **–ar** verbs and another one for verbs in **–er** and **–ir**. The first person plural **nosotros/as** of **–ar** and **-ir** verbs is the same as for the present tense. Here are the preterite forms of three regular verbs: **trabajar** *to work*, **conocer** *to know, meet*, **vivir** *to live*.

yo	trabaj**é**	conoc**í**	viv**í**
tú	trabaj**aste**	conoc**iste**	viv**iste**
él/ella/Vd.	trabaj**ó**	conoc**ió**	viv**ió**
nosotros/as	trabaj**amos**	conoc**imos**	viv**imos**
vosotros/as	trabaj**asteis**	conoc**isteis**	viv**isteis**
ellos/ellas/Vds.	trabaj**aron**	conoc**ieron**	viv**ieron**

Trabajé dos años en Jamaica.	*I worked for two years in Jamaica.*
Conocí a Julia en el año 2000.	*I met Julia in the year 2000.*
Vivimos juntos varios años.	*We lived for several years together.*

3 Spelling-changing verbs

A few verbs change their spelling - the consonant before the verb ending - in the first person singular of the preterite tense.

a Verbs ending in **–gar** change 'g' tu **gu** before 'e': **Llegué** (from **llegar**) **ayer** , *I arrived yesterday.*

b Those in **–car** change 'c' to **que**: **Lo busqué** (from **buscar**), *I looked for it.*

c Verbs ending in **–zar**, for example **empezar**, *to begin, start,* change 'z' to c before 'e': **Empecé anoche** *I started last night.*

For irregular preterite forms see Unit 16.

4 Time phrases associated with the preterite

The following words and expressions are normally associated with the preterite. Try learning them by using them in sentences with regular verbs:

anoche	*last night*
ayer	*yesterday*
anteayer/antes de ayer (**antier** in some Latin American countries)	*the day before yesterday*
el lunes/mes/año/verano/ invierno pasado	*last Monday/month/year/ summer/winter*
la semana/Navidad/ primavera pasada	*last week/Christmas/spring*
en 1945, en el sesenta y tres, en los (años) ochenta	*in 1945, in (the year) sixty-three, in the eighties*
hace un año/mucho tiempo	*a year/long time ago.*

5 ¿Cuánto tiempo llevas...? *How long have you been...?*

In Unit 11 you learned to use the construction **hace + que + present tense** verb to say how long you have been doing something: **Hace un mes que trabajo aquí,** *I've been working here for a month.* An alternative way of expressing the same is by using a construction with **llevar** followed by a *time phrase* and the **–ando** or **–iendo** form of the verb (known as *gerund*) corresponding to the '-*ing*' form in English (see Unit 14).

¿Cuánto tiempo llevas trabajando aquí/ estudiando español?	*How long have you been working here/studying Spanish?*

Llevo un año trabajando   *I've been working here/*
    aquí/estudiando español.   *studying Spanish for a year.*

If the context is clear, especially with verbs such as **vivir, trabajar, estudiar,** the **-ando** or **–iendo** form of the verb may be left out.

Lleva seis meses en la   *He/she's been in the company/*
    empresa/en esta   *in this university for six*
    universidad.   *months.*

Llevamos mucho tiempo   *We've been a long time in this*
    en esta casa.   *house.*

6 ¿Cuánto tiempo hace? *How long ago?*

To ask or say how long ago something happened use **hace** with a verb in the *preterite tense.*

¿Cuánto tiempo hace que   *How long ago did you arrive*
    llegaste a España?   *in Spain?*

Llegué hace dos años. *Or*   *I arrived two years ago.*

Hace dos años que llegué.

7 Personal 'a'

Note the use of 'a' before a name or a word referring to a person in sentences like the following. This is a feature of Spanish that has no equivalent in English:

Conocí **a** Luis hace dos años.   *I met Luis two years ago.*

Invité **a** todos mis amigos.   *I invited all my friends.*

Practice

1 La historia de mi vida

Isabel, a journalist, tells her life-story. Can you match the pictures with the sentences?

a Me casé con Antonio   **d** Terminé la carrera
    en 2004.   a los 23.

b Entré en la universidad   **e** Empecé el colegio a los
    a la edad de 18 años.   6 años.

c Nací en Aranjuez el 7 de   **f** Empecé a trabajar como
    mayo de 1976.   periodista en enero de 2000.

entrar	(here) to start	la carrera	career
a la edad de	at the age of	como	as

2 Con relación a su anuncio ...

Sebastián, an unemployed hotel receptionist, wrote the following letter in reply to a job advertisement. Complete the letter by changing the infinitives in brackets into the right form of the *preterite tense*.

Muy señor mío:

Me llamo Sebastián García Robles e hice estudios de hostelería en el Instituto Mediterráneo de Málaga, los que (terminar) en 1994. Entre 1995 y 2001 (trabajar) como recepcionista en el Hotel Andaluz de Marbella. En junio de 2002 (trasladarse) a Alicante e (ingresar) en el grupo hotelero Iberotur. (Desempeñar) el puesto de recepcionista en el Hotel Don Jaime, cargo que (ocupar) hasta diciembre de 2005, fecha en que (perder) mi empleo por reducción de plantilla ...

hice (from **hacer**)	*I did*	**el puesto/cargo**	*post*
trasladarse	*to move*	**ocupar**	*to hold* (job)
ingresar	*to join*	**perder**	*to lose*
desempeñar	*to hold* (job)	**la plantilla**	*workforce*

i En cartas formales o comerciales, como la anterior, se utiliza la expresión **Muy señor/a mío/a** *Dear Sir/Madam*. También puedes utilizar la expresión **Distinguido/a señor/a** o **Estimado/a señor/a** *Dear Sir/Madam*. La fórmula más común para terminar una carta formal es **Atentamente** o **Muy atentamente** *Yours sincerely*.

Note the use of a colon (dos puntos) instead of a comma (una coma) after the salutation, as in **Muy señor mío:**

3 Una entrevista

You have been asked to conduct a formal interview in Spanish. How would you say the following? Use the *usted* form of the verb.

a Where were you born?

b When were you born?

c What did you study?

d When did you finish your studies (**los estudios**)?

e Where do you work now?

f How long have you been working there? (use **llevar**)

g Where did you work before?

4 ¿Cuánto tiempo llevas...?

How would you ask Soledad how long she has been doing each of the following, and how would she reply?

4.1 First, match the drawings with the phrases below.

a vivir en Londres: dos años
b estudiar inglés: un año y medio
c hacer atletismo: tres años
d trabajar como enfermera: un año

4.2 Now ask and answer for her using the construction with **llevar**. Use the 'tú' form of the verb.

▶ 5 ¿Cuánto tiempo hace...?

María, Rafael, Fátima, and José, all left their countries to go and live somewhere else. Listen to their stories and answer the questions which follow.

a When was each person born?
b How long ago did María marry Antonio?
c How long ago did Rafael emigrate to Argentina?
d Where were his children born?
e How long ago did Fátima's parents arrive in Spain?
f How long has she been working as a bilingual secretary?
g How long ago did José arrive in Spain?
h Where did he work first and where is he working now?

emigrar	*to emigrate*
secretariado bilingüe	*bilingual secretarial course*

6 ¿Quién es?

Here is part of the life story of a famous Spanish actor. Can you guess who he is? First, complete the text by filling in the blanks with the preterite tense of the verbs in brackets.

(*Nacer*) ...... en Málaga en 1961. (*Filmar*) ...... cinco películas con el director español Pedro Almodóvar. (*Dejar*) ...... España y *(triunfar)* ...... en Hollywood con películas tales como *Philadelphia, La casa de los espíritus* y *Los reyes del mambo.* (*Casarse*) ...... con la actriz Melanie Grifith, y en 1996 (ellos) *(tener)* ...... su primer hijo. (*Ser*) ...... el narrador en *Evita,* del director de cine Alan Parker. En 1999 (*realizar*) ...... su primer trabajo como director en la película *Locos en Alabama*, cuyo tema es el racismo. En esta película *(actuar)* ...... con su esposa Melanie Grifith. En el año 2003 (*obtener*) ...... un gran triunfo en Broadway con la obra musical *Nine*, por la cual fue nominado al premio *Tony.*

dejar	*to leave*
triunfar	*to succeed*
tales como	*such as*
realizar	*to carry out*
cuyo/a	*whose*
actuar	*to act*
obtener	*to obtain* (like 'tener')
la obra musical	*musical*
el premio	*prize*

7 Mi biografía

As part of a magazine project, you have been asked to write about the life of Rosa Ramírez, a famous photographer. Use the following information given by her to write your text, making all necessary changes to verbs and other grammatical words. Begin like this: " Se llama Rosa Ramírez, nació...."

Me llamo Rosa Ramírez, nací en León el 6 de mayo de 1975, pero llegué a Madrid hace varios años. Soy fotógrafa, estoy casada y tengo dos hijos. Estudié fotografía en Madrid y terminé los estudios en 1997. En

1999 conocí a Julio, mi marido, y nos casamos un año después. Fernando, nuestro primer hijo, nació en octubre del año 2002 y dos años más tarde nació nuestra hija Francisca. Mi marido es guitarrista y lleva dos años tocando con un grupo de música *rock*.

8 Ahora tú

You have been asked to provide information about your own life. Use the above and the previous activities as a model to write about yourself.

16 me gustó muchísimo

I liked it very much

In this unit you will learn how to:

- talk about a past holiday or journey
- say what you thought of something or someone
- talk about the weather

▶ 1 ¿Dónde fuiste?

Elisa, Julio, Laura and Manuel talk about their holidays.

1.1 Among the following sentences there are three actions which are not mentioned in the dialogue. Listen to the conversation and try to spot them.

a I didn't do anything special.
b I went home.
c My boyfriend came home from Marbella.
d I went to Mexico.
e I was in Mexico for two years.
f I was in Mexico two years ago.

Elisa	¿Qué hicisteis en las vacaciones?
Julio	Yo no hice nada especial. Me quedé en casa.
Laura	Pues, yo pasé mis vacaciones en Marbella. Estuve en casa de mi novio. Y tú Elisa, ¿dónde fuiste?
Elisa	Fui a México con Tomás. Estuvimos dos semanas allí.
Julio	¿Qué os pareció México? ¿Os gustó?
Elisa	Sí, nos encantó. Nos pareció un país interesantísimo. Fueron unas vacaciones estupendas.
Manuel	Yo estuve en México hace dos años y me gustó muchísimo.

estuve en Marbella con mi novio

1.2 Now read the dialogue and find the past tense forms (*the preterite*, Unit 15) of the following verbs: **estar, pasar, gustar, hacer, ir, ser, encantar, quedarse, parecer.**

1.3 Read the dialogue again and say in which way the meaning of the following two words is intensified: **interesante, mucho.**

> **pasar** *to spend* (time)   **parecer** *to seem*

▶ 2 ¿Qué tal el tiempo?

Elisa tells Julio about the weather, **el tiempo,** in Mexico City. Note the use of **hacer,** *to do, make,* to refer to the weather.

2.1 What does Elisa say about the weather and why does she think they were lucky? Listen and find out.

Julio ¿Qué tal el tiempo en la Ciudad de México?

Elisa Me pareció muy agradable. No hace mucho calor, aunque en julio llueve a menudo. Pero tuvimos suerte, sólo llovió una vez.

Julio Aquí hizo muchísimo calor.

2.2 Read the dialogue now and find the Spanish for the following phrases: 'it's not very hot', 'it often rains', 'it rained only once', 'it was very hot'.

agradable	*pleasant*
aunque	*although*
tuvimos (from **tener**) **suerte**	*we were lucky*

How do you say it?

Talking about a past holiday or journey

a To ask people what they did you can say

¿Qué hiciste/hizo Vd. en tus/sus vacaciones?	*What did you do on your holidays?*
¿Qué hicisteis el verano pasado?	*What did you do last summer?*

b To say what you did you can say

Me quedé/nos quedamos en casa.	*I/we stayed at home.*
No hice/hicimos nada.	*I/we didn't do anything.*
Fui/fuimos a China.	*I/we went to China.*
Pasé/pasamos unos días en Florida.	*I/we spent a few days in Florida.*

Saying what you thought of something or someone

¿Qué te/le pareció la ciudad/ la gente?	*What did you think of the city/the people?*
Me pareció muy caro(a)/ agradable.	*It seemed very expensive/ pleasant (to me)*
¿Qué os/les pareció?	*What did you think of it?*
Nos pareció muy bonita.	*It seemed very pretty (to us)*

Talking about the weather

Hace (mucho) calor/frío.	*It's (very) hot/cold.*
Hizo (muchísimo) calor/frío.	*It was (very) hot/cold.*

Grammar

1 Saying what you did: *irregular preterite forms*

The number of irregular verbs in the preterite tense is small but some of these are very common, so try to learn them as they come up. Many of them have similar forms, and that should help you to memorize them. Note that in the preterite tense there is no difference in form between **ser** *to be* and **ir** *to go*.

estar *to be*
estuve, estuviste, estuvo, estuvimos, estuvisteis, estuvieron

tener *to have*
tuve, tuviste, tuvo, tuvimos, tuvisteis, tuvieron

andar *to walk*
anduve, anduviste, anduvo, anduvimos, anduvisteis, anduvieron

poder *to be able to, can*
pude, pudiste, pudo, pudimos, pudisteis, pudieron

ser *to be,* **ir** *to go*
fui, fuiste, fue, fuimos, fuisteis, fueron

ver *to see*
vi, viste, vio, vimos, visteis, vieron

hacer *to do, make*
hice, hiciste, hizo, hicimos, hicisteis, hicieron

decir *to say, tell*
dije, dijiste, dijo, dijimos, dijisteis, dijeron

venir *to come*
vine, viniste, vino, vinimos, vinisteis, vinieron

Anduvimos por el río.	*We walked along the river.*
Miguel no pudo venir.	*Miguel couldn't come.*
Fue un viaje interesante.	*It was an interesting journey.*
Vi sitios maravillosos.	*I saw marvellous places.*
¿Qué te dijeron?	*What did they tell you?*
Ella vino sola.	*She came on her own.*

The preterite form of **hay** *there is/are* (from **haber**) is **hubo** *there was/were*. For other irregular preterite forms see **Irregular verbs** on page 302.

2 Parecer *to seem*

Parecer *to seem*, functions in the same way as **gustar** and **encantar** (see Unit 13), that is, with the third person of the verb, singular or plural, preceded by one of the following pronouns: **me, te, le, nos, os, les**: "¿Qué te pareció La Habana?" *'What did you think of Havana?'* (literally, *'What to you seemed Havana'?*), "Me pareció interesante" *'It seemed interesting'* (literally, *'To me it seemed interesting'*, "Los cubanos nos parecieron simpáticos" *'Cubans seemed nice'* (literally, *'Cubans to us seemed nice'*).

3 Talking about the weather

a Using 'hacer'

Hace calor/frío/viento.	*It's warm/cold/windy.*
Hace bueno.	*The weather is good.*
Hace buen/mal tiempo.	*The weather is good /bad.*
Ayer hizo sol/frío.	*Yesterday it was sunny/cold.*

b Using 'estar' and 'haber'

Está/estuvo nublado/cubierto.	*It is/was cloudy/overcast.*
Está lloviendo/nevando.	*It's raining/snowing.*
Hay/hubo niebla.	*It is/was foggy.*
Hay/hubo tormenta.	*There is/was a storm.*

c Llover (o>ue) *to rain*, **nevar** (e>ie) *to snow*

Llueve/llovió mucho.	*It rains/rained a lot.*
No nieva/nevó.	*It doesn't/didn't snow.*

4 Using *-ísimo/-ísima*

a -ísimo or -ísima can be added to adjectives to intensify their meaning. If the word you want to emphasize ends in a consonant, just add -ísimo (m) or -ísima (f), and -s for plural: **fácil** *easy*, **facilísimo/a(s)** *very easy*. If it ends in a vowel, remove this and add -ísimo/a(s): **caro/a(s)** *expensive*, **carísimo/a(s)** *very expensive*. Some adverbs, for example **mucho, poco,** can also take -ísimo, in which case this is invariable: **me gustó muchísimo** *I liked it very much.*

b Words ending in -co or -ca and -go or -ga become -**quísimo/a** and -**guísimo/a** respectively, in order to keep the sound of the -c or -g : **rico** *rich*, **riquísimo/a(s)** *very rich*, **largo** *long*, **larguísimo/a(s)** *very long*.

A number of adjectives do not accept **-ísimo/-ísima** so you should not use it unless you are sure. The alternative of course is to use words such as **muy** *very*, **bastante** *quite, rather*, **demasiado** *too*: **muy/bastante/demasiado difícil** *very/quite/too difficult.*

Practice

1 Un email

Antonia was sent by her company to Mexico. Here's an e-mail she sent to a colleague back home. Can you put the verbs in brackets in the appropriate form of the preterite tense?

Hola Carmen:

¿Qué tal estás? Yo, estupendamente. Llegué a la Ciudad de México hace tres días. El avión (salir) a la hora y el vuelo (ser) estupendo. El primer día (yo) no (hacer) nada especial, (cenar) algo ligero y (acostarse). Anteayer (tener) una reunión con nuestros socios y por la tarde (estar) en el Museo de Antropología, que me (gustar) muchísimo. Ayer al mediodía (ir) a un mercado e (hacer) algunas compras. Por la noche, unos amigos mexicanos (venir) a recogerme al hotel y (ir) juntos a cenar. (Yo) lo (pasar) muy bien. Los mexicanos que (yo) (conocer) (parecer) simpatiquísimos...

yo (estoy) estupendamente	*I feel great*
algo ligero	*something light*
el/la socio/a	*partner*
recoger	*to pick up*
juntos/as	*together*
pasarlo bien	*to have a good time*

2 ¿Qué hizo?

Can you say what Alejandro did when he went on holiday to the Caribbean, **el Caribe**? Match the drawings with the verbs and put these in the appropriate form of the preterite tense.

a (salir) a bailar **d** (conocer) a una chica guapísima
b (ir) a pescar **e** (hacer) vela
c (nadar) muchísimo **f** (tomar) el sol

| la/el chico/a | *girl/boy* | guapo/a | *pretty, good looking* |

3 ¿Qué hicieron?

Here are some of the things María Teresa and Agustín did while on holiday in Egypt, **Egipto**. Choose an appropriate verb from the list to complete each sentence, using the preterite tense: **ver, hacer, ir, tener, parecer, estar, andar**.

a Agustín y yo ..... de vacaciones a Egipto.
b ..... una semana en el Cairo y otra semana en Luxor.
c En el Cairo ..... las pirámides y la Esfinge.
d También ..... por los mercados, que ..... interesantísimos.
e ..... un viaje maravilloso por el río Nilo.
f ..... muchísima suerte con el tiempo. No hizo demasiado calor.

---

las pirámides *the pyramids*   **la Esfinge** *the Sphynx*

---

4 Fui a los Estados Unidos

A Spanish-speaking friend has just returned from a holiday in the United States. How would you ask him/her the following?

a Where did you go?
b How long were you there?
c Did you stay with friends?
d What did you do there?
e What did you think of the place?
f Was it very hot?

5 Ahora tú

Use the previous activities as a model to write a brief account of a real or imaginary holiday or a journey that you made. Don't forget to say what the weather was like and what you thought of the place.

6 ¿Qué tal el tiempo?

6.1 You and a Spanish-speaking colleague will be travelling through Spain on business, so you want to know what the weather is like in the places you'll visit. First match each weather symbol with an appropriate phrase.

a hace viento
b está nublado
c está nevando
d hace sol
e hay tormenta
f está lloviendo
g está cubierto
h hay niebla

6.2 Now look at the weather map and answer your colleague's questions.

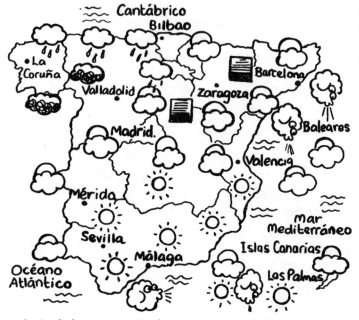

a ¿Qué tal el tiempo en Málaga?   **c** Y en Bilbao, ¿qué tal?
b ¿Y en Baleares?   **d** ¿Y en Zaragoza?

▶ **7 Misión hispanoamericana**

Your next assignment will be in Argentina. On your cable TV you hear a weather report for Buenos Aires, the capital city. Look at the key words below and then listen to the report several times and answer the following questions.

a Which one of the following expressions describes the weather in Buenos Aires yesterday? : *it was cloudy, it was a sunny day, it was very hot.*

b What will the weather be like today?

c At what time of day is Buenos Aires likely to have rain and strong wind tomorrow?

d What will the weather be like after midday?

e What will be the minimum and maximum temperatures tomorrow?

el sol/de sol	*sun, sunny*
la temperatura	*temperature*
los grados	*degrees*
la lluvia	*rain*
fuerte	*strong*
las perspectivas	*prospects*

hace mucho frío

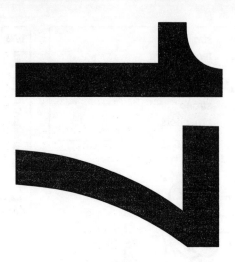

17

eran muy simpáticos
they were very nice

In this unit you will learn how to:

- ask for and give reasons
- ask and say what someone was like
- ask and say what a place or something was like

▶ 1 ¿Por qué?

Rocío, Blanca and Daniel describe people they knew.

1.1 Below are some of the words used by them to describe people. They include masculine and feminine forms. How many of them can you recognize? Check their meanings first, then listen to the dialogues and tick them as you hear them. Note the key expressions **era** *he/she/it was, you were* (formal, sing), **eran** *they were, you were* (formal, pl), **¿por qué?** *why?*, **porque** *because*.

agresivo/a	generoso/a	irresponsable
antipático/a	guapo/a	machista
divertido/a	horrible	reservado/a
estricto/a	insoportable	tímido/a
feo/a	inteligente	trabajador/a

a Rocío

Daniel ¿Por qué dejaste tu trabajo, Rocío?

Rocío Porque mi jefe era insoportable. Tenía un carácter muy agresivo. Mis compañeros de trabajo eran muy simpáticos, pero mi jefe no, todo lo contrario, él era muy antipático. ¡Era feo, era horrible! Además, mi sueldo era muy bajo.

b Blanca

Rocío ¿Por qué te divorciaste de Santiago, Blanca?

Blanca Mira, Santiago era muy guapo, era inteligente y divertido y tenía un gran sentido del humor, pero era muy irresponsable y demasiado machista.

c Daniel

Blanca ¿Cómo era tu madre, Daniel?

Daniel Mi madre era una persona reservada, un poco tímida, trabajadora, generosa, dedicada a su familia y bastante estricta con sus hijos.

1.2 Now read the dialogues and answer these questions:

a Which of the words in exercise 1.1 describe Rocío's former boss?

b Which fit Santiago and which Daniel's mother?

c What expressions are used in the dialogues to say *my colleagues, on the contrary, a great sense of humour?*

además	*besides*	**bajo/a**	*low*
el sueldo	*salary*	**dedicado/a a**	*devoted to*

▶ 2 ¿Qué tal era el hotel?

After leaving her job and her boss Rocío took a holiday with her family. In this dialogue Rocío describes the hotel where she stayed.

2.1 Which of the two hotels below is the one where they stayed?

Listen and find out and, as you do, note the following verb forms:

era (from **ser**) *it was*, **estaba** (from **estar**) *it was* (location), **tenía** (from **tener**) *it had*, **había** (from **haber**) *there was/were*.

Daniel   ¿Qué tal era el hotel donde estuviste?

Rocío   Era estupendo. Era un hotel de cuatro estrellas, estaba a cien metros de la playa, tenía piscina, un buen restaurante, vistas al mar y aparcamiento. Las habitaciones eran muy cómodas y había aire acondicionado y televisión por cable.

2.2 A friend of yours may be travelling to the same hotel. Read the dialogue and explain what the hotel was like.

vista(s) al mar	*seaview*	**el aparcamiento**	*carpark*

How do you say it?

Asking for and giving reasons

¿Por qué dejó su trabajo/se divorció?	*Why did she/he leave her/his job/got divorced?*
Porque su jefe/marido/mujer era insoportable.	*Because her/his boss/her husband/his wife was unbearable.*

Asking and saying what someone was like

¿Cómo era tu madre/ abuelo?	*What was your mother/ grandfather like?*
Era alta(o)/guapa(o).	*She/he was tall/good looking.*
Tenía sentido del humor/ paciencia.	*She/he had a sense of humour/ patience.*

Asking and saying what a place or something was like

¿Qué tal/cómo era el hotel/ el apartamento?	*What was the hotel/ apartment like?*
Era cómodo, tenía servicio de Internet, había garaje.	*It was comfortable, it had Internet facilities, there was a garage.*
Estaba en el centro de la ciudad.	*It was in the centre of the city.*
¿Qué tal era tu sueldo?	*What was your salary like?*
Era bajo/malo/bueno.	*It was low/bad/good.*

Grammar

1 Describing people, places and things in relation to the past: *the imperfect tense (1)*

Usage

a To describe people, places or things in relation to the past you need the *imperfect tense*. Unlike the preterite (Units 15 and 16), the imperfect cannot be used to refer to an action which was completed at a definite point in the past. In **Mi abuela era muy culta** *My grandmother was very cultured*, there is no concern for time, except to show that one is referring to a past experience. Compare this with **Mi abuela murió el año pasado** *My* *grandmother died last year*, which signals an event that took place at a specific point in the past, for which you require the *preterite tense*.

b The imperfect tense often accompanies the preterite, as a kind of framework or description behind the actions that took place: **Dejé** (preterite) **mi trabajo porque mi sueldo era** (imperfect) **muy bajo** *I left my job because my salary was very low*. For more examples see paragraph **b** below. For other uses of the imperfect see Unit 18 and paragraph 12 of **Grammar summary**.

Formation

a Regular verbs

There are two sets of endings for the imperfect tense, one for **–ar** verbs and another one for **–er** and **–ir** verbs. The first and third person singular are the same for all three. Here are two examples, one for each set:

	estar *to be*	**tener** *to have*
yo	est**aba**	ten**ía**
tú	est**abas**	ten**ías**
él, ella, Vd.	est**aba**	ten**ía**
nosotros/as	est**ábamos**	ten**íamos**
vosotros/as	est**abais**	ten**íais**
ellos/ellas, Vds.	est**aban**	ten**ían**

b Irregular verbs

There are only three irregular verbs in the imperfect tense: **ser** *to be*, **ver** *to see* and **ir** *to go*. Below is the imperfect form of **ser**. For **ver** and **ir** see Unit 18.

ser *to be*	
yo	era
tú	eras
él, ella, Vd.	era
nosotros/as	éramos
vosotros/as	erais
ellos, ellas, Vds.	eran

Read the passage below which combines the use of the preterite with that of the imperfect tense.

Fue la primera ciudad que visitamos en nuestro viaje. No *era* una ciudad grande, pero *era* una ciudad atractiva y *tenía* muchos sitios de interés turístico. *Había* un museo de arte colonial que nos gustó mucho y la catedral, que *era* de estilo neogótico, *era* imponente.

El hotel donde *estábamos* – no recuerdo cómo se *llamaba* - *estaba* en las afueras de la ciudad. Estuvimos dos días allí antes de continuar nuestro viaje. En aquel tiempo Elena y yo *éramos* muy jóvenes...

estilo neogótico	*neogothic style*
imponente	*imposing*
recordar (o>ue)	*to remember*
las afueras	*outskirts*

2 Time phrases associated with the imperfect tense

The following expressions are often used with the imperfect, although depending on the context they may be found with other forms of the past, for example the preterite: **antes** *before*, **entonces** *at that time*, **en esa/aquella época** *at that time*, **en esos/aquellos años** *in those years,* **de pequeño(a)/joven** *when I/he/she was young.*

Practice

1 ¿Por qué?

Match each question with an appropriate answer using **¿por qué?** or **porque**.

a ¿..... dejaste el curso?
b ¿..... decidiste estudiar español?
c ¿.....vendió su ordenador/computador(a) (LAm)?
d ¿.....no hicieron el crucero por el Caribe?
e ¿..... se mudaron de casa?
f ¿.....no viniste en el coche/auto, carro (LAm)?

1 ..... el viaje era muy caro.
2 ..... la calle donde estaba era muy ruidosa.
3 ..... la profesora era muy aburrida.
4 ..... mi novio/a habla español.
5 ..... tenía una avería.
6 ..... no tenía suficiente memoria.

el curso	course	**ruidoso/a**	noisy
el crucero	cruise	**aburrido/a**	boring
mudarse	to move	**la avería**	breakdown

2 Palabra por palabra

Here are some words used for describing people's characters. How many of them do you know or can you guess? Look them up in your dictionary if necessary and then give the opposite of each word.

a divertido/a
b triste
c audaz
d tonto/a
e modesto/a
f cortés
g optimista

h simpático/a
i fuerte
j desagradable
k trabajador/a
l irresponsable
m inmaduro/a
n inseguro/a

3 Sopa de letras

Can you spot the opposites of the words listed above in the word square? The completed word square is at the end of the unit.

A	K	X	A	B	U	R	R	I	D	O
R	D	P	N	J	I	O	P	L	M	N
R	E	E	T	B	S	N	G	H	T	P
O	S	S	I	H	G	E	A	T	Y	E
G	C	I	P	A	L	E	G	R	E	R
A	O	M	A	O	M	K	R	U	F	E
N	R	I	T	W	N	A	A	Y	R	Z
T	T	S	I	D	J	S	D	H	H	O
E	E	T	C	E	P	P	A	U	Q	S
U	S	A	O	B	P	P	B	B	R	O
H	T	I	M	I	D	O	L	K	L	O
I	N	T	E	L	I	G	E	N	T	E

▶ 4 ¿Cómo era Roberto?

Pepe describes Roberto, someone he once knew. Listen to Pepe's account several times and answer the questions which follow.

a Where did Pepe and Roberto meet?
b What was Roberto's profession?
c How does Pepe describe him?
d What happened to Roberto?

How would you relate Pepe's account to someone else in Spanish? Listen again before you do it.

la capacidad	capacity	**la relación**	relationship
alegre	cheerful, happy	**una carta**	a letter
extrovertido/a	extrovert	**nos conocimos**	we met

5 Ahora tú

Write a short description of someone you knew. Try using words from the dialogues and the previous activities, and others suitable for the person you wish to describe.

6 La casa de Marta

Look at this plan of the house where Marta used to live and then complete the description below with one of the following verbs, using the imperfect tense: **estar, haber, ser, tener.**

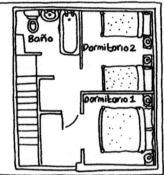

Mi casa no (a) _____ ni grande ni pequeña, pero (b) _____ muy cómoda. La casa (c) _____ dos plantas. En la planta baja (d) _____ el salón comedor y la cocina y en la primera planta (e) _____ los dos dormitorios y el baño. En uno de los dormitorios (f) _____ una cama matrimonial y en el otro (g) _____ dos camas. La calle donde (h) _____ (i) _____ bastante tranquila y cerca de la casa (j) _____ tiendas y un supermercado. Mis vecinos (k) _____ gente muy simpática y el barrio no (l) _____ malo.

| **la planta** (or **el piso**) | *floor* |
| **el salón comedor** | *sitting room-dining room* |

Note the use of three negatives in **Mi casa no ..... ni grande ni pequeña** *My house ... neither big nor small.*

7 Ahora tú

Use the activity above as a model to describe a place where you used to live. Here are some words you might need:

el garaje	*garage*
el jardín del frente/de atrás	*front/back garden*
el patio	*courtyard, patio*

Answer to Activity 3

A	K	X	A	B	U	R	R	I	D	O
R	D	P	N	J	I	O	P	L	M	N
R	E	E	T	B	S	N	G	H	T	P
O	S	S	I	H	G	E	A	T	Y	E
G	C	I	P	A	L	E	G	R	E	R
A	O	M	A	O	M	K	R	U	F	E
N	R	I	T	W	N	A	A	Y	R	Z
T	T	S	I	D	J	S	D	H	H	O
E	E	T	C	E	P	P	A	U	Q	S
U	S	A	O	B	P	P	B	B	R	O
H	T	I	M	I	D	O	L	K	L	O
I	N	T	E	L	I	G	E	N	T	E

18

¿qué hacías allí?

what were you doing there?

In this unit you will learn how to:

- say where you used to live
- say what work you used to do
- talk about things you did regularly in the past

▶ 1 ¿Dónde vivías antes?

At a party Rodolfo meets Elena. Elena tells Rodolfo about her life in Alicante before arriving in Barcelona.

1.1 How long was Elena in Alicante and what was she doing there? Listen and find out.

Rodolfo	¿Dónde vivías antes de llegar a Barcelona?
Elena	Vivía en Alicante. Estuve cinco años allí.
Rodolfo	¿Qué hacías en Alicante?
Elena	Trabajaba en una agencia de viajes. Era la encargada de ventas.
Rodolfo	¿Vivías sola?
Elena	No, compartía un piso con un amigo. Nos llevábamos muy bien.

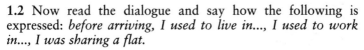

trabajaba en una agencia de viajes

1.2 Now read the dialogue and say how the following is expressed: *before arriving, I used to live in..., I used to work in..., I was sharing a flat.*

el/la encargado/a de ventas	*sales manager* (literally, *the one in charge of...*)
solo/a	*on my/your own, alone*
compartir	*to share*
llevarse bien	*to get on well*

▶ 2 Me encantaba

Rodolfo asks Elena whether she liked living in Alicante.

2.1 What does Elena say with regard to her friends there? She mentions three things she used to do with her friends. What were they? Listen and find out.

Rodolfo ¿Te gustaba vivir en Alicante?

Elena Sí, me encantaba. Tenía muy buenos amigos allí. Los veía prácticamente todos los días, salíamos de copas o a cenar, los fines de semana íbamos a bailar... Lo pasábamos estupendamente.

Rodolfo Y el trabajo, ¿qué tal?

Elena No estaba mal. No ganaba mucho, pero la vida no era tan cara como aquí.

los fines de semana
iba a bailar

2.2 What does Elena say about her job in Alicante? And about her salary? How does she express both ideas? Read and find out.

pasarlo bien/estupendamente	*to have a good/great time*
ganar	*to earn*
la vida	*life*

How do you say it?

Asking people where they used to live, and responding

¿Dónde vivías/vivía Vd.? *Where did you live/were you living?*

Vivía en Florencia. *I lived/used to live/was living in Florence.*

Asking people what work they used to do, and responding

¿Dónde trabajabas/trabajaba Vd.? *Where did you work/were you working?*

¿En qué trabajabas/trabajaba Vd.? *What work did you do?*

¿Qué hacías/hacía Vd.? *What did you do/were you doing?*

Trabajaba en un banco. *I used to work/was working in a bank.*

Era contable/secretario/a. *I was an accountant/secretary.*

Talking about things you did regularly in the past

Salía/salíamos mucho. *I/we used to go out a lot.*

Iba/íbamos al teatro/a conciertos. *I/we used to go to the theatre/concerts.*

Veía/veíamos televisión. *I/we used to watch television.*

Grammar

1 Saying what you used to do or were doing:
the imperfect tense (2)

In unit 17 you learned to use the imperfect tense to describe people and places you knew in the past. This unit focuses on the use of the *imperfect* to refer to:

a a state or an action which continued in the past over an unspecified period.

En aquel tiempo María vivía conmigo.	*At that time María lived/used to live/was living with me.*
Ella trabajaba en radio y televisión.	*She worked/used to work/was working on radio and television.*

Note that if a definite period of time is mentioned, even when the action took place over a long period, the *preterite* and not the imperfect must be used (see units 15 and 16): 'Estuve allí cinco años', '*I was there for five years*'.

b habits or repeated events in the past

Siempre salíamos por la noche.	*We always went out at night.*
Me llamaba todos los días.	*He/she used to call me everyday.*

2 Irregular verbs in the imperfect tense

Other than **ser** (see Unit 17), only **ir** *to go*, and **ver** *to see*, are irregular in the imperfect tense. Note that the endings for **ver** are the same as those of regular –**er** and –**ir** verbs (see Unit 17).

	ir	ver
yo	iba	veía
tú	ibas	veías
él/ella/Vd.	iba	veía
nosotros/as	íbamos	veíamos
vosotros/as	ibais	veíais
ellos/ellas/Vds.	iban	veían

| Él iba al pueblo todos los veranos. | *He went/used to go to the village every summer.* |
| Yo la veía a menudo. | *I saw/used to see her often.* |

3 Adverbs in *–mente*

Words such as *practically, regularly*, are called adverbs (see also **Glossary of grammatical terms**). In English, adverbs often end in *–ly*, and the Spanish equivalent of this is **–mente**. In English you simply add *–ly* to the adjective to form the adverb, for example *practical – practically*. In Spanish the rule is as follows:

If the adjective ends in **–o**, for example **práctico**, change the **–o** (masculine) to **–a** (feminine) and add **–mente**: **práctica – prácticamente**. If the adjective does not have a feminine form, simply add **–mente**: **fácil – fácilmente**. Note that if the adjective has a written accent, the adverb must keep the accent.

There are many adverbs which do not end in **–mente**, for example **bien** *well*, **mal** *badly*, **aquí** *here*, **allí** *there*, **antes** *before*, **ahora** *now*.

4 Preposition + infinitive

Note that in the phrase **antes de llegar** *before arriving*, Spanish uses the infinitive, whereas English uses the gerund, the *–ing* form of the verb. The general rule in Spanish is that verbs which follow a preposition (words like **a, de, para, sin**) must be in the *infinitive*, which often translates in English with the gerund: **después de salir** *after going out*, **para oír mejor** *to/in order to hear better*, **sin recordar nada** *without remembering anything*, **al empezar** *on starting*.

Practice

1 ¿Qué hacía Pablo?

Pablo remembers his childhood years. How would he tell someone what he used to do? Match the drawings with the phrases below, and put the verbs in the right form of the imperfect tense.

a (dormir) la siesta	**d** (hacer) los deberes
b (jugar) con mi pelota	**e** (levantarse) a las 8.00
c (ir) a la escuela	**f** (comer) con mi madre

2 Cuando tenía 18 años …

Elvira, from Jaén, tells a friend about her life when she was eighteen. Put the infinitives in the right form of the imperfect tense.

Cuando (yo) tenía dieciocho años …

(Vivir) con mis padres en Jaén.
(Trabajar) como dependienta en un supermercado.
(Ir) al trabajo en bicicleta.
(Empezar) a las 9.00 y (salir) a las 7.00.
(Ganar) 40.000 pesetas mensuales, unos 240 euros de ahora.
(Estar) soltera.
(Tener) un novio que (llamarse) Manuel.
Manuel y yo (verse) por la tarde, (dar) largos paseos y (hablar) de amor.

mensual(es)	*monthly* (sing/pl)
dar un paseo	*to go for a walk*
verse	*to see one another*
el amor	*love*

3 Ahora tú

¿Dónde vivías cuando eras pequeño/a? ¿Qué hacía tu padre? ¿Y tu madre? ¿Quién te llevaba a la escuela? ¿Te gustaba ir a la escuela? ¿Dónde pasabas tus vacaciones? ¿Qué hacías allí?

| ¿quién? | who | la escuela | school |

▶ **4 ¿A qué se dedicaban?**

Begoña, Esteban and Víctor talk about their previous and present jobs. Can you say what they used to do and what they do now? Listen and fill in the gaps with the appropriate names and change the infinitives in brackets into the right tense, the *present* or the *imperfect*.

_____ a   (Ser) intérprete. (Trabajar) para la Unión Europea.
_____ b   (Ser) maestra. (Trabajar) en un colegio.
_____ c   (Trabajar) en un restaurante. (Ser) camarero.
_____ d   (Estar) sin trabajo.
_____ e   (Ser) estudiante. (Estudiar) lenguas.
_____ f   (Ser) programador. (Trabajar) en una empresa de programación.

la Unión Europea	European Union
el/la maestro/a	teacher (primary school)
el/la programador/a (de ordenadores)	computer programmer
la programación	programming

5 ¿Qué hacían Delia y Pepe?

Delia and Pepe had similar duties in the company where they both worked. Can you say what they were? Choose from the phrases in the box below and write an appropriate sentence under each drawing indicating what they used to do, e.g. **asistir a reuniones – Asistían a reuniones.**

mandar faxes, servir café a los clientes,
contestar el teléfono, trabajar en el ordenador,
leer la correspondencia, atender al público

6 Asistíamos a reuniones

How would Delia and Pepe tell someone else what they used to do? Begin like this: **Asistíamos a reuniones …**

7 Una entrevista

You've been asked to interview a Spanish-speaking person who is applying for a job. How would you ask the following in Spanish? Choose between the *imperfect* or the *preterite tense*, as appropriate, using the formal Vd.

a What work did you do before?
b How long did you work there?
c How much were you earning?
d Why did you leave your job?

8 Ahora tú

¿A qué te dedicabas antes?
¿Trabajabas o estudiabas?
¿Dónde trabajabas/estudiabas?
¿Qué hacías en tu tiempo libre?

---

el tiempo libre   *spare time*

19

¿qué has hecho?

what have you done?

In this unit you will learn how to:
- talk about past events related to the present
- complain about a service
- claim lost property

▶ 1 He ido al museo

In this unit you will learn the Spanish equivalent of phrases such as *I have been to the museum, What have you done?*, which are expressed through the *perfect tense.* In Dialogue 1 you will hear María Luisa talk to Patricia, whom she has met on a city tour, about some of the things they have done.

1.1 Each of the sentences below contains some wrong information. First, look at the phrases in the vocabulary box, then listen to the conversation and put them right.

a He estado varias veces aquí.

b Es la segunda vez que vengo.

c He ido a la catedral, pero todavía no he visto el museo.

d Por la noche he salido con unas amigas a cenar.

Mª Luisa	¿Es la primera vez que vienes aquí?
Patricia	No, he estado dos veces aquí. ¿Y tú?
Mª Luisa	Es la primera vez que vengo. ¿Has visitado el museo y la catedral?
Patricia	Esta mañana he ido al museo, pero todavía no he visto la catedral. Me han dicho que es maravillosa. Y tú, ¿qué has hecho hoy?
Mª Luisa	Por la mañana no he hecho nada especial. Por la tarde, he salido con unos amigos a comer.

1.2 How would you express the following in Spanish? Refer back to the dialogue and the vocabulary below.

a This is the second time I come to Spain.

b Today I have been (gone) to the market.

c I haven't seen the ruins (las ruinas) yet.

d I've been told they are very interesting.

he estado	*I have been*
he ido	*I have been* (literally, *gone*)
todavía no	*not yet*
he visto	*I have seen*
me han dicho	*I've been told*
he hecho	*I have done*

▶ 2 He olvidado mi paraguas

Mª Luisa has left her umbrella in the restaurant where she had lunch with her friends, and she goes back to claim it.

2.1 How does Mª Luisa describe her umbrella? Listen to the dialogue and note the following key words and phrases: **he olvidado** (from **olvidar**) *I have forgotten*, **el paraguas** *umbrella*, **de cuadros** *checked*.

Patricia   Perdone, esta tarde he comido aquí con unos amigos y he olvidado mi paraguas. Es un paraguas azul, de cuadros.

Camarero ¿Es este su paraguas?

Patricia   Sí, es ese. Muchísimas gracias.

Camarero No hay de qué, señora.

2.2 What expressions are used in the dialogue for *I've had lunch here, Is this your umbrella?, Yes, that's it.*

olvidar	*to forget, leave behind*
no hay de qué	*you're welcome!*

▶ 3 Hemos pedido una habitación exterior

Marta, who is staying at a hotel with her husband, phones the hotel reception to complain about the room they have been given.

3.1 What is Marta's complaint? Listen and find out.

Recepcionista Recepción, ¿dígame?

Marta   Hola, llamo de la habitación trescientos diez. Mi marido y yo hemos pedido una habitación exterior y ustedes nos han dado una interior. Además, el aire acondicionado no funciona y faltan toallas.

Recepcionista Usted perdone, señora. Ahora mismo les doy otra habitación.

3.2 What expressions are used in the dialogue to say: *I'm calling from..., it doesn't work, I do apologize, I'll give you another room right now.*

hemos pedido	*we have asked for*
nos han dado	*you have given us*
exterior	*outward-facing*
interior	*facing a central patio*
faltar	*not to be enough, to be lacking*

How do you say it?

Talking about past events related to the present

¿Has visitado el museo?	*Have you visited the museum?* (inf)
¿Ha visto la catedral?	*Have you seen the cathedral?* (formal)
He/hemos estado/ido allí.	*I/we have been there.*

Complaining about a service

El aire acondicionado/la calefacción no funciona.	*The air conditioning/heating doesn't work.*
Falta champú.	*There's not enough/There's no shampoo.*
Faltan toallas.	*There are not enough/There are no towels.*
No hay toalla de manos/baño.	*There's no hand/bath towel.*

Claiming lost property

| He olvidado mi bolso/la cartera (LAm) | *I've forgotten/left my handbag.* |
| (Me) he dejado la cartera/el maletín. | *I've left/forgotten my briefcase.* |

Grammar

1 Talking about past events related to the present: *the perfect tense*

Usage

a The Spanish *perfect tense*, like the English perfect, is used for past events which have taken place in a period of time that has not yet ended, that is, a past which is somehow related to the present.

He estado dos veces aquí.	*I've been here twice* (until now).
Todavía no han visitado el Palacio Real.	*They still haven't visited the Royal Palace* (so far).
Ya ha salido.	*He/she has already left.*

b Events which have taken place in the recent or the immediate past are usually expressed in Peninsular Spanish with the perfect tense. Here, English may use the preterite tense.

Esta tarde he visto a Eva.	*I've seen/saw Eva this afternoon.*
Hoy hemos ido al teatro.	*Today we've been/ went to the theatre.*
Han llegado hace un momento.	*They arrived a moment ago.*
¿Has oído ese ruido?	*Did you hear/Have you heard that noise?*

c There are regional differences in the use of the perfect tense, especially in the Spanish-speaking countries of Latin America where, overall, the tendency is to use the preterite tense in contexts where Peninsular Spanish would show preference for the perfect, for example:

Hoy fui al palacio de gobierno.	*Today I went/have been to the government palace.*
Esa película ya la vi.	*I've already seen that film.*

instead of,

Hoy he ido al palacio de gobierno.
Esa película ya la he visto.

Formation

The perfect tense is formed with the present tense of the auxiliary verb **haber** *to have*, and a *past participle*, which is that part of the verb which in English usually ends in '- ed'. In Spanish, the endings of past participles are **–ado** for **–ar** verbs, and **–ido** for verbs in **–er** and **–ir**. In the perfect tense these past participles are invariable. Here are the perfect tense forms of three regular verbs: **estar** *to be,* **comer** *to eat,* **ir** *to go.*

yo	he	estado	comido	ido
tú	has	estado	comido	ido
él, ella, Vd.	ha	estado	comido	ido
nosotros/as	hemos	estado	comido	ido
vosotros/as	habéis	estado	comido	ido
ellos, ellas, Vds.	han	estado	comido	ido

2 Irregular past participles

The following are the most common irregular forms:

abrir – abierto *open*   **morir – muerto** *dead*
decir – dicho *said*   **poner – puesto** *put*
escribir – escrito *written*   **romper – roto** *broken*
freír – frito *fried*   **ver – visto** *seen*
hacer – hecho *done, made*   **volver – vuelto** *returned, come back*

3 Time phrases associated with the perfect tense

Among time phrases associated with the perfect tense we find:

hoy	*today*
esta mañana/tarde/semana	*this morning/ afternoon/week*
esta noche	*tonight*
este mes/año	*this month/year*
alguna vez	*ever*
nunca	*never*
ya	*already*
todavía/aún	*yet*

¿Te ha llamado alguna vez?	*Has he/she ever called you?*
Nunca lo ha hecho.	*He/she has never done it.*
Todavía/aún no han vuelto.	*They haven't come back yet.*

4 Impersonal sentences with the third person plural

A simple way to form *impersonal sentences*, that is, sentences in which you do not need to specify the identity of the person who performed the action expressed by the verb, is to use the third person plural of the verb.

Me han dicho que es importante.   *I've been told it's important.*

Aceptaron mi reclamación.   *They accepted my complaint.*

Practice

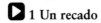 **1 Un recado**

Your boss does business with Spain and Latin America. On your answerphone this morning you find a message from María Bravo, from Mexico. Listen and make a note of it in English to pass it on to your boss.

> **encontrar** *to find*   **aplazar** *to put off*

2 ¿Qué han hecho?

What have the following people done this summer? Fill in the blanks in these sentences with an appropriate verb from the list, using the perfect tense.

> mudarse viajar abrir pintar quedarse hacer volver pasar

a Patricia _____ un curso de inglés intensivo.
b Marta y Victoria _____ sus vacaciones en Marruecos.
c Agustín _____ a Londres a visitar a unos amigos.
d Mónica _____ a Chile, después de vivir tres años en Europa.
e Esteban y Rosa María _____ a un nuevo piso.
f Yo no tenía dinero y _____ en casa.
g Pilar y yo _____ nuestro piso.
h José Manuel y Juan Carlos _____ una pequeña tienda de ropa.

> **mudarse** *to move (house)*   **pintar** *to paint*

3 ¿De qué se queja?

Laura and her husband had booked a hotel room through an agency, but on arrival they were greatly disappointed and complained to the hotel manager. Something went wrong.

3.1 Listen to the conversation several times, and say which of the two ads below fits in their expectations.

HOTEL EXCELSIOR *

Vara del Rey, 17, San Antonio, Tel.: 971 34 01 85

Situado en pleno centro de San Antonio a escasos minutos de la playa, hotel de ambiente y explotación familiar, todas sus habitaciones cuentan con baño o ducha. Asimismo dispone de salón social y de televisión, al igual que de bar y restaurante.

HOTEL CONDES *

Zona Comercial Carabela, Puerto de Alcudia, Tel.: 971 54 54 92

Situado a 100 mt. de la orilla del mar, en un lugar perfecto donde podrá practicar toda clase de deportes acuáticos. Dispone de una gran piscina y solarium, salón de T.V y vídeo, bares en el interior y en la terraza y zona especial para niños entre los jardines. Las habitaciones disponen todas de baño completo y terraza con vistas al mar.

3.2 Listen again a few times and say whether the following statements are true or false (**verdadero o falso**).

a El recepcionista les ha dado una habitación con vistas a un aparcamiento.

b Laura y su marido han estado dos veces en esa ciudad.

c Es la segunda vez que les pasa algo así.

¡Esto es el colmo!	*This is the last straw!*
¡Es increíble!	*This is incredible!*
contar con (o>ue)	*to have*
disponer de	*to have*

4 Palabra por palabra

Here are some of the things that might go wrong in your hotel room. How many of them can you guess? Look up the words you don't know.

a La calefacción, el aire acondicionado, la televisión, el grifo del agua caliente/fría ... no funciona.
b El váter, el lavabo, la bañera ... está atascado/a.
c Falta jabón, champú, papel higiénico.
d No hay suficientes toallas/mantas.

5 Ahora tú

It's your first day in your hotel room and you call reception to complain about some of the facilities in the room. How would you say the following?

a The heating doesn't work.
b The washbasin is blocked.
c There is no soap in the bathroom.
d I need more blankets on my bed.

6 Objetos perdidos

Margarita left something behind in señor Palma's office. What did she leave and how does she describe it? Read and find out.

Margarita   Perdone, he estado en el despacho del señor Palma esta mañana y he dejado una cartera con unos documentos. Es una cartera negra, de piel. ¿Puede decirme si la han encontrado? Es muy importante.

Recepcionista   Sí, señora. Su cartera está aquí en la recepción.

los objetos perdidos	lost property
el despacho	office

7 Ahora tú

You were in a bar with a friend at midday, and after leaving the place you realized that you had left something behind. Choose from the following and tell the waiter what you have lost, and ask whether he has found it.

8 ¿Ha llamado usted al director del banco?

You have a busy day at the office today and your Spanish boss is checking your progress. Here is a list of the things you needed to do, with a tick for those you have already done. How would your boss ask whether you have done each of the following? And how would you reply? Follow the examples.

Ejemplos:

– ¿Ha llamado Vd. al director del banco?
– *No, todavía no lo he llamado.*
– ¿Ha contestado Vd. la carta de Ángela Salas?
– *Sí, ya la he contestado.*

a	*Llamar al director del banco*	✗
b	*Contestar la carta de Ángela Salas*	✓
c	*Pedir hora con el doctor Prado*	✓
d	*Escribir a los distribuidores en Nueva York*	✓
e	*Hacer el pedido de material de oficina*	✗
f	*Ver a la señora Martínez*	✓
g	*Abrir la caja con las mercancías*	✗

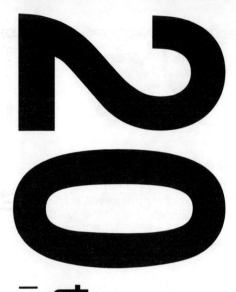

20

te veré mañana

I'll see you tomorrow

In this chapter you will learn how to:
- confirm travel arrangements
- cancel a hotel reservation
- talk about the future
- express conditions

▶ 1 Iré al aeropuerto a recogerte

Ángel is flying to Madrid to visit his friend Ana. In a phone call to her he confirms his travel arrangements.

1.1 When is Ángel leaving and when is he arriving in Madrid? Listen and find out.

Ana   ¿Sí, dígame?

Ángel Hola, Ana. Soy Ángel.

Ana   Ángel, ¡qué sorpresa! ¿Qué tal estás?

Ángel Muy bien. Mira, te llamaba para confirmar mi viaje. Salgo esta tarde y llego a Madrid mañana a las ocho y media.

Ana   ¡Hombre, me alegro! Iré al aeropuerto a recogerte. Supongo que traerás mucho equipaje.

Ángel Sí, bastante.

Ana   Bueno, le pediré el coche a Rafael. El mío es demasiado pequeño.

Ángel Gracias, Ana. ¿Qué tal está el tiempo en Madrid?

Ana   Estupendo. Seguro que mañana hará calor.

Ángel Bueno, Ana. Te veré mañana, entonces. Si el vuelo se retrasa, te llamaré.

Ana   Vale, Ángel. Hasta mañana y buen viaje. Un beso.

Le pediré el coche a Rafael. El mío es demasiado pequeño.

1.2 Now read the dialogue and focus attention on those verbs that refer to the future, for example **salgo** *I'm leaving*, **llego** *I'm arriving*. These are in the present tense, but there are others, such as **iré** *I'll go*, **traerás** *you'll bring*, which are in the *future tense*. Try to spot them and then answer the following questions.

a What does Ana promise to do?
b Whose car is Ana borrowing and why?
c What will Ángel do if his flight is delayed?
d What expression does Ana use to say '*It's sure to be warm tomorrow*'.

¡qué sorpresa!	*what a surprise!*
alegrarse/me alegro	*to be/I'm glad*
suponer/supongo	*to/I suppose*
mío/a	*mine* (m/f)
bueno	(here) *OK*
si se retrasa (from **retrasarse**)	*if it's delayed*

i **¡Hombre!** This expression, meaning literally *man*, is used frequently in Spanish, especially in Spain, to convey different types of emotions, so its exact meaning will depend on the context, for example *come on!, cheer up!, you bet!*

▶ 2 No podremos viajar

Julio is cancelling a hotel reservation he had made for him and his wife.

2.1 Listen to the dialogue and try to spot the expressions meaning the following:

a I was calling about ...   c We won't be able to travel.
b a reservation in the name of ... d We'll have to cancel it.

Recepcionista	Hotel Foresta, ¿dígame?
Julio	Buenas tardes. Llamaba por una reserva que hice para dos personas a nombre de Julio Pérez, para el 10 de octubre. No podremos viajar en esa fecha y tendremos que anularla. Lo siento.
Recepcionista	Perdone, ¿me puede repetir su nombre, por favor?
Julio	Julio Pérez.
Recepcionista	Sí, sí, aquí está. Muy bien, señor, su reserva está anulada.

2.2 Your holiday plans have changed and you need to cancel a hotel reservation. How would you express the following in Spanish?

Good evening. I was phoning about a reservation I made in the name of ... for 20th August. I won't be able to travel on that date and I'll have to cancel it. I'm very sorry.

no podremos (from **poder**)	*we won't be able to*
tendremos que (from **tener**)	*we'll have to*

How do you say it?

Confirming travel arrangements

Salgo/Llego (pasado) mañana/el lunes

I'm leaving/arriving (the day after) tomorrow/on Monday

Saldremos/Llegaremos esta noche/el 15.

We'll leave/arrive tonight/on the 15th.

Cancelling a hotel reservation

Llamo/Llamaba para anular una reserva.

I am/was calling to cancel a reservation.

No podré/podremos viajar.

I/we won't be able to travel.

Talking about the future

Te veré mañana.

I'll see you tomorrow.

Seguro que hará calor.

It's sure to be warm.

Expressing conditions

Si el vuelo se retrasa, te llamaré.

If the flight is delayed I'll call you.

Si no viajo hoy, viajaré el domingo.

If I don't travel today I'll travel on Sunday.

Seguro que mañana hará calor.

Grammar

1 Talking about the future

As in English, in Spanish you can refer to the future in more than one way.

a Using **ir a** + *infinitive* (see Unit 13): **Voy a viajar a Perú** *I'm going to travel to Peru.*

b Using the *present tense*, especially with verbs indicating movement, but also with some other verbs: **Llegan dentro de dos días** *They are arriving in two days'time*, **¿Qué película ponen mañana?** *What film are they showing tomorrow?*

c Using the future tense: **Le pediré el coche a Rafael** *I'll borrow Rafael's car.*

2 The future tense

Usage

The use of the future tense to refer to future actions and events has become relatively uncommon in everyday spoken language, where the tendency now is to use **ir a** + *infinitive* or the *present tense* (see 1 above), but it remains common when expressing

a Supposition (including supposition in the present), certainty and predictions

Supongo/Me imagino que vendrás.	*I suppose/imagine you'll come.*
Ahora estará durmiendo.	*He/she must be sleeping now.*
Seguro que nos invitarán.	*I'm sure they'll invite us.*

b Promises and determination

Te prometo que lo haré.	*I promise you I'll do it.*
Se lo diré.	*I'll tell him/her.*

c The idea of '*I wonder...*'

¿Qué hora será?	*I wonder what time it is.*
¿Dónde estarán?	*I wonder where they are.*

The future tense remains common in all forms of writing, especially so in more formal styles and in the language of the press.

El presidente será recibido por las autoridades.	*The president will be received by the authorities.*

Formation

a Regular verbs

The future is formed with the *whole of the infinitive*, to which the endings are added, the same for –ar, -er and –ir verbs. Here are the future forms of three regular verbs **llamar** *to call*, **ver** *to see*, **ir** *to go*. Note that all forms, except the first person plural **nosotros/as** have a written accent.

yo	llamaré	veré	iré
tú	llamarás	verás	irás
él, ella, Vd.	llamará	verá	irá
nosotros/as	llamaremos	veremos	iremos
vosotros/as	llamaréis	veréis	iréis
ellos, ellas, Vds.	llamarán	verán	irán

b Irregular verbs

The endings of irregular verbs are the same as those of regular ones. Here is a list of the most common:

decir *to say, tell*: diré, dirás, dirá, diremos, diréis, dirán.

hacer *to do, make*: haré, harás, hará, haremos, haréis, harán.

poder *to be able, can*: podré, podrás, podrá, podremos, podréis, podrán.

poner *to put*: pondré, pondrás, pondrá, pondremos, pondréis, pondrán.

querer *to want, love*: querré, querrás, querrá, querremos, querréis, querrán.

saber *to know*: sabré, sabrás, sabrá, sabremos, sabréis, sabrán.

salir *to leave, go out*: saldré, saldrás, saldrá, saldremos, saldréis, saldrán.

tener *to have*: tendré, tendrás, tendrá, tendremos, tendréis, tendrán.

venir *to come*: vendré, vendrás, vendrá, vendremos, vendréis, vendrán.

The future form of **haber** is **habrá** *there will be* (**hay** in the present tense).

3 Si... *If...*

To express ideas such as *If I can I'll go, If it rains we'll stay at home,* use the construction **si** + *present tense* + *future tense*: **Si puedo, iré; Si llueve, nos quedaremos en casa.** In the spoken language, the future tense is sometimes replaced by the *present tense*: **Si puedo, voy; Si llueve, nos quedamos en casa.**

4 Mío, tuyo, suyo... *Mine, yours, his, hers, its...*

You are already familiar with words like **mí** *my,* **tu** *your* (inf), **su** *your (formal), his, her, its,* the *short form* of possessives (see Unit 3). Words like **mío, tuyo, suyo,** etc, correspond to the *long forms* of possessives, and they agreee in *gender* (m or f) and *number* (sing or pl) with the *thing possessed,* not with the *possessor.* The following are all their forms:

singular	plural	
mío/a	míos/as	*mine*
tuyo/a	tuyos/as	*yours* (inf)
suyo/a	suyos/as	*his/hers/its/yours* (formal)
nuestro/a	nuestros/as	*ours*
vuestro/a	vuestros/as	*yours* (inf)
suyo/a	suyos/as	*theirs/yours* (formal)

Long forms are normally preceded by **el, la, los** or **las**:

Mi impresora no funciona, usaré la tuya.	*My printer doesn't work, I'll use yours.*
Estos son tus billetes. ¿Dónde están los míos?	*These are your tickets. Where are mine?*

El, la, los, las are not needed in sentences which translate in English as *of mine, of yours,* etc.: **Son amigos nuestros** *They are friends of ours.*

El, la, los, las are also omitted after the verb 'ser', unless identification is also implied: **Esta casa es mía** *This house is mine* (implying *possession* only), **Esta casa es la mía (no la otra)** *This is my house (not the other one)* (implying *possession* and *identification,* with the emphasis on **esta**). The second example could equally be expressed as **Mi casa es esta (no la otra)** *My house is this one (not the other one).*

Practice

1 Un viaje de negocios

Álvaro García is travelling to South America on business. In an e-mail to his business contacts he confirms his journey. Fill in the gaps in the text with one of the following verbs: **quedarse, llevar, llamar, llegar, salir**. Use the future tense.

> quedarse   llevar   llamar   llegar   salir

> Estimada señora Álvarez:
>
> Con relación a mi próxima visita a Santiago, me es muy grato informarle que _____ de Madrid en el vuelo AB 145, el jueves 28 de abril a las 10:45 de la noche y que _____ a Santiago el viernes 29 a las 7:00 de la mañana, hora local. _____ en el hotel San Carlos en la calle La Concepción, y la _____ por teléfono esa misma mañana para confirmar nuestra reunión. _____ toda la documentación que usted me ha solicitado.
>
> Atentamente,
>
> Álvaro García

me es muy grato	*I have pleasure in*
esa misma mañana (literally)	*that same morning* (emphatic)

i **Estimado/a señor/señora** *Dear Sir/Madam* es más personal que **Muy señor/a mío/mía** *Dear Sir/Madam* y se utiliza frecuentemente en correspondencia comercial con **el apellido** *surname* de la persona (see e-mail above). También se utiliza con **el nombre de pila** *first name*, en correspondencia a personas a las que no se conoce bien, por ejemplo **Estimada Victoria** *Dear Victoria*.

▶ 2 Mensajes en el contestador

Mónica, from Seville, found two recorded messages in her answerphone, one from her friend María and another one from Mark. What did each say? Listen and find out.

3 Si ...

Paco is speculating about his future at work. Form conditional sentences by matching the phrases on the left with those on the right.

a	Si tengo que trabajar horas extras	1	trabajaré como programador
b	Si no me aumentan el sueldo	2	podré irme a Estados Unidos
c	Si hago un curso de informática	3	me apuntaré para cobrar el paro
d	Si aprendo inglés	4	pediré un aumento de sueldo
e	Si no encuentro trabajo	5	buscaré otro trabajo

---

apuntarse para cobrar el paro   *to go on the dole*

---

4 Seguro que te las pedirán

Your friend Ángela is uncertain about getting the job she applied for, but you try to reassure her. Look at the first sentence, which has been done for you, and reply to each of Ángela's statements in a similar way.

a Si me *piden* referencias tendré que dar tu nombre.
  Seguro que te las pedirán.
b Si me *entrevistan* tendré que prepararme muy bien.
  Estoy seguro/a de que ...
c Si me *ofrecen* el puesto lo aceptaré.
  Seguramente ...
d Si el sueldo no *es* muy bueno pediré más dinero.
  Estoy seguro/a de que ...
e Si me *dan* un coche de la empresa elegiré un Mercedes.
  Seguro que...

5 Supongo que sí

While doing a Spanish course in Salamanca, Peter will be staying with a Spanish family. Everyone in the family is speculating about Peter. Rephrase their questions, using the expressions given to you. The first sentence has been done for you.

a	¿Conoce Salamanca?	Supongo que conocerá Salamanca.
b	¿Viene solo?	Me imagino que ...
c	¿Tiene nuestra dirección?	Supongo que ...
d	¿Sabe cómo llegar aquí?	Me imagino que ...
e	¿Entiende algo de español?	Supongo que ...

6 Está mal aparcado

Fill in the gaps with a possessive, using either short forms like **mi, tu, su,** or long forms such as **mío, tuyo, suyo,** as appropriate. Use **el, la, los** or **las** where necessary.

a   b

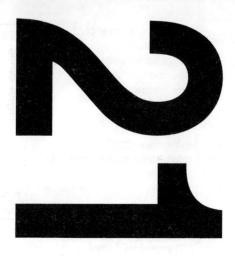

21

me encantaría

I'd love to

In this unit you will learn how to:
- make suggestions
- say what you would like to do
- arrange to meet someone
- invite someone and accept or decline an invitation

▶ 1 ¿Qué te apetece ver?

Margarita and her friend Santiago make arrangements to go out.

1.1 Listen to the dialogue several times and answer the questions below. Key expressions here are **¿qué te parece si ...?** *what about ...?*, **¿qué te apetece ...?** *what would you like/do you feel like ...?*, **me gustaría ...** *I'd like (to) ...*, **me encantaría ...** *I'd love to ...*, **tengo que ...** *I have to ...*, **podríamos quedar ...** *we could meet ...*

a What does Margarita suggest doing this evening?
b Where and when do she and Santiago arrange to meet?
c Why is Antonio not coming with them?

Margarita	¿Qué te parece si vamos al cine esta noche?
Santiago	Sí, sí, vamos. ¿Qué te apetece ver?
Margarita	Me gustaría ver *Sin palabras*. ¿La has visto?
Santiago	No, pero me gustaría verla. ¿Sabes dónde la ponen?
Margarita	En el cine Plaza. Empieza a las diez. Podríamos quedar delante del cine sobre las nueve y media. ¿Te parece bien?
Santiago	Vale, me parece bien.
Margarita	¿Vienes con nosotros, Antonio?
Antonio	Me encantaría, pero tengo que trabajar, si no iría.

1.2 Now read the dialogue and then try putting the following sentences in Spanish:

a What about going to the theatre tomorrow?
b I'd like to see *Historia de dos vidas*.
c I've seen the play (**la obra**), but I'd love to see it again (**otra vez**).
d We could meet right here (**aquí mismo**) about 7.45.

vamos	let's go
poner	to show (a film)
quedar	to arrange to meet
sobre	about, around (with the time)
si no iría	otherwise I'd go

▶ 2 ¿Queréis venir a cenar a casa?

Margarita invites Antonio and Santiago for dinner at her house.

2.1 Who accepts the invitation and who doesn't? What expression does each person use in reply to the invitation? Listen and find out. A key expression here is **tener un compromiso** to *have an engagement*.

Margarita ¿Queréis venir a cenar a casa el viernes? He invitado a Sara también.

Antonio Yo, encantado, gracias.

Santiago Me encantaría, pero no puedo. Tengo un compromiso. ¿Otro día, quizá?

Margarita Sí, sí, otro día.

2.2 Now read the dialogue and use some of the expressions in it to give the Spanish for the following:

a Would you like to come to my house on Saturday? I have a party (**una fiesta**) and I have invited other friends. (Use the **vosotros** form.)

b I'd love to but I can't. I have an engagement with some friends from the office. Next time (**la próxima vez**) perhaps?

| encantado/a | I'll be delighted (said by a man/woman) |
| quizá, quizás | perhaps |

How do you say it?

Making suggestions

¿Qué te/le parece si (vamos a ...)? *What about (going to...)?*

¿Qué tal si (cenamos en ...)? *What about (having dinner at...)?*

| ¿Qué os parece invitar a Mercedes? | *What about inviting Mercedes?* |
| Podríamos ir a tomar una copa, ¿qué te parece? | *We could go and have a drink, what do you think?* |

Asking people what they would like to do, and responding

| ¿Qué te/le gustaría/apetece (hacer)? | *What would you like (to do)?* |
| Me gustaría/apetece (salir un rato). | *I'd like (to go out for a while).* |

Arranging to meet someone

¿A qué hora/Dónde quedamos?	*What time/Where shall we meet?*
Podríamos quedar en (la puerta).	*We could meet at (the entrance).*
¿Quedamos (aquí mismo)?	*Shall we meet (right here)?*

Inviting someone, and accepting or declining an invitation

¿Quieres/quiere Vd. venir a (cenar)?	*Would you like to come for (dinner)?*
Encantado/a.	*I'll be delighted.*
Me encantaría, pero no puedo.	*I'd love to, but I can't.*
Tengo un/otro compromiso.	*I have an/another engagement.*
Tengo que (trabajar/estudiar).	*I have to (work /study).*

Grammar

1 The conditional tense

Usage

a In the sentence *I would buy it but I don't have money*, *'would buy'* is *conditional*. As the name implies, the conditional tense is used to refer to actions or events which might take place given certain conditions (in the example above, *If I had money...*). Spanish expresses conditions in a similar way: **Lo compraría, pero no tengo dinero.**

b The conditional tense is also used with verbs such as **poder** *to be able to, can,* **deber** *to have to, must,* followed by the *infinitive*:

Podríamos quedar en la esquina.			*We could meet at the corner.*
Deberías decírselo.			*You should tell him/her.*

c It is also used for politeness in sentences like the following:

¿Le/te importaría no fumar?	*Would you mind not smoking?*
¿Le gustaría venir a mi fiesta de cumpleaños?	*Would you like to come to my birthday party?*

Formation

Like the future tense (see Unit 20), the conditional is formed with the whole infinitive, to which the endings are added, the same for **–ar, -er** and **–ir** verbs. Here is the conditional of three regular verbs, **invitar** *to invite*, **ser** *to be*, **ir** *to go*. Note that the first and third person singular have the same forms and that all forms have a written accent.

yo	invitaría	sería	iría
tú	invitarías	serías	irías
él, ella, Vd.	invitaría	sería	iría
nosotros/as	invitaríamos	seríamos	iríamos
vosotros/as	invitaríais	seríais	iríais
ellos, ellas, Vds.	invitarían	serían	irían

Yo los invitaría a todos.	*I'd invite them all.*
Hoy no puedo, otro día sería mejor.	*Today I can't, another day would be better.*
Iríamos con vosotros, pero estamos ocupados.	*We'd go with you but we are busy.*

2 Irregular conditional forms

Irregular conditional forms are the same as those for the future tense (see Unit 20), their endings being no different from those of regular verbs.

decir *to say, tell*: diría, dirías, diría, diríamos, diríais, dirían.

hacer *to do, make*: haría, harías, haría, haríamos, haríais, harían.

poder *to be able to, can*: podría, podrías, podría, podríamos, podríais, podrían.

poner *to put*: pondría, pondrías, pondría, pondríamos, pondríais, pondrían.

querer *to want, love*: querría, querrías, querría, querríamos, querríais, querrían.

saber *to know*: sabría, sabrías, sabría, sabríamos, sabríais, sabrían.

salir *to leave, go out*: saldría, saldrías, saldría, saldríamos, saldríais, saldrían.

tener *to have*: tendría, tendrías, tendría, tendríamos, tendríais, tendrían.

venir *to come*: vendría, vendrías, vendría, vendríamos, vendríais, vendrían.

The conditional form of **haber** is **habría** (**hay**, in the present tense) *there would be.*

3 **Apetecer** *to appeal, to feel like, to fancy* **parecer** *to seem*

a To say something appeals to you or you feel like something or doing something, use **apetecer**, in a construction similar to that with **gustar** *to like* (see Unit 13), in which the person to whom something is appealing goes before **apetecer**: **Me apetece un helado** *I feel like an ice cream* (literally, *To me appeals an ice cream*). As with **gustar**, **apetecer** will be preceded by one of the following pronouns: **me, te, le, nos, os, les** (see Units 8 and 13). Here are some more examples:

¿Te apetece dar un paseo?	*Do you feel like going for a walk?*
Me apetece un café bien caliente.	*I fancy a very hot coffee.*

Apetecer is used especially in Spain but is rather uncommon in Latin America. The alternative, of course is to use **querer** or **gustar**, which are used in all countries: **¿Qué quieres/te gustaría hacer?** *What do you want/would like to do?*

b Parecer, *to seem* (see Unit also 16) functions in the same way above, so a suggestion such as **¿Qué te parece si vamos al fútbol?** *What about going to the football?* translates literally as *What to you it seems if we go to the football?*. Here are some more examples of the use of **parecer** in suggestions:

| ¿Qué te/le parece si la llamamos? | What about calling her/if we call her? |
| ¿Qué os parece comenzar mañana? | What about starting tomorrow? |

Practice

1 ¿Qué haría Maite?

Maite is busy at the office today and she is dreaming about the things she would do if she did not have to work. Change the infinitives into the appropriate form of the conditional tense.

Yo
a (Hacer) la compra.
b (Lavar) la ropa.
c (Escribir) algunas cartas.
d (Llamar) a mi novio.

Mi novio y yo
e (Salir) en el coche.
f (Ver) alguna exposición.
g (Tener) tiempo para ir a nadar.
h (Poder) ir a bailar.

2 Pensaba quedarme en casa

It's Saturday and you are making plans for the evening, so you phone a Spanish friend and make arrangements to see a play. Fill in your part of the conversation by following the guidelines below.

– ¿Dígame?
– *Say who you are and ask your friend if he/she has any plans for the evening.*
– No, niguno. Pensaba quedarme en casa. ¿Por qué?
– *Suggest going to the theatre together.*
– ¿Qué te apetece ver?
– *Choose from the plays below and say which one you would like to see. Ask whether he/she has seen it.*
– No, no la he visto, pero me encantaría verla.
– *Say it is on at the Olimpia and that it starts at 7.00. Suggest meeting in the cafe opposite the theatre at 6.30. Ask if that is all right with him/her.*
– Sí, me parece bien.

LAS ESTRELLAS DE LA GUIA DEL OCIO

	Alberto de la Hera	Eduardo Haro Tecglen	Enrique Centeno	Lorenzo L. Sancho
✓ Novedad	Guía del Ocio	El País	Diario 16	ABC
OBRAS EN CARTEL				
1. Mi pobre Marat ✓	★★★★	—	—	★★★★★
2. La evitable ascensión ✓	★★★★	—	★★★★	★★★
3. La zapatera prodigiosa ✓	★★★	★★★★	★★★★	—
4. Terror y miseria ...	★★★	★★★	★★★★	★★★★★
5. Los padres terribles ✓	★★★★	★★★	—	★★★★
6. Amor, coraje y compasión	★★★	★★	★★★★	★★

★★★★★ **Excepcional**   ★★★★ **Muy buena**   ★★★ **Buena**   ★★ **Regular**   ★ **Mala**

▶ 3 Unas invitaciones

Lucía, señor Flores, and Mario, each have an invitation. Where are they being invited? Which of them accepts the invitation, and what excuse is given by those who decline it? Listen and fill in the box below.

Nombre	Invitación	¿Acepta o no?	Excusa
Lucía			
Sr. Flores			
Mario			

el cóctel	*cocktail party*	**nuevo/a**	*new*
la bienvenida	*welcome*	**celebrar**	*to celebrate*

4 Una invitación informal

This morning your receive an e-mail from a Spanish colleague. Where is he inviting you, and where and at what time does he suggest you meet?

¡Hola!

Tengo dos entradas para ver a Joaquín Cortés. ¿Te gustaría venir conmigo? La función es a las 8:00 y podríamos quedar en el bar que está al lado del teatro a las 7:30. Después de la función, si te apetece, me gustaría invitarte a cenar.

¿Qué te parece? Llámame.

Rafael

5 Ahora tú

Write an e-mail to your Spanish friend inviting him/her somewhere. Choose something that interests you or one of the following and suggest a place and a time you can meet:

(una función de) ballet/ópera
un concierto (de rock/jazz/música clásica)
una obra de teatro
(un) partido de fútbol/tenis/rugby
una carrera de coches/caballos

la obra de teatro	*play*	**la carrera**	*race*
el partido	*game*	**el caballo**	*horse*

6 Una invitación formal

On a visit to a Spanish-speaking country you and your travelling companion receive a formal invitation. Your colleague does not understand Spanish so he/she asks you to translate it for him/her.

La Cámara de Comercio de Santa Cruz tiene el agrado de invitarle a la ceremonia de inauguración de sus nuevas oficinas.

El acto de apertura, en el que participarán las autoridades locales, se realizará en la Avenida del Libertador, 52, el martes 25 de mayo a las 19:30.

la **Cámara de Comercio**	*Chamber of Commerce*
tener el agrado de	*to have pleasure in*
la apertura	*opening*
realizarse	*to take place*

i Read this passage dealing with invitations and punctuality among Spanish and Latin American people, and find out how their customs differ from those in your country.

En España y en Latinoamérica, en invitaciones y citas de tipo formal, cuando no hay una relación íntima o de amistad con los anfitriones, la gente es más o menos puntual. Pero, si el que invita es un amigo o pariente, la puntualidad no suele ser la norma. ¿Un amigo te ha invitado a una fiesta para las 9:00 o las 10:00? Pues, si llegas a la hora tu amigo seguramente se sorprenderá, y quizás él mismo no estará preparado para recibirte a esa hora. Media hora o incluso una hora de retraso se considera normal. En algunos países de habla española se utiliza la expresión **hora inglesa** cuando se espera puntualidad, por ejemplo **Quedamos a las seis, pero a las seis hora inglesa, ¿eh?** *So, six o'clock it is, but six o'clock sharp, OK?*

22

¿le sirvo un poco más?

shall I give you some more?

In this unit you will learn how to:
- talk about what you had done
- express compliments
- offer something and respond to an offer
- express gratitude and pleasure

▶ 1 ¿Qué le parece la ciudad?

On a business trip to Mérida in Mexico, Laura, from Spain, meets Victoria. The relationship is formal and this is reflected in the language of the dialogues below.

1.1 Had Laura been to Mérida before? What does she think of the city? Listen and find out.

Victoria   ¿Había estado aquí antes?
Laura   Había estado en la Ciudad de México, pero nunca había venido a Mérida.
Victoria   ¿Qué le parece la ciudad?
Laura   Me encanta. Es una ciudad preciosa.

1.2 Read the dialogue, study the vocabulary and new expressions, and then translate the following into Spanish.

a Had you been to Spain before?
b I had been in Barcelona, but I'd never come to Granada.
c What do you think of the hotel?
d I like it. It's a very good hotel.

había estado	*I/you/ he/she had been*
había venido	*I/you /he/she had come*
precioso/a	*beautiful*

▶ 2 Está buenísimo

Victoria and her husband invite Laura for dinner and she compliments her hosts on the meal.

2.1 Listen to the conversation and focus attention on the phrases used by Laura to describe the dish, and on how she's been offered some more food or something more to drink. As you listen, try completing the following sentences.

a El pescado está _____.
b Está _____.
c ¿Le sirvo _____?
d ¿Quiere _____ vino?

Laura	El pescado está buenísimo.
Victoria	Es una especialidad mexicana. ¿No lo había comido nunca antes?
Laura	No, nunca, está delicioso.
Victoria	¿Le sirvo un poco más?
Laura	No, gracias.
Victoria	¿De verdad?
Laura	De verdad, gracias.
Jorge	¿Quiere un poco más de vino?
Laura	Sí, gracias, pero sólo un poco.

2.2 Read the dialogue and study the expressions you might need when being invited for a meal or when playing host to a Spanish-speaking person. Then try saying the following in Spanish:

a The *paella* is very good.
b The chicken is delicious.
c Shall I give you some more dessert? (formal)
d Would you like some more coffee? (formal)

la especialidad	*especialty*
había comido	*I/you/he/she had eaten*
servir (e>i)	*to serve*
¿de verdad?	*Are you sure?, really? (literally truly?)*
de verdad	*I'm sure, really*

▶ 3 ¡Qué tarde es!

Laura is leaving and she and her hosts exchange some compliments.

3.1 Choose from the following expressions to complete the sentences in the bubbles below, then listen to the conversation to see whether you were right.

a tenerla en nuestra casa   **c** la invitación
b de haberla conocido   **d** muy amables

Laura	¡Uy, qué tarde es! Debo irme. Muchas gracias por la invitación. Han sido ustedes muy amables.
Jorge	Ha sido un placer tenerla en nuestra casa. Me alegro mucho de haberla conocido.
Victoria	Gracias por haber venido. ¡Que tenga un buen viaje!
Laura	Adiós, y muchísimas gracias.

3.2 Read the dialogue and find the expressions meaning the following:

a How late it is!
b I must go.

c Thank you for coming.
d Have a nice journey!

amable	*kind*
el placer	*pleasure*
me alegro (from **alegrarse**)	*I'm glad*
haber	*to have* (auxiliary verb)

i En España cuando se quiere invitar a una persona, especialmente a una persona a la que no se conoce bien, generalmente se la invita a un restaurante u otro sitio similar. La mayor parte de la vida social en España y en la mayoría de los países latinoamericanos tiene lugar en sitios públicos, tales como restaurantes, bares o cafés. La invitación a comer o cenar en casa generalmente está reservada para amigos más íntimos o parientes, y en ocasiones más especiales. En algunos países de Latinoamérica, sin embargo, la gente acostumbra invitar a sus amigos y conocidos a casa con más frecuencia.

Si la invitación es para comer o cenar en casa de un amigo, no es obligación llevar algo, pero si quieres hacerlo, puedes llevar una botella de vino o el postre. Pero, si la relación es formal, tendrás que llevar algo, por ejemplo champán o flores o bombones (*chocolates*) para la señora de la casa.

How do you say it?

Talking about what you had done

Nunca había estado/venido aquí.	*I/you* (formal)/*he/she had never been/come here.*
No lo habíamos comido antes.	*We hadn't eaten it before.*

Expressing compliments about food

Esto/el pescado está muy bueno/buenísimo/ delicioso.	*This/the fish is very good/ delicious.*

Expressing gratitude and pleasure

Gracias por la invitación/ la comida.	*Thanks for the invitation/the meal.*
Ha sido Vd. muy amable.	*You've been very kind.* (formal)
Ha sido un placer/gusto	*It's been a pleasure.* (formal)

Offering something and responding to an offer

¿Te/le sirvo un poco más?	*Shall I give you some more?* (inf/ formal)
¿De verdad?/¿De veras?	*Are you sure?/Really?*
De verdad/De veras.	*I'm sure/Really.*
Sí, gracias/por favor.	*Yes, thank you/ please.*

Grammar

1 Saying what you had done: *the pluperfect tense*

To express ideas such as *I had never visited Argentina, We hadn't seen it,* you need the *pluperfect tense.* This is formed with the imperfect of **haber** (see Unit 17) and a *past participle* (see Unit 19): **Nunca había visitado Argentina, No lo/la habíamos visto.** Below is the pluperfect tense of **estar** *to be,* **comer** *to eat,* **venir** *to come.* Note that, as for the imperfect, the first and third person singular are the same.

yo	había	estado	comido	venido
tú	habías	estado	comido	venido
él, ella, Vd.	había	estado	comido	venido
nosotros/as	habíamos	estado	comido	venido
vosotros/as	habíais	estado	comido	venido
ellos, ellas,Vds.	habían	estado	comido	venido

For irregular past participles see Unit 19.

Había estado ocupado/a.	*I/you/he/she had been busy.*
Todavía no habían comido.	*They hadn't eaten yet.*
¿Por qué no habías venido a verme?	*Why hadn't you come to see me?*

2 Offering something: *Shall I ...?, Would you like ...?*

To offer someone something, as in *Shall I bring you something to drink?*, Spanish uses the present tense in a construction in which the person being offered something comes first: **¿Te traigo algo para beber?** (literally, *To you I bring something to drink?*). Here are some more examples:

| ¿Le(s) sirvo (un poco) más (de) té? | *Shall I give you some more tea?* (formal, sing/pl) |
| ¿Te/os doy un bocadillo? | *Shall I give you a sandwich?* (inf, sing/pl) |

Alternative ways of offering someone something are through the use of **querer** in the *present tense* or the *conditional*.

| ¿Quiere(s) un poco más de ensalada? | *Do you want some more salad?* (formal/inf) |
| ¿Querría usted algún licor? | *Would you like a liqueur?* (formal) |

3 Exclamations

To say *how,* as in *How late it is!, How kind you are!, How difficult it is!* use **qué**: **¡Qué tarde es!, ¡Qué amable es usted!, ¡Qué difícil es!** Note the use of a double exclamation mark and a written accent on **qué**.

Practice

1 Lo que había hecho Francisco

Here are some of the things Francisco had done before he got married. Match the drawings with the phrases below, then use the verbs in brackets to say what he had done.

a (escribir) un libro de poemas
b (terminar) la carrera de medicina
c (viajar) por el mundo
d (aprender) a conducir
e (hacer) el servicio militar
f (estudiar) guitarra clásica

2 ¿Qué había ocurrido?

Events which were prior to some past event or state, and which are somehow related, are normally expressed with the *pluperfect tense*, for example **El campo estaba muy verde. Había llovido mucho.** *The country was very green. It had rained a lot.* Now match the phrases below and form similar sentences.

a La llamé a su casa.

b Lo/le reconocí inmediatamente.

c Hablaba español perfectamente.

d Estaban muy cansados.

1 Lo había estudiado en el colegio.

2 Ya había salido.

3 Habían andado muchas horas.

4 Habíamos trabajado juntos.

▶ 3 Una invitación formal

You are visiting a Spanish-speaking country and during your stay you are invited for lunch. Follow the guidelines and fill in your part of the conversation.

Mujer ¿Había estado aquí antes?

Tú *Say you had never been here before. Add that it is a very nice country.*

Mujer Gracias.

Tú *(The main course consists of* mariscos, *seafood.) Tell your hosts that the* mariscos *are very good.*

Marido Es un plato típico de aquí.

Tú *Say they are delicious.*

Mujer ¿Le sirvo un poco más?

Tú *Say yes, but just a little.*

Marido ¿Le pongo un poco más de vino?

Tú *Say no, thank you.*

Marido ¿De verdad?

Tú *Say yes, sure, thank you, you can't drink any more because you have to drive* (conducir)*.*

4 Ahora tú

You are having a formal dinner party with people you don't know well. How would you offer your guests more of the following? Try varying the expressions you use.

5 ¿Qué dirías tú?

Each of these sentences contains one mistake. Can you spot it?

a Muchas gracias para tu regalo. Es precioso.
b Gracias, señora. Has sido usted muy amable.
c Me alegro mucho haberte conocido, Antonio.
d Ha sido un placer conocerlo, señora.

> **el regalo** *present*

6 Una carta de agradecimiento *(A thank-you letter)*

On her return to Spain, Laura sent a thank-you letter to her host in Mexico. Fill in the gaps in her letter with one of the following words.

> placer   visita   marido   poder   agradecer   estancia

Estimada Victoria:

Quisiera _____ a usted y a su _____ las muchas atenciones que tuvieron conmigo durante mi _____ en México. Fue realmente un _____ haberlos conocido y espero _____ corresponder de igual forma durante su próxima _____ a España.

Atentamente

Laura Sánchez

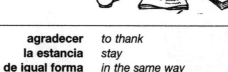

> **agradecer**   *to thank*
> **la estancia**   *stay*
> **de igual forma** *in the same way*

i Thank-you letters are much less common in Spanish than in English, except in more formal situations such as the one above. In more informal relationships people, especially the young, normally dispense with such formalities.

23

siga todo recto
go straight on

**In this unit you will learn
how to:**
- ask for directions (2)
- give directions (2)
- give instructions

▶ 1 Gire a la derecha

1 In dialogue one, as in dialogue two, you'll hear people asking for and giving directions.

1.1 Agustín, who is outside the Telefónica (16 on the map) on avenida Tejada, stops his car to ask for directions. What place is he looking for? Listen and try to follow the directions on the map. Key phrases here are **siga todo recto** *go straight on,* **when you get to ...** *al llegar ...,* **gire a la derecha/izquierda** *turn right/left.*

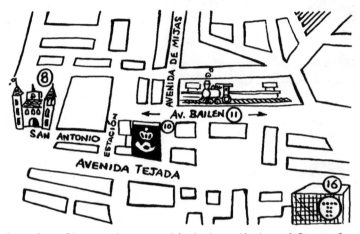

Agustín	Oiga, por favor, ¿podría decirme dónde está Correos?
Señora	Mire, siga todo recto y al llegar a la avenida de Mijas gire a la derecha. Correos está en la calle de Bailén, la segunda a la izquierda.
Agustín	¿Hay que tomar la avenida de Mijas, me ha dicho?
Señora	Sí, tome la cuarta calle a la derecha.
Agustín	Gracias.
Señora	De nada.

1.2 Read the dialogue now, study the vocabulary and try saying the following in Spanish.

– *Could you tell me where the museum is?*
– *Go straight on and when you reach Cervantes Street turn left. The museum is on San Alfonso Avenue, the third on the right.*

---

hay que...   *you have/one has to...*

▶ 2 Suba usted por esa escalera

Back at his hotel, Agustín asks the hotel receptionist how to get to the restaurant.

2.1 Listen to the conversation a few times and say whether the following statements are true or false (**verdaderos o falsos**).

a Para ir al restaurante hay que bajar al primer piso.
b El restaurante está en el pasillo de la izquierda.
c Está enfrente del bar.

Agustín	Perdone, ¿dónde está el restaurante, por favor?
Recepcionista	Suba usted por esa escalera hasta el primer piso y tome el pasillo de la izquierda. El restaurante está pasado el bar.
Agustín	Gracias.

2.2 Now complete the following sentence without looking at the dialogue; then read this and check if you were right:

Suba usted _____ esa escalera _____ el primer piso y tome el pasillo _____ la izquierda.

la escalera	*stairs*	**el pasillo**	*corridor*
hasta	*to/up to*	**pasado**	*past*

▶ 3 Hágalo después de la señal

Agustín phoned a doctor's surgery to make an appointment, but he got a recorded message.

3.1 Listen to the recorded message several times, each time focusing attention on a different point.

a ¿Cuál es el horario de atención al público del doctor García?
b ¿A qué número hay que llamar para urgencias?
c ¿Qué número hay que marcar para anular una cita?

Contestador: Esta es la consulta del doctor Ignacio García. Lamentamos no poder atender a su llamada en este momento. Nuestro horario de atención es de 9:00 a 11:30 de la mañana y por la tarde de 4:00 a 6:00. Para urgencias, llame al 952 642 21 09. Para anular una cita, marque el 952 759 55 32. Para pedir hora con el doctor, indíquenos su nombre y número de teléfono y le confirmaremos su cita. Hágalo después de la señal. Gracias.

3.2 Formal instructions can also be given with the infinitive, for example **dejar** instead of **deje** su número de teléfono, *leave your telephone number*. Now read the dialogue and try to identify the verb forms corresponding to these infinitives, and study the way in which they have been used:

a marcar   e indicar
b llamar   d hacer

la consulta	*surgery*
lamentar	*to regret*
la señal	*signal*
pedir hora	*to ask for an appointment*

How do you say it?

Asking for directions

¿Podría decirme dónde está ..../el museo?
Could you tell me where it is/the museum is?

¿Sabe Vd. dónde está .../ el ayuntamiento?
Do you know where it is/the town hall is?

Giving directions formally

Siga todo recto/de frente/ derecho. (LAm)
Go straight on.

Gire/Tuerza/Doble a la izquierda.
Turn left.

Tome/Coja la primera calle .....
Take the first street/turning.....

Suba/Baje por esa escalera.
Go up/down those stairs.

Está pasada la recepción/ pasado el bar.
It's past the reception/the bar.

Giving instructions formally

Llame al/Marque el (número .....)
Call/Dial (number .....)

Grammar

1 Giving directions and instructions:
the imperative

Usage

a Directions and instructions are usually given in English through the *imperative* or command form of the verb: *Turn left, Go straight on, Dial 999*. In Spanish there are two main ways of giving directions and instructions, one is with the *present tense* (see Unit 4), the other with the *imperative*. Compare the following sentences in which the first verb form corresponds to the present tense, the other to the imperative (both for **Vd.**): **Gira/Gire a la izquierda, Sigue/Siga de frente, Marca/Marque el 999**. Both forms are just as frequent in this context.

b The imperative has a number of other uses, both in English and Spanish. It is used to give orders or commands, *Do it now!*, **¡Hágalo ahora!**, in certain forms of requests, *Come in, please* **Pase, por favor** and in suggestions, *Speak to her* **Hable con ella**. The present tense is musch less common in this context.

Formation

Spanish uses different imperative forms, depending on whether you are addressing someone formally or informally (*formal* and *informal* imperative forms), and whether you are talking to one or more than one person (*singular* and *plural* forms). Informal imperatives also have different *positive* and *negative* forms. This unit focuses on the *formal imperative*. For the informal imperative see Unit 24.

a The imperative for **usted** is formed with the *stem* of the first person singular of the *present tense* (**yo**) to which the endings are added: **-e** for **-ar** verbs and **-a** for verbs in **-er** and **-ir**. For the **ustedes** form add **-n**. Stem-changing and most irregular verbs follow the same rule. Here are some examples, of which the first three correspond to regular verbs.

Infinitive	Present tense	Imperative (sing/pl)
tomar *to take*	tomo	tome/n
beber *to drink*	bebo	beba/n
subir *to go up*	subo	suba/n
seguir *to go on*	sigo	siga/n
torcer *to turn*	tuerzo	tuerza/n
decir *to say, tell*	digo	diga/n

Tome(n) la primera calle a la derecha. — *Take the first street on the right.*

Suba(n) por aquí. — *Go up this way.*

Siga/(n) hasta el primer semáforo. — *Go on as far as the first traffic light.*

Tuerza(n) a la izquierda. — *Turn left.*

b A few verbs change their spelling in the imperative in order to keep the same consonant sound as the infinitive. Among these we find:

Infinitive	Present tense	Imperative (sing/pl)
buscar *to look for*	busco	busque/n
marcar *to dial*	marco	marque/n
coger *to take*	cojo	coja/n
llegar *to arrive*	llego	llegue/n

Coja(n) la primera a la derecha. — *Take the first on the right.*

Marque(n) el 100. — *Dial 100.*

c Some irregular imperatives have forms which do *not* follow the pattern of the present tense.

Infinitive	Present tense	Imperative (sing/pl)
dar *to give*	doy	dé/n
estar *to be*	estoy	esté/n
ir *to go*	voy	vaya/n
saber *to know*	sé	sepa/n
ser *to be*	soy	sea/n

Dé(n) la vuelta aquí.	*Turn round here.*
Vaya(n) despacio.	*Go slowly.*
Sea(n) prudente(s).	*Be careful!*

d For *negative* formal imperatives simply place **no** before the verb: **No beba si va a conducir** *Don't drink if you are going to drive*, **No diga/haga nada** *Don't say/do anything*.

To make the imperative sound less abrupt, as in commands or requests, you are advised to use polite forms such as **por favor** *please*, **si no le importa** *if you don't mind*, **si es tan amable** *if you would be so kind*.

Envíemelo por email, si no le importa.   *Send it to me by e-mail, if you don't mind.*

2 Position of pronouns with imperatives

Pronouns like **me, te, lo/a, le,** etc., are attached to the end of positive imperatives but precede negative ones: **Démelos, por favor** *Give them to me, please*, **No me los dé** *Don't give them to me*, **¡Hágalo!** *Do it!*, **¡No lo haga!** *Don't do it!*

A written accent is usually necessary to show that the stress remains in the same position when the pronoun is added, as in **haga - hágalo, diga - dígame.**

Practice

1 Señales de tráfico

Can you match the following traffic signs with their meanings opposite?

a Gire a la derecha.
b No toque la bocina.
c Ceda el paso.
d Cruce de peatones. Conduzca con cuidado.

e Zona de escuela. Disminuya la velocidad.
f Cruce ferroviario. Pare, mire y escuche.
g No adelantar.
h No entrar.

▶ 2 Está una calle más arriba

Look at this map showing some hotels in a South American town and then listen to the directions given to a tourist who is trying to find a hotel. In which hotel is the tourist now and which one is he looking for?

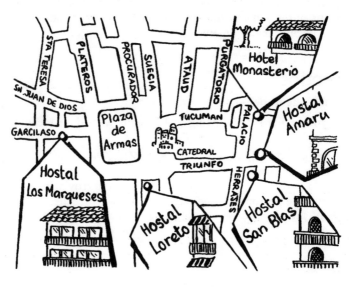

al salir	*when you leave/on leaving*
doble (from **doblar**)	*to turn*
más arriba	*further up*

3 Hay una desviación

Read this email with directions sent to Antonia by someone she is visiting, and fill in the gaps with the appropriate formal imperative forms of these verbs: **tomar, subir, seguir, preguntar, girar.**

_____ usted de frente por la avenida de Suel y al llegar a la carretera nacional 340 _____ usted a la izquierda en dirección al aeropuerto. Antes de llegar al aeropuerto hay una desviación hacia Santa Clara. _____ usted esa desviación y _____ todo recto hasta llegar a una estación de servicio. Nuestra fábrica está pasada la estación de servicio. _____ usted hasta nuestras oficinas, que están en la tercera planta, y _____ por mí en recepción.

la carretera	*road, highway*
la desviación	*diversion*
hacia	*towards*
hasta	*until, as far as*
la planta	*floor*

4 ¿Sabe usted dónde hay un banco?

A Spanish-speaker asks you for directions in your own town. Use the guidelines below to complete your part of the conversation.

– Perdone, ¿sabe usted dónde hay un banco?
– *Say yes and tell him/her to go straight on and take the third turning on the left, then take the first turning on the right and go straight on as far as the end of the road. The bank is opposite the station.*

5 Ahora tú

You are outside the church, **la iglesia,** on calle San Antonio (8 on the map on page 239) when someone approaches you to ask for directions to the station (11 on the map).

How would you reply?

– Perdone, ¿podría decirme dónde está la estación?

6 Tráigamela, por favor

Read this brief exchange between Elsa and her boss.

Elsa ¿Le traigo la correspondencia de hoy? (sí)
Jefe/a Sí, tráigamela, por favor.
Elsa ¿Abro la ventana? (no)
Jefe/a No, no la abra.

How would Elsa's boss reply to each of the following?

Follow the examples, using written accents where appropriate.

a ¿Envío el fax?(sí)
b ¿Llamo a la secretaria? (sí)
c ¿Hago el pedido? (no)
d ¿Le paso las carpetas? (sí)
e ¿Contesto el mail? (no)
f ¿Le enseño el informe? (sí)

¿envío el fax?

hacer un pedido	*to place an order*
la carpeta	*file*
enseñar	*to show*
el informe	*report*

24

me duele la cabeza

I have a headache

In this unit you will learn how to:
- say how you feel
- describe minor ailments
- make requests
- give advice

▶ 1 Un dolor de cabeza

Marta is feeling unwell and she describes her symptoms to her friend Luis.

1.1 Listen to the conversation a few times and, without looking at the text below, try completing these sentences:

a Por favor, _____ una aspirina.

b _____ muchísima sed.

c Sí, _____ un momento.

Luis	¿Qué te pasa?
Marta	Tengo un dolor de cabeza horrible.
Luis	¿Quieres tomar algo?
Marta	Sí, por favor tráeme una aspirina y un vaso de agua. Tengo muchísima sed.
Luis	Sí, espera un momento. Vuelvo en seguida.

1.2 Now read the text and find the phrases which mean the following:

a What's wrong with you?

b I'll be right back

la cabeza	*head*
el vaso	*glass*
tener sed	*to be thirsty*

▶ 2 Tengo mucho calor

Luis comes back to Marta after some time.

2.1 Listen to the conversation and answer these questions:

a How is Marta feeling now?
b Why does she ask Luis to open the window?
c What does Luis suggest she does?

Luis ¿Te encuentras mejor?
Marta No, no me encuentro bien. Me duele la cabeza todavía y tengo mucho calor. Por favor, abre la ventana un poco.
Luis Sí, claro. Mira, ¿por qué no descansas un rato? Trata de dormir. Te hará bien. No te levantes.
Marta ¿Podrías apagar la luz, por favor? Y no me esperes para cenar.
Luis Muy bien. No comas nada hasta mañana.

2.2 Now read the dialogue and find phrases which are similar in meaning to the following:

a No estoy bien.　　**c** ¿Puedes abrir la ventana?
b Tengo dolor de cabeza.　　**d** Tienes que descansar.

encontrarse (o>ue)	to feel
apagar la luz	to turn off the light
tratar de	to try to
descansar	to rest

How do you say it?

Saying how you feel

No me encuentro bien.　　*I don't feel well*
Tengo sed/calor.　　*I'm thirsty/hot.*

Describing minor ailments

Me duele la cabeza/el estómago.　　*I have a headache/a stomach ache.*
Tengo dolor de cabeza/ estómago/muelas/garganta.　　*I have a headache/stomach ache/toothache/sore throat.*

Making requests

Tráeme una aspirina/un vaso de agua. — *Bring me an aspirin/a glass of water.*

Abre/cierra la ventana/puerta. — *Open/close the window/door.*

¿Podrías apagar/encender la luz? — *Could you turn off/on the light?*

Giving advice

Trata de descansar/dormir. — *Try to rest/sleep.*

No te levantes/comas. — *Don't get up/eat.*

Grammar

1 The informal imperative or command: *tú* and *vosotros*

In Unit 23 you learnt to use the *formal imperative* or *command* form, for **usted** and **ustedes**. In this unit you will learn to use the *informal imperative*, for **tú** and **vosotros**. Unlike the formal imperative, which has similar positive and negative forms, for example **tome** *take*, **no tome** *don't take*, the informal one has different positive and negative forms.

Formation

a The **tú** form of the *positive* imperative or command is like the **tú** form of the present tense, but *without* the **–s**.

tú esper**as** *you wait*	espera *wait*
tú com**es** *you eat*	come *eat*
tú abr**es** *you open*	abre *open*

b For the **vosotros** form, replace the **–ar** of the infinitive with **–d**.

esper**ar**	esper**ad**
com**er**	com**ed**
abr**ir**	abr**id**

c Stem-changing verbs, for example **cerrar** (e>ie) *to shut, close*, **volver** (o>ue) *to come back*, make a similar change in the **tú** form of the imperative: cierra *shut, close*, vuelve *come back*. The endings are the same as for regular verbs in **a** above.

d A few verbs have irregular *positive* imperative or command forms for **tú**. For **vosotros** follow the pattern in **b** above.

decir	di	*say*
hacer	haz	*do, make*
ir	ve	*go*
poner	pon	*put*

salir	sal	*go/get out*
ser	sé	*be*
tener	ten	*have*
venir	ven	*come*

e *Negative* imperatives for **tú** and **vosotros** are different from positive ones. The general rule is as follows: verbs ending in **–ar** take **–e** and those in **–er** and **–ir** take **–a**.

esperar	no esperes – no esperéis	*don't wait*
comer	no comas – no comáis	*don't eat*
abrir	no abras – no abráis	*don't open*

f Some verbs form the *negative* informal imperative in a different way (See *irregular imperatives* Unit 23).

dar *to give*	no des – no deis	*don't give*
estar *to be*	no estés – no estéis	*don't be*
ir *to go*	no vayas – no vayáis	*don't go*
ser *to be*	no seas – no seáis	*don't be*

g Verbs ending in **–car** and **–gar**, **–ger** and **–gir** change their spelling in the negative imperative form in order to keep the same consonant sound of the infinitive.

bus**car** *to look for*	no bus**ques**/no bus**quéis**	*don't look for*
lle**gar** *to arrive*	no lle**gues**/no lle**guéis**	*don't arrive*
co**ger** *to take, catch*	no co**jas**/no co**jáis**	*don't take/catch*
ele**gir** *to choose*	no eli**jas**/no eli**jáis**	*don't choose*

Look at the examples which follow and see how they fit the rules above.

Espera un momento.	*Wait a moment.*
Come sólo un poco.	*Eat just a little.*
Abrid las ventanas.	*Open the windows.*
Ve a por un médico.	*Go and get a doctor.*
Haz lo que digo.	*Do as I say.*
Ponlo aquí.	*Put it here.*
Ten paciencia.	*Have patience.*
No nos esperes.	*Don't wait for us.*
No vayáis en el coche.	*Don't go in the car.*
No lleguéis tarde.	*Don't be late.*

2 Position of pronouns with imperatives

Just as with formal commands, pronouns are attached to the end of positive forms but precede negative ones (see Unit 23): **Hazlo** *Do it* , **No lo hagas** *Don't do it.*

3 Me duele... *It hurts...,*
Tengo dolor de... *I have a pain in...*

a Doler *to hurt,* is used in a construction similar to that with **gustar** (see Unit 13), in which the person who is affected by the pain goes before the verb. So you literally say '*to me, to you*', etc. '*it hurts*': **Me duele la cabeza** *I have a headache* (literally, *To me hurts the head*). If what hurts is plural, **doler** has to be plural: **Me duelen los pies** *My feet ache* (literally, *To me hurt the feet*)

Note that in place of the English possessive, as in *my feet, my back* etc., Spanish uses a definite article: **los pies, la espalda.** The use of **me, te, le,** etc. makes the use of a possessive unnecessary.

This construction with **doler** is much more common than that with **tener dolor de ...** below and it can be used with most parts of the body.

b Tener dolor de... *to have a pain in...* can replace **doler** in expressions such as **Tengo dolor de cabeza/estómago/muelas/espalda** *I have a headache/stomach/tooth/back ache.* With other parts of the body most speakers will use **doler** so, if in doubt, use this.

4 'Tener' for 'to be'

Note the use of **tener** for *to be* in expressions like the following:

Tengo hambre/sed/frío/calor. *I'm hungry/thirsty/cold/hot.*

Other expressions of this kind are

tener cuidado	*to be careful*
tener éxito	*to be successful*
tener miedo	*to be afraid*
tener paciencia	*to be patient*
tener razón	*to be right*
tener sueño	*to be sleepy*
tener suerte	*to be lucky*
tener vergüenza	*to be ashamed*

Practice

1 Las dolencias más comunes

Look at the chart below which lists the most common complaints in different European countries, including Spain, and compare the figures. How many words can you guess? Which countries seem the most healthy, according to the chart?

Las dolencias más comunes en Europa

%	España	Bélgica	Alemania	Italia	Países Bajos	Francia	Reino Unido
Fiebre/resfriado	70	69	51	65	51	64	81
Dolor de cabeza	48	43	35	46	35	49	63
Fatiga	31	40	14	29	14	47	45
Reumatismo	33	34	32	49	32	43	38
Ansiedad/insomnio	41	42	25	37	25	41	39
Problemas digestivos	27	32	22	33	22	34	28

Fuente: Secodip.

▶ 2 Una visita al doctor

You will hear two conversations between a patient and a doctor. Listen to the dialogues and answer the following questions.

a Which of the complaints in the chart do you associate with the patients' symptoms?
b What does each doctor advise the patient to do or what does he or she prescribe?

me siento (from **sentirse** e>ie to feel)	I feel (myself)
intranquilo/a	anxious
estresado/a	under stress
a ver ...	let's see ...
estomacal	stomach (adjective)
recetar	to prescribe
la pastilla	tablet, pill

3 Describe los síntomas

On a visit to a Spanish-speaking country you go to the doctor because you are feeling unwell. Describe your symptoms by filling in the gaps with one of these verbs:

| tener | tener dolor | sentirse/encontrarse | doler |

a No _____ bien.
b _____ la cabeza.
c _____ de estómago.
d _____ un poco de fiebre.
e _____ todo el cuerpo.
f _____ muy cansado/a.

| **el cuerpo** | body |

4 Un día de mucho calor

The heat seems to have affected you during your stay in a Spanish-speaking country, so you ask a friend for help. Follow the guidelines below and fill in your part of the conversation.

Amigo/a ¿Qué te pasa?
Tú *Tell your friend that you are not feeling well.*
Amigo/a ¿Qué tienes?
Tú *Say that you have a terrible headache and you are feverish.*
Amigo/a ¿Quieres tomar algo?
Tú *Ask your friend to bring you a glass of mineral water. Say you are very thirsty.*
Amigo/a Muy bien. ¿Quieres algo más?
Tú *Ask your friend to open the door. Say you are very hot.*
Amigo/a ¿Quieres comer algo?
Tú *Say no, thank you, you are not hungry.*

5 Consulta abierta

Two readers of a health magazine wrote to the editor seeking help with their problems. What are their problems? Read the letters and find out.

✉ Un problema de peso

Me llamo Isabel, tengo 45 años y tengo un problema común a mucha gente: no logro bajar de peso. Soy muy sociable y me encanta salir a comer con mis amigos. A veces me pongo a régimen durante unos días y bajo algunos kilos, pero no soy constante y subo de peso otra vez. Necesito una solución definitiva para terminar con este problema. ¿Qué puedo hacer?

Isabel

✉ Dolores de cabeza crónicos

Me llamo Ricardo, tengo 28 años y trabajo en un banco desde hace un año. Mi problema es que al final del día siento un dolor de cabeza devastador en la parte superior izquierda de la cabeza que me incapacita para todo. Después siento náuseas, que normalmente acaban en vómitos. He tratado de poner fin a este problema tomando analgésicos, pero no he tenido éxito. ¡Por favor ayúdenme y díganme qué puedo hacer!

Ricardo

el peso	*weight*
lograr	*to manage*
bajar/subir de peso	*to lose/gain weight*
ponerse a régimen	*to go on a diet*
sentir (e>ie)	*to feel*
acabar en	*to end up in*
poner fin	*to put an end*
ayudar	*to help*

6 ¿Qué consejos les darías?

Consider these words of advice. Which would be suitable for Isabel and which for Ricardo? Classify them accordingly using 'I' for Isabel and 'R' for Ricardo.

a No trabajes demasiado.
b No comas en exceso.
c Reduce el consumo de azúcar y grasas.
d Haz gimnasia o yoga para controlar tu estrés.
e Busca otro trabajo.
f Cambia tu dieta.

el azúcar *sugar*	**las grasas** *fat*	

i En España la mayoría de la gente recibe atención médica a través de **la Seguridad Social**, *social security*. Otros utilizan **la sanidad privada**, *private health services*. Los visitantes de otros países de la Unión Europea pueden recibir atención médica a través de la Seguridad Social. En caso de accidente u otra emergencia se puede recibir atención rápida en una **Casa de Socorro** o en un **Puesto de Socorro**, *first-aid post*.

la mayoría *majority*	**a través de** *through*	

25

quería alquilar un piso

I'd like to rent a flat

In this unit you will learn how to:
- say what sort of place or person you want
- express hope
- express uncertainty

▶ 1 ¿Qué tipo de piso busca?

Paloma would like to rent a flat and she makes enquiries at an estate agent.

1.1 What kind of flat is Paloma looking for and how much is she prepared to pay? Listen and reply. Key words here are **alquilar** *to rent*, **el piso** *flat*, **buscar** *to look for*, **amueblado** *furnished*.

Empleado	Buenos días. ¿Qué desea?
Paloma	Buenos días. Quería alquilar un piso.
Empleado	¿Qué tipo de piso busca usted? Tenemos varios.
Paloma	Pues, busco algo que esté cerca del centro, que tenga tres o cuatro dormitorios, y que no sea demasiado caro. No quiero pagar más de 800 euros mensuales. Y lo prefiero amueblado.
Empleado	Muy bien, veré lo que tenemos. Siéntese, por favor.

1.2 Now read the dialogue, then look at the advertisement below and say which of the flats listed in it might suit Paloma.

INMOBILIARIA SU CASA
Compra-Venta, Alquiler, Pisos, Locales

• **En urbanización cerca de Vendrell.** Torre de una planta en alquiler, 2 dormitorios, por todo el año, alquiler mensual 600 €).
• **Piso en alquiler.** Cornellá. 3 dorm., 650 €.

• **Piso en alquiler.** Amueblado, 3 dorm., San Ildefonso, 700 €.
• **San Ildefonso.** Planta baja en alquiler, 680 €, 2 dorm.
• **Piso.** En venta, 2 dorm., San Ildefonso, precio de 150.000 €.
• **Parcela en Vallirana.** Urbanización Can Prunera, 1300 m2, 90.000 €.

Suspiro, 2, 3ª, izq. – **T. 93 364 44 68** – Cornellá

1.3 ¿Qué tipo de piso o casa buscas tú? Adapt Paloma's part and state your own requirements, for example "cerca de la playa/en el campo, 2/3 dormitorios/garaje/jardín, que no cueste más de ..., amueblado/sin amueblar".

---

siéntese/siéntate	*sit down* (from **sentarse** e>ie, formal /inf)
la inmobiliaria	*estate agent*
el local	*premises*
la urbanización	*housing development*
la torre	*villa*
de una planta	*one-storey*
la parcela	*plot*

▶2 Espero que encuentres a alguien

Paloma has rented a flat and is looking for someone to share it with her.

2.1 What sort of person is Paloma looking for? Listen to a conversation between her and her friend Teresa and say whether the statements below are true or false (**verdaderos o falsos**). Key words here are **compartir** to *share*, **alguien** *someone*, **la edad** *age*, **fumar** to *smoke*.

a Paloma busca a alguien que tenga su misma edad.
b Quiere una persona que trabaje en casa.
c Prefiere una persona que no fume y que sea vegetariana.
d Quiere una persona que tenga gatos.

Paloma	Estoy buscando a alguien para compartir el piso. Si sabes de alguna persona, dímelo.
Teresa	¿Qué tipo de persona buscas?
Paloma	Pues, quiero una persona de mi edad, que trabaje fuera de casa, que no fume, que sea vegetariana... y que le gusten los gatos, como a mí.
Teresa	Espero que encuentres a alguien, pero no creo que sea fácil.

2.2 Read the dialogue and find the expressions meaning **I hope you'll find someone, I don't think it'll be easy.**

2.3 Ahora tú

Imagine you want to share the place where you live. Adapt Paloma's part and say what sort of person you are looking for. Here are some ideas: "(ser) joven/mayor, estudiante/ profesional, tranquilo/a, (tener) sentido del humor, (gustar) los deportes".

dímelo	*let me know* (literally *tell me it*)
fuera de	*away from*
el gato	*cat*
como a mí	*like me*

ℹ En España, es común que muchos jóvenes de veinte, veinticinco o incluso (*even*) treinta años vivan con sus padres. La imposibilidad de encontrar un empleo (*job*) limita su independencia. La vivienda (*housing*) es cara en las grandes ciudades como Madrid y Barcelona, y los jóvenes que trabajan a menudo prefieren compartir un piso con amigos, al menos (*at least*) en los primeros años.

En Latinoamérica, por tradición, es normal que los jóvenes, tanto hombres como mujeres, vivan con sus padres hasta el momento de casarse. Los jóvenes latinoamericanos, en general, son menos independientes que los españoles, y los padres son más estrictos con sus hijos.

tanto hombres como mujeres	*men as well as women*

How do you say it?

Saying what sort of place you want

Quiero un piso que tenga dos dormitorios.	*I want a flat with* (literally *which has*) *two bedrooms.*
Busco una casa que no sea demasiado cara.	*I'm looking for a house which is not too expensive.*
Prefiero que esté cerca de la playa.	*I prefer it to be near the beach.*

Saying what sort of person you want

Busco a alguien que no fume.	*I'm looking for someone who doesn't smoke.*
Quiero una persona que trabaje fuera de casa.	*I want a person who works away from home.*
Prefiero una persona que hable español.	*I prefer a person who speaks Spanish.*

Expressing hope

Espero que encuentres a alguien.	*I hope you find someone.*
Esperamos que sea agradable.	*We hope he/she/it will be pleasant.*

Expressing uncertainty

No creo que sea fácil/difícil.   *I don't think it will be easy/difficult.*

No creo que tenga garaje.   *I don't think it has a garage.*

Grammar

1 The subjunctive

Sentences such as **Busco un apartamento que esté cerca de la oficina** *I'm looking for an apartment which is near the office*, **No creo que sea difícil** *I don't think it'll be difficult,* like the rest of the examples above, refer to something which is hypothetical or unertain, something which may or may not become a reality. To express ideas such as these, Spanish uses a special form of the verb which is known 'technically'as *subjunctive.* The subjunctive is not a tense. It is described as a *mood* of the verb, itself comprising tenses of its own, just as the tenses you have learnt so far are part of the *indicative mood.* The subjunctive is used very rarely in modern English, but there are remnants of it in sentences such as the following: *I insist that he **come*** **Insisto en que *venga*,** *If I **were** you* **Yo en tu lugar** (literally, *I in your place*)

The subjunctive is very common in all forms of Spanish, spoken and written, formal and informal. Of the tenses of the subjunctive, the *present subjunctive* is the one used most, and the only one covered in this book. Look at the notes below to see how this is used and what its forms are.

2 The present subjunctive

Formation

The *present subjunctive* is formed by removing the –o of the first person singular of the ordinary present tense (or *present indicative*), to which the endings are added: –e for –ar verbs and –a for verbs in –er and –ir , just as for the formal imperative, with stem-changing and most irregular verbs following the same rule (see Unit 23)

Here are the full forms of **hablar** *to speak,* **comer** *to eat,* **vivir** *to live.*

yo	hable	coma	viva
tú	hables	comas	vivas
él, ella, Vd.	hable	coma	viva
nosotros/as	hablemos	comamos	vivamos
vosotros/as	habléis	comáis	viváis
ellos, ellas, Vds.	hablen	coman	vivan

A few verbs form the present subjunctive in a different way:

Infinitive	Present subjunctive
dar *to give*	dé, des, dé, demos, deis, den
estar *to be*	esté, estés, esté, estemos, estéis, estén
haber *to have* (auxiliary verb)	haya, hayas, haya, hayamos, hayáis, hayan
ir *to go*	vaya, vayas, vaya, vayamos, vayáis, vayan
saber *to know*	sepa, sepas, sepa, sepamos, sepáis, sepan
ser *to be*	sea, seas, sea, seamos, seáis, sean

Usage

a The subjunctive normally occurs in a construction with a *main verb*, for example **quiero** *I want*, followed by **que** *that, which, who*, and the subjunctive verb.

Quiero un hotel que no **sea** muy caro.	*I want a hotel which is not too expensive.*
Necesitan una persona que les **ayude**.	*They need a person who can help them.*

b It is used after verbs and expressions indicating possibility, wishes and requests, and thinking, the latter in negative sentences only.

Puede que lo **encuentres**.	*You may find it.* (possibility)
Quiero que me **llames**.	*I want you to call me.* (wish or request)
No creo que **vayan**.	*I don't think they'll go.* (thinking)

c It occurs after verbs and expressions indicating some kind of emotion and hope.

Me molesta que me **interrumpan.**	*It bothers me to be interrupted.*
Me alegro de que **vengan.**	*I'm glad they are coming.*
Espero que **sea** cierto.	*I hope it's true.*

d It is also used after impersonal expressions such as **es normal** *it is normal*, **es importante** *it is important*, **es extraño** *it is strange*.

Es normal que **vivan** con los padres.	*It is normal for them to live with their parents.*
Es importante que lo **hagáis.**	*It's important that you should do it.*
Es extraño que no **estén** en casa.	*It's strange that they are not at home.*

e It is required after **cuando** *when*, and other time expressions referring to the future, and after **para que** *so that* and with similar expressions indicating purpose.

Cuando **llegue** María se lo diré.	*When María arrives I'll tell her.*
Allí está para que lo **veas.**	*There it is so that you can see it.*

Practice

1 Buscando un lugar donde vivir

Look at the advertisements below placed by people looking for a flat or room to rent or let, or someone to share.

1.1 Can you give the contact name or telephone number for each of the following?

a an English teacher wanting to share a flat
b someone offering a room to a vegetarian and non-smoker
c a student of French looking for accommodation with a French family
d someone offering a large, sunny room to a female
e someone looking for a two-bedroom flat to rent
f someone looking for free accommodation for a weekend

INMOBILIARIA

Pisos

▲ **Busco familia** francesa que viva en Francia y que me alquile una habitación durante diez meses. Soy estudiante de francés. T. 642 65 54 21. Luisa.

▲ **Busco piso** en alquiler. Zona Sagrada Familia. Dos habitaciones, sala, cocina y baño. Pago máximo 420 € /mes. Persona responsable.
T. 94 418 50 05. Begoña.

▲ **Necesito sitio** gratis en Sitges, para pasar un fin de semana durante el Festival de Cinema Fantàstic. No molestaré.
T. 644 30 65 96 (de 17 a 20 h.). Carlota

▲ **Profesora de** inglés busca habitación en piso compartido. Preferiblemente zona centro. T. 93 330 16 87 (horas de oficina).

○ **Busco chica**, para compartir piso. Zona Valle Hebrón. Habitación grande y soleada. Urge a partir de octubre.
T. 93 357 26 71 (a partir 21h.)

○ **Busco chica** estudiante, para compartir piso junto Metro Marina. Precio: 240 € /mes+ gastos. T. 93 300 99 44 (de 21 a 22.30 h.).

○ **Llogo pis** zona Hospital de Sant Pau, 3 habitacions, cuna, menjador, gran terrassa i assolejat. Preu: 540 € /mes.
T. 973 44 04 57 (tardes).

○ **Sitges. Alquilo** habitación muy tranquila. Preferiblemente a persona vegetariana y no fumadora. T. 977 894 69 05 (noches).

1.2 One of the advertisements is in Catalan. Can you spot it? Give the contact number.

2 Estudiante busca familia española

One of your friends is travelling to Salamanca to do a Spanish course and would like to stay with a family. His/her Spanish is not very good, and he/she needs help to compose the following advertisement. Try making sense of what he/she wants by changing the verbs in brackets into the appropriate form of the present subjunctive.

Estudiante busca habitación con familia española

Estudiante de habla inglesa de 20 años busca familia española que (vivir) en Salamanca y que me (alquilar) una habitación durante el mes de agosto. Prefiero una familia en la que (hay) otras personas de mi edad que (poder) ayudarme con mi español. Preferiblemente un sitio que (estar) cerca de la universidad.
T. +44 (0)20 7741 3462.

3 Ahora tú

You will be spending some time in a Spanish-speaking country in order to improve your Spanish, and would like to share a flat with someone. Write an advertisement like those in Activity 1, or a note like the one above, saying what you are looking for.

4 No creo que …, Espero que …

Raúl and his flatmates are trying to choose another person to share their flat. His friend Juan hopes the person they are discussing will be the right one, but Carmen is rather pessimistic. Follow the example and answer for Juan and Carmen.

Raúl	¿Pagará puntualmente?
Juan	Espero que pague puntualmente.
Carmen	No creo que pague puntualmente.

a ¿Será sociable?
b ¿Estará dispuesto a hacer la limpieza?
c ¿Sabrá cocinar?
d ¿Tendrá sentido del humor?
e ¿Le gustarán los animales domésticos?
f ¿Se llevará bien con nosotros?

¿le gustarán los animales domésticos?

dispuesto/a a	*willing to*
los animales domésticos	*pets*
hacer la limpieza	*to clean (up)*
llevarse bien con	*to get on well with*

5 Los requisitos más importantes

Julio's company needs a new public relations employee and he has been asked to draw a list of possible requirements. Here are some notes he's jotted down. Give the English for each of the requirements listed by him and then complete the sentences using the present subjunctive in place of the infinitives.

a Es imprescindible que … (*saber* idiomas, *tener* carnet de conducir, *tener* experiencia y *ser* capaz de relacionarse bien con la gente).

b Es importante que ... (*ser* creativo y dinámico, *tener* buena presencia y *haber* terminado sus estudios superiores).

c Es necesario que ... (*tener* conocimientos de informática, *contar* con vehículo propio, *estar* dispuesto a viajar y *poder* incorporarse de inmediato a la empresa).

imprescindible	*essential*
conducir	*to drive*
capaz	*capable*
la presencia	*appearance*
los estudios superiores	*higher education*
la informática	*computing*
contar (o>ue) **con**	*to have*
estar dispuesto/a a	*to be willing*
incorporarse a	*to join*

▶ 6 ¿Qué tipo de persona buscan?

6.1 Julio and Isabel are discussing the requirements for the new employee their company is seeking. Which of the requirements in Activity 5 are mentioned by them? Listen to the conversation and tick them as you hear them.

veamos	*let's see*	**preferiblemente**	*preferably*

7 Una historia personal

In Spain, as in other industrialized nations, the people most affected by *unemployment*, **el desempleo**, are *the young,* **los jóvenes**. Read about José and about his experience with job-hunting and, as you do, try answering the following questions.

a What are José's qualifications?
b How is he described?
c What actions has he taken in order to get a job?
d Why hasn't he been able to get one?
e How does he feel?

José tiene veintinueve años, hizo la carrera de empresariales en Madrid y tiene un máster de una universidad en los Estados Unidos. José habla y escribe perfectamente inglés y francés. Es extrovertido y simpático, pero nunca ha conseguido un empleo. Nunca ha trabajado en una oficina, no ha tenido jamás un jefe ni compañeros de trabajo. Simplemente, no encuentra empleo, aunque ha ido muchas veces al *Instituto Nacional de Empleo*, ha enviado su currículum docenas de veces, ha leído cientos de anuncios de empleo en los periódicos, pero no ha tenido éxito. En unas empresas le piden experiencia, en otras le dicen que con sus títulos no pueden pagarle el salario que corresponde. José no sabe qué hacer, está desesperado.

(las ciencias) empresariales (f, pl)	*business studies*
conseguir (e>i)	*to get*
jamás	*never* (stronger than **nunca**)
compañero/a de trabajo	*colleague*
aunque	*although*
el Instituto Nacional de Empleo (m)	*Department of Employment*
el anuncio de empleo (m)	*job advertisement*
el éxito	*success*
pedir (e>i)	*to ask for*
el título	*qualification, degree*

i Note that **la oficina** and **el despacho** both translate *office* in English, but in Spanish they mean different things. **Oficina** describes an office in general terms, a place where a number of people work, while **despacho** refers to the actual room where someone works. In some Latin American countries the word **oficina** conveys both meanings.

Congratulations on completing *Teach Yourself Spanish*!

We hope you have enjoyed working your way through the course. We are always keen to receive feedback from people who have used our course, so why not contact us and let us know your reactions? We'll be particularly pleased to receive your praise, but we should also like to know if things could be improved. We always welcome comments and suggestions, and we do our best to incorporate constructive suggestions into later editions.

You can contact us through the publishers at:
Teach Yourself Books, Hodder Headline Ltd,
338 Euston Road, London NW1 3BH, UK

We hope you will want to build on your knowledge of Spanish and have made a few suggestions to help you do this in the section entitled **Taking it further**, on page 283.

¡Buena suerte!
Juan Kattán-Ibarra

Units 1–5

1 Fill in the gaps in this dialogue with an appropriate question word.

a '¿ _____ se llama usted?' 'Maricarmen García.'
b '¿ _____ está?' 'Muy bien, gracias, ¿y usted?'
c '¿De _____ es usted?' 'De Bilbao.'
d '¿ _____ número de teléfono tiene?' 'El 209 1520.'
e 'Y el teléfono de su oficina, ¿ _____ es?' 'El 312 2104.'
f '¿ _____ vive?' 'En la calle de San Pablo.'
g '¿ _____ va a tomar?' 'Quiero pescado con patatas fritas.'

(Units 1, 2, 3, 4, 5)

2 Fill in the gaps in this dialogue with the correct form of **ser** and **estar**.

Jaime   Hola, ¿cómo _____ (tú)?
Eloísa   (Yo) _____ muy bien, gracias.
Jaime   Ésta _____ Mónica, una amiga.
Eloísa   Hola, ¿qué tal? (Tú) no _____ española, ¿verdad?
Mónica   No, _____ argentina. _____ de Salta.
Eloísa   ¿Dónde _____ Salta?
Mónica   _____ en el norte de Argentina.

(Units 1, 2, 4)

3 You'll be meeting a group of Spanish speakers, so be prepared to exchange greetings and some personal information.

a Say 'good afternoon', and give your name and nationality.
b Spell your name and surname.
c Say what languages you speak.
d Tell someone you are pleased to meet him/her. (Give two alternatives.)
e Introduce Sarah Johnson, a colleague, to someone you don't know well.

f Say where you live and what your telephone number is.

(Antes de empezar, Units 3, 4)

4 You arrive in a hotel in a Spanish-speaking country. Use the guidelines below to fill in your part of the conversation with the hotel receptionist.

– ¿Dígame?
– *Good evening. I´d like a single room with a bathroom for two nights.*
– Muy bien.
– *Is breakfast included?*
– No, el desayuno es aparte. Son cuatro euros.
– *Where can I have dinner?*
– Aquí mismo. Hay un restaurante en el primer piso.
– *Is there a bank nearby? I´d like to change some money.*
– *(The receptionist is speaking too fast.) Can you speak more slowly, please.*

(Antes de empezar, Units 3, 4)

5 Which place or street in the map below does each of the following sentences refer to? You are at the corner of Defensa and México, looking towards calle San Juan.

a Hay uno al final de la calle Defensa, a la derecha.
b Está enfrente del banco.
c Está a la izquierda, al lado del supermercado.
d Está en la esquina de Defensa a Estados Unidos.
e Está en la calle Defensa, casi esquina a Independencia, a la izquierda.
f Es la tercera calle.
g Es la segunda calle.

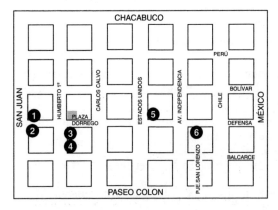

1 banco
2 iglesia
3 museo
4 supermercado
5 Hotel Nacional
6 correos

(Unit 4)

6 Change the verbs in italics into the appropriate form of the present tense.

a (Nosotros) *querer* el menú del día.
b (Yo) *querer* pescado a la plancha con patatas fritas.
c ¿Qué *querer* tú?
d ¿Me *traer* (usted) pollo con puré?
e ¿Qué *tener* (usted) de postre?
f Nosotros *tener* flan, helados y melón.
g Por favor, ¿nos *traer* (usted) dos cafés?

(Unit 2, 3, 5)

Units 6–10

1 Answer the questions below with **Es la ...**, **Son las ...**, **A la/las ...**, as appropriate. Use the times in brackets.

a Por favor, ¿qué hora es? (1.15)
b ¿Qué hora es? (2.40)
c ¿A qué hora sale el próximo tren para Salamanca? (5.45)
d ¿Y a qué hora llega? (6.30)
e ¿Tienes hora? (4.10)
f ¿A qué hora cierra la tienda? (1.00)

(Unit 6)

2 Study this exchange between a customer and a shop assistant, then write similar dialogues using the words below.

– ¿Cuánto cuestan esos melones?
– ¿Estos?
– Sí, esos.

a (las) manzanas
b (el) aceite de oliva
c (la) mantequilla
d (los) melocotones

(Unit 7)

3 Fill in the gaps in these sentences with one or more of these words: **me, le, les, lo, los, la, las, nos**. Add an accent where appropriate.

a Perdone, estas camisetas, ¿en qué color _____ tiene?
b Esta chaqueta es muy bonita. ¿Puedo probar _____?
c ¿Cómo _____ quedan esos zapatos, señor?
d Estos zapatos _____ quedan muy bien. _____ _____ llevo.
e Por favor, de _____ un billete de ida y vuelta para Málaga.

f Quisiéramos alquilar un coche. ¿Qué coche _____ recomienda?

g ¿Quieren ustedes un coche económico? Pues, _____ recomiendo este.

(Units 8, 9)

4 Rita and Ramón are planning a holiday and they are comparing two possible hotels, rating these from 1 to 5, with 5 being the highest mark and 1 the lowest. Look at the chart below and write comparative sentences with the following words, using expressions like **más ... que, mejor, tan ... como**, as appropriate.

a cerca	**d** barato
b vistas	**e** grande
c tranquilo	**f** cómodo

(Unit 10)

	Hotel Costa Azul	Hotel Playa Blanca
precio	5	3
comodidad	4	2
cercanía a la playa	1	4
tranquilidad	3	3
tamaño de las habitaciones	4	4
vistas	3	4

5 Rosa wrote to someone about herself and her family. Change the infinitives in brackets into the right form of the present tense.

Me llamo Rosa, (tener) 28 años, (estar) casada y (tener) un hijo de dos años. (Ser) enfermera y (trabajar) en un hospital. Mi marido se llama Antonio, (tener) 30 años, (ser) contable y (trabajar) en un banco. Antonio y yo (estar) casados desde hace cuatro años y (vivir) en Toledo desde hace tres años y medio.

(Unit 10)

6 How would you express the following in Spanish?

a Are you single or married? (use the 'tú' form)

b How old are you? (use the 'usted' form)

c I´m forty five years old.

d How many children do you have? (use the 'tú' form)

e I have three. The oldest is 20, and the youngest is 15.

(Unit 10)

Units 11–15

1 How would you express the following in Spanish?

a What do you do for a living? (Use the 'usted' form)

b How long have you been working there? (Use the 'usted' form)

c I've been working there for almost five years.

d What are your working hours? (use the 'usted' form)

e Silvia is an engineer and works in Valencia. She works from 9.00 to 5.00, from Monday to Friday.

f Luis is a shop assistant. He works in a shop. His wife is a receptionist. She has been working in a hotel for eight years.

(Unit 11)

2 Antonio wrote to a friend describing his daily routine. Fill in the gaps with a verb from the list, using the appropriate form of the present tense. Do not repeat any.

almorza	desayunar	leer	levantarse	trabajar	ver
	volver	ducharse	llegar	salir	

Normalmente _____ a las siete de la mañana, luego _____ Después de ducharme, _____, normalmente un café y unas tostadas. A las ocho y media _____ para el trabajo y _____ allí sobre las nueve. Al mediodía _____ con unos colegas en un restaurante cerca de la oficina. Por la tarde _____ desde las tres hasta las siete. A las siete _____ a casa, _____ el periódico o _____ la televisión un rato.

(Unit 12)

3 In an e-mail to a new Spanish-speaking acquaintance Pat wrote about the things she and her family like to do in their spare time. Can you help Pat by putting the verbs in brackets in the right form?

A mí (encantar) los deportes. El tenis, especialmente (gustar) mucho. Pero a mi marido no (gustar) nada los deportes. A él (gustar) leer y ver la televisión. A mis hijos (fascina) la televisión también. A nosotros (encantar) salir fuera de la ciudad los fines de semana. Y a ti, ¿qué (gustar) hacer en tu tiempo libre?

(Unit 13)

4 Everyone has an assignment at the office today. How would you ask the following people what they are going to do, and how would they reply? Use the appropriate form of **ir a** + infinitive.

Use the informal form of the verb (for **tú** and **vosotros/as**):

a Paco   escribir un informe
b María y Pepe   contestar unas cartas

Use the formal form of the verb (for **usted** and **ustedes**):

a Señora Martínez   recibir a un cliente
b Señor Díaz y señorita Pérez   realizar unas entrevistas

(Unit 13)

5 You are left in charge of the phone at Anglohispania, a company which does trade with Spain and Latin America, and you need to make some calls yourself. How would you express the following in Spanish?

a Hello?
b You've got the wrong number.
c Who's calling?
d I'll put you through right away.
e He'll be with you right away.
f Do you want to leave a message?
g I'd like to speak to señor Julián.
h Can you put me through to señora Lira?
i I'd like to arrange an interview with the manager.
j Please tell him/her that I phoned.

(Unit 14)

6 Change the verbs in brackets into the appropriate form: the present tense, the preterite, or the gerund (the *-ando/-iendo* form of the verb).

Me llamo Julia Montes, soy argentina. (Nacer) en Buenos Aires en 1975 y (llegar) a España con mis padres en 1990. A los 21 años (casarse) con José, un español. José y yo nos (conocer) en unas vacaciones en Marruecos y nos (casarse) un año después. Yo soy profesora de francés y (llevar) un año y medio (dar) clases en una esuela de lenguas. José es antropólogo y (llevar) tres años (trabajar) en un museo. José y yo (tener) dos hijos. Ahora José y yo (vivir) en Barcelona, pero antes (vivir) un año en Valencia. En Valencia (nacer) Ana, nuestra primera hija.

(Unit 15)

Units 16–20

1 After his return from a holiday in Cuba, Emilio sent an e-mail to a friend, describing it. Change the infinitives in brackets into the proper form of the preterite tense.

Querida Marta:

Hace sólo una semana que (*regresar*) de Cuba y no te imaginas lo bien que lo (*pasar*). (*Estar*) una semana en La Habana. Es una ciudad muy interesante. Me (*encantar*). También (*ir*) a Varadero. Allí (*quedarse*) en casa de Alejandro, un amigo cubano. Alejandro y yo (*visitar*) Trinidad, una ciudad colonial, y luego (*volver*) juntos a La Habana, donde yo (*tomar*) el avión para regresar a España. (*Llegar*) a Madrid el sábado por la tarde y el lunes pasado (empezar) a trabajar.

(Unit 16)

2 Víctor remembers the time he met Elisa. Complete his account by choosing the right verb, the preterite or the imperfect tense.

(Yo) (conocí/conocía) a Elisa en el año 1951, cuando (yo) (tuve/tenía) sólo veinte años. En aquel tiempo (yo) (estuve/estaba) en la universidad. Elisa (fue/era) mi nueva vecina, (tuvo/tenía) diecisiete años, y (vivió/vivía) con su madre, que (trabajó/trabajaba) en Correos. Recuerdo el primer día que la (vi/veía). (Yo) (fui/iba) a la universidad y ella (volvió/volvía) de la compra. La (saludé/saludaba) al pasar, pero no me (respondió/respondía). Días más tarde la (vi/veía) otra vez y le (hablé/hablaba). Ése (fue/era) nuestro primer encuentro ...

(Units 15, 16, 17, 18)

3 Julio and his colleagues Rafael and Silvia are talking about what they have done at the office today. Choose an appropriate verb from the list to complete the sentences below. The first sentence in each column has been done for you.

> hablar   entrevistar   hacer   ir   enviar
> volver   escribir   asistir

Julio

a   He llegado a la oficina a las 8.30.

b   _____ muchas llamadas telefónicas.

c   _____ varios mails.

d   _____ con varios clientes.

e   _____ a dos reuniones.

Rafael y Silvia

f   Hemos despachado varios pedidos.

g   _____ muchísimas cartas.

h   _____ a tres personas para un nuevo puesto.

i   _____ al aeropuerto.

j   _____ a casa muy cansados.

(Unit 19)

4 How would you tell someone else what Julio and his colleagues Rafael and Silvia have done? Change the verbs above into the right form.

(Unit 19)

5 Ana is planning a holiday, and she tells a friend what she will do. Fill in the gaps in the following sentences with an appropriate verb from the box, using the future tense.

> hacer   quedarse   ir   llegar   viajar   volver   salir

a   Este año _____ de vacaciones a Buenos Aires.

b   _____ de Madrid el día 23.

c   _____ en Iberia.

d   El avión _____ escala en San Pablo.

e   _____ a Buenos Aires al día siguiente.

f   _____ en casa de unos amigos argentinos.

g   _____ a Madrid el 7 de agosto.

(Unit 20)

6 How would you tell someone what Ana will do? Change the verbs into the appropriate form.

(Unit 20)

1 José and his friends Raquel and Pablo are talking about the things they would do if they won a big prize in the lottery. Speak for them by changing the infinitives in brackets into the appropriate form of the conditional tense (Unit 21).

José
a No (trabajar) más.
b (Hacer) un viaje alrededor del mundo.
c (Comprar) una casa para mí y otra para mis padres.
d (Poner) el dinero en un banco y (vivir) de los intereses.

Raquel y Pablo
e (Poder) pagar todas nuestras deudas.
f (Enviar) a nuestros hijos a los mejores colegios.
g (Ayudar) a nuestras familias.
h (Irse) a vivir al mejor barrio de la ciudad.

(Unit 21)

2 A Spanish-speaking person is visiting your place of work and you are having lunch with them. How would you express the following in Spanish? The relationship is formal.

a Had you been to (*your own country or town*) before?
b What do you think of the city?
c Shall I give you some more?
d Would you like some more wine?
e I'll take you to your hotel in my car.
f I'm very glad to have met you.

(Unit 22)

3 You are staying in a hotel at the corner of Antonio Varas and Diagonal Oriente and you need to visit a place at number 1436 on Eduardo de la Barra. A note with directions has been left for you at reception, but these are wrong. Look at the map and correct them.

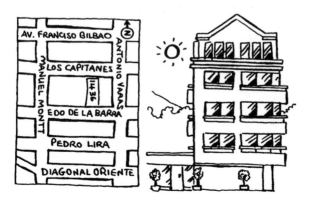

Siga todo recto por Antonio Varas y al llegar a Eduardo de la Barra gire a la derecha. El número 1436 está a la izquierda, entre Antonio Varas y Los Capitanes.

(Unit 23)

4 Some Spanish-speaking people are visiting your place of work and they are asking for directions. How would you express the following? Use the formal form.

a Go straight on and then take the third turning on the left. The bank is at the end of that street.

b Go up those stairs to the first floor. The toilets are on the right, past the telephones.

(Unit 23)

5 Match each statement on the left with the most appropriate request or advice on the right.

a Tengo sed	1 Abre la ventana, por favor.
b Tengo hambre	2 Ve al dentista.
c Tengo frío	3 Tráeme algo para beber.
d Tengo calor	4 Por favor, dame una aspirina.
e Tengo dolor de cabeza	5 Ponte un jersey.
f Me duelen las muelas	6 Come algo.

(Unit 24)

6 Merche and Nicolás are each looking for the ideal partner. What sort of person does each want? Complete the sentences below with the appropriate form of each of the verbs in brackets, making other changes where necessary.

a Merche busca un novio que (ser) inteligente, (tener) sentido del humor, no (fumar) y la (querer) de verdad.

b Nicolás quiere una novia que (ser) guapa, (saber) varios idiomas, (llevarse) bien con él y (estar) dispuesta a casarse.

(Unit 25)

Units 1–5

1 a ¿Cómo? b ¿Cómo? c ¿dónde? d ¿Qué? e ¿Cuál?
f ¿Dónde? g ¿Qué?
2 estás; estoy; es; eres; soy; soy; está; Está
3 a Buenas tardes, me llamo (*your name*), soy
(*nationality*).
b See alphabet in Unit 3. c Hablo (*languages*). d Mucho
gusto/Encantado/a. e Le presento a Sarah Johnson, una
compañera de trabajo/colega. f Vivo en (*place*) y mi
(número de) teléfono es el (Nº).
4 Buenas tardes/noches. Quisiera una habitación individual
con baño para dos noches./¿Está incluido el
desayuno?/¿Dónde puedo/se puede cenar?/ ¿Hay un
banco por aquí? Quisiera cambiar dinero./¿Puede hablar
más despacio, por favor?
5 a un banco b la iglesia c el museo d el Hotel Nacional
e correos f Estados Unidos g Avenida Independencia
6 a queremos b quiero c quieres d trae e tiene f tenemos
g trae

Units 6–10

1 a Es la una y cuarto. b Son las tres menos veinte. c A las
seis menos cuarto. d A las seis y media. e Son las cuatro
y diez. f A la una.
2 a ¿Cuánto cuestan esas manzanas? - ¿Estas? - Sí, esas.
b ¿Cuánto cuesta ese aceite de oliva? - ¿Este? - Sí, ese.
c ¿Cuánto cuesta esa mantequilla? - ¿Esta? - Sí, esa.
d ¿Cuánto cuestan esos melocotones? - ¿Estos? - Sí, esos.

3 **a** las **b** probármela **c** le **d** me/me los **e** deme **f** nos **g** les

4 **a** El hotel P.B. está más cerca de la playa que el hotel C.A.
b ... P.B. tiene mejores vistas que el hotel C.A. **c** ... C.A. es
tan tranquilo como el hotel P.B. **d** ... C.A. es más barato
que el hotel P.B. **e** Las habitaciones del hotel C.A. son tan
grandes como las habitaciones del hotel P.B. **f** C.A. es más
cómodo que el hotel P.B.

5 tengo; estoy; tengo; soy; trabajo; tiene; es; trabaja;
estamos; vivimos.

6 **a** ¿Estás soltero o casado? **b** ¿Cuántos años tiene (usted)?
c Tengo cuarenta y cinco años. **d** ¿Cuántos hijos tienes?
e Tengo tres. El mayor tiene 20 y el menor tiene 15.
f Luis es dependiente. Trabaja en una tienda. Su mujer es
receptionista. Trabaja en un hotel desde hace ocho añas.

Units 11–15

1 **a** ¿A qué se dedica (usted)? **b** ¿Cuánto tiempo hace que
trabaja allí? **c** Trabajo allí desde hace casi cinco
años./Hace casi cinco años que trabajo allí. **d** ¿Qué
horario de trabajo tiene?/¿Cuál es su horario de trabajo?
e Silvia es ingeniera y trabaja en Valencia. Trabaja de 9:00
a 5:00, de lunes a viernes.

2 me levanto – me ducho – desayuno – salgo – llego –
almuerzo – trabajo – vuelvo – leo – veo.

3 me encantan – me gusta – le gustan – le gusta – les fascina
– nos encanta – te gusta.

4 **a** ¿Qué vas a hacer? Voy a escribir ... **b** ¿Qué vais a hacer?
Vamos a contestar ... **c** ¿Qué va a hacer Vd.? Voy a recibir
... **d** ¿Qué van a hacer Vds.? Vamos a realizar ...

5 **a** ¿Dígame? **b** Se ha equivocado de número. **c** ¿De parte de
quién? **d** En seguida le pongo. **e** En seguida se pone.
f ¿Quiere dejar algún recado? **g** Quisiera hablar con el ...
h ¿Me puede poner con la ...? **i** Quisiera/ Quería
solicitar/concertar una entrevista con el/la gerente. **j** Por
favor, dígale que he llamado.

6 nací – llegué – me casé – nos conocimos – nos casamos –
llevo – dando – lleva – trabajando - tenemos – vivimos –
vivimos – nació

Units 16–20

1 regresé – pasé – estuve – encantó – fui – me quedé – visitamos – volvimos – tomé – llegué – empecé.
2 conocí – tenía – estaba – era – tenía – vivía – trabajaba – vi – iba – volvía – saludé – respondió – vi – hablé – fue
3 a *See example.* b he hecho c he enviado d he hablado e he asistido f *See example.* g hemos escrito – enviado h entrevistado i hemos ido j hemos vuelto
4 *Examples*: Julio ha llegado, ha hecho, etc. Rafael y Silvia han despachado, han escrito, etc.
5 a iré b saldré c viajaré d hará e llegaré f me quedaré g volveré
6 a irá b saldrá c viajará d hará e llegará f se quedará g volverá

Units 21–5

1 a trabajaría b haría c compraría d pondría/viviría e podríamos f enviaríamos g ayudaríamos h nos iríamos
2 a ¿Había estado en (*place*) antes? b ¿Qué le parece la ciudad? c ¿Le sirvo (un poco) más? d ¿Quiere (un poco) más (de) vino? e Lo/la llevaré a su hotel en mi coche. f Me alegro de haberlo/la conocido.
3 ... gire a la izquierda ... está a la derecha ... entre Antonio Varas y Manuel Montt
4 a Siga todo recto/de frente y luego tome la tercera (calle) a la izquierda. El banco está al final de esa calle. b Suba por esas escaleras hasta el primer piso. Los servicios están a la derecha pasados los teléfonos.
5 a-3 b-6 c-5 d-1 e-4 f-2
6 a ... sea – tenga – fume – quiera b ... sea – sepa – se lleve – esté

taking it further

Sources of authentic Spanish

Spanish newspapers and magazine

El País (http://www.elpais.es); *El Mundo* (http://www.el-mundo.es/); *La Vanguardia* (http://www.lavanguardia.es); *ABC* (http://www.abc.es); *El Periódico* (http://www.elperiodico.es/)

For general information, including Spanish current affairs and world news, try the following magazines: *Cambio 16, Tiempo, Tribuna, etc.*

For light reading and entertainment you might like to look at *Hola, Quo, Mía, Pronto, Lecturas, Semana, etc.* These are by far the most popular amongst Spaniards and, as a beginner, you may find some of the articles easier to follow.

Latin American newspapers and magazines

Latin American newspapers and magazines will be more difficult to find outside each country, but if you have internet facilities you will be able to access their websites, although they may be special net versions. The following is a list of some main Latin American newspapers:

Argentina: *La Nación* (http://lanacion.com.ar/) *Clarín* (http://www.clarin.com)

Chile: *El Mercurio* (http://www.elmercurio.cl/)

Colombia: *El Espectador* (http://www.elespectador.com/)

Cuba: *Granma* (http://www.granma.cu/)

México: *El Universal* (http://www.el-universal.com.mx/)

Perú: *El Comercio* (http:/elcomercioperu.com.pe/); *Correo* (http://www.correoperu.com.pe/)

Radio and television

An excellent way to improve your understanding of spoken Spanish is to listen to radio and watch television. On medium wave after dark and via satellite you will be able to gain access to *Radio Nacional de España, Televisión Española (TVE)* and other stations. And for spoken Latin American Spanish, you may like to tune in to the *BBC Spanish Latin American Service*, which can be heard on short wave.

Travelling in Spain and Latin America

Travelling in a Spanish-speaking country is probably the best way to practice what you have learnt and improve your command of the spoken language. If you are planning to do this, there are a number of good guidebooks which will help you to plan your journey. The well-known *Lonely Planet* covers not just specific countries, but also main regions and cities, including Spain and Latin America. For the latter, the *Mexico and Central American Handbook* and the *South American Handbook* have a long tradition amongst travellers in the region. *Time Out, Michelin, Fodor's,* among several others, have also become well established in the travelling market.

For travellers in Spain, the following websites may prove useful, with information such as tourist attractions, accommodation, travel, restaurants, etc:

Travelling to Spain: http://www.SiSpain/english/ travelli/

Spain Today (local section of the *Europe Today* travel guide): http://www.wtg-online.com/data/esp/esp.asp

All about Spain: http://www.red2000.com/

Páginas amarillas del viajero (yellow pages for travellers): http://www.spaindata.com/data/1index.shtml

Spanish National Tourist Office: http://www.tourspain.co.uk

Railway travel in Spain: horarios.renfe.es/hir/ingles.html

Madrid metro: http://www.metromadrid.es

Travellers in Latin America will find useful information in:

Travel.org – Latin America): http://www.travel.org/latin.htm/;

Latin America – travel notes: http://www.travelnotes.org/LatinAmerica/index.htm

Culture and history

Internet users interested in Spain may like to try the following sites:

España en la Red (Spain on the net): http://www.msn.es/homepage.asp

Historia – Sí Spain: http://www.sispain. org/spanish/history

Sí – Spain: http://www.sispain.org/spanish/index.htm/

Historia – Sí Spain: http://www.sispain.org/spanish/history

About.com – Spanish culture: http://spanisculture.about.com/

For Latin America go to:

Latin American History:
http://www.ltinsynergy.org/ latinamericahistory.htm

For Spanish language, the *Instituto Cervantes* a worldwide organization, offers courses in Spanish and promotes Spanish culture in general; the *Hispanic Council*, in the United Kingdom, based in London, may be able to help you with enquiries about Spanish language courses and aspects of life in Spain. For information on Latin American Spanish you can contact the *Hispanic Council* or the embassy of the country you are interested in.

For the *Instituto Cervantes* go to: http://cervantes.es

For other related information, including Latin America, go to:

http://www.spanish.about.com
http://www.spanish-language.org
http://www.spanishabroad.com
http://planeta.com/schoolist.html

Working in Spain and Latin America

For an overview of job prospects in Spain and Latin America, including teaching go to:

http://www.transitionsabroad.com/listings/work/esl/teachingeng lishinspain.html

http://www.transitionsabroad.com/listings/work/esl/articles/wor kinlatinamerica.html

http://www.tefllogue.com/finding-a-job/working-in-latin-america-an-overview.html

http://www.4icj.com/Latin-America

adjectives Adjectives are used to provide more information about nouns, e.g. That school is very *good*. **Ese colegio es muy *bueno*.** The *new* hotel is *excellent*. **El *nuevo* hotel es *excelente*.**

adverbs Adverbs tend to provide more information about verbs. He left *quietly*. **Salió *silenciosamente*.** But adverbs can also provide more information on adjectives: It was *totally* unnecessary. **Era *totalmente* innecesario.** In English, adverbs often (but not always) end in **-ly**. The equivalent of this in Spanish is **-mente**.

articles There are two types of articles, *definite* and *indefinite*. In English, the definite article is *the* – **el/la/los/las** in Spanish. *A*, **un/una**, are the indefinite articles.

comparative When we make comparisons we need the comparative form of the adjective. In English this usually means adding *-er* to the adjective or putting *more* in front of it. This shirt is *cheaper than* that one. **Esta camisa es *más* barata *que* esa.** This blouse is *more* expensive *than* that one. **Esta blusa es *más* cara *que* esa.** See also **superlative**.

demonstratives Words like *this este*, *that ese*, *these estos*, *those esos* are called **demonstratives**.

gender In English, gender is usually linked to male and female persons or animals, so, for example, we refer to a man as *he* and to a woman as *she*. Objects and beings of an indeterminate sex are referred to as having *neuter* gender. So, for instance, we refer to a table as *it*. In Spanish, nouns referring to female persons are feminine and those referring to male people are masculine. But all nouns are either masculine or feminine in Spanish and this has nothing to do with sex. **La mesa** *table*, **la mano** *hand*, are feminine, while **el mes** *month*, **el día** *day*, are masculine. While there are some rules to help you, you have to accept that the gender of every noun has to be learned.

imperative The imperative is the form of the verb used to give directions, instructions, orders or commands: *Turn* right at the corner. *Gire* **a la derecha en la esquina.** First *dial* 020. **Primero** *marque* **el 020.**

infinitive The infinitive is the basic form of the verb. This is the form that you will find entered in the dictionary. In Spanish, infinitives end in -ar, -er, and -ir, e.g. habl*ar to speak*, com*er to eat*, viv*ir to live*.

irregular verbs Life would be considerably easier if all verbs behaved in a regular fashion. Unfortunately, Spanish, like other European languages, has verbs which do not behave according to a set pattern and which are therefore commonly referred to as irregular verbs.

nouns Nouns are words like *house* **casa**, *bread* **pan** and *wealth* **riqueza.** They are often called 'naming words'.

number The term is used to indicate whether something is *singular* or *plural*. See **singular.**

object The term *object* expresses the 'receiving end' relationship between a noun and a verb. So, for instance, the thief is said to be at the receiving end of the arrest in the sentence 'The policeman arrested *the thief*'. **El policía arrestó *al ladrón*.** The thief is therefore said to be the *object* of the sentence.

In sentences such as 'My mother gave *the driver some money*', the phrase '*some money*' is said to be the *direct object*, because the money is actually what the mother gave. The phrase '*the driver*' is said to be the *indirect object* because the driver was the recipient of the giving.

plural See **singular.**

personal pronouns As their name suggests, personal pronouns refer to persons, e.g. *I* **yo**, *you* **tú, usted,** *he* **él,** *she* **ella,** etc. See **pronouns.**

possessives Words like *my* **mi,** *your* **tu, su,** *our* **nuestro** are called possessives. So are words such as *mine* **mío,** *yours* **tuyo, suyo,** etc.

pronouns Pronouns fulfil a similar function to nouns and often stand in the place of nouns which have already been mentioned, e.g. My *girlfriend* (noun) is twenty-five years old. *She* (pronoun) is very pretty. **Mi *novia* tiene veinticinco años. *Ella* es muy guapa.**

prepositions Words like *in* en, *for* por, para, *between* entre, are called prepositions. Prepositions often tell us about the position of something. They are normally followed by a noun or a pronoun, e.g. The bank is *between* the school and the church. **El banco está *entre* el colegio y la iglesia.** This present is *for* you. **Este regalo es *para* ti.**

reflexive pronouns Words such as *myself* me, *yourself* te, se, *ourselves* nos, are called reflexive pronouns.

reflexive verbs When the subject and the object of a verb are one and the same, the verb is said to be reflexive, e.g. *I washed myself* before going out. ***Me lavé* antes de salir.** *We enjoyed ourselves* very much. ***Nos divertimos* mucho.**

singular The terms *singular* and *plural* are used to make the contrast between 'one' and 'more than one', e.g. *book/books* **libro/libros,** *city/cities* **ciudad/ciudades.**

subject The term *subject* expresses a relationship between a noun and a verb. So, for instance, in the sentence 'My mother gave the driver some money', because it is the mother who does the giving, the mother is said to be the subject of the verb *to give,* **dar.**

subjunctive mood The so-called subjunctive mood is used very rarely in modern English, but there are remnants of it in such sentences as If I *were* you. **Yo en tu lugar.** I insist that he *come.* **Insisto en que *venga*.** Spanish uses the subjunctive much more frequently than English.

superlative The superlative is used for the most extreme version of a comparison. This shirt is the *cheapest* of all. **Esta camisa es *la más barata* de todas.** This blouse is the most expensive of all. **Esta blusa es *la más cara* de todas.** See also **comparative**.

tense Most languages use changes in the verb to indicate an aspect of time. These changes in the verb are traditionally referred to as tense, and the tenses may be *present, past* or *future,* e.g., They *went* out. **Salieron** (*past*). She *is* at home. ***Está* en casa** (*present*). We *will go* to the cinema ***Iremos* al cine** (*future*).

verbs Verbs often communicate actions, e.g., *to play* **jugar,** states, e.g. *to exist* **existir,** and sensations, e.g. *to see* **ver.** A verb may also be defined by its role in the sentence, and usually has a subject, e.g. My head (*subject*) aches (*verb*). **Me duele la cabeza.**

grammar summary

Essentials of grammar

1 Definite articles (Units 2, 3)

	Masculine Feminine	
Singular	el hotel *the hotel*	la habitación *the room*
Plural	los hoteles *the hotels*	las habitaciones *the rooms*

2 Contractions (Unit 2)

a + el = al   Voy **al** estadio.   *I'm going to the stadium.*
de + el = del Vengo **del** trabajo. *I'm coming from work.*

3 Indefinite articles (Unit 2, 11)

	Masculine Feminine	
Singular	**un** coche *a car*	**una** casa *a house*
Plural	**unos** coches *some cars*	**unas** casas *some houses*

4 Nouns: masculine and feminine, singular and plural (Units 2, 3, 10)

a In Spanish, all nouns are either masculine or feminine. Nouns ending in –o are usually masculine, while those ending in –a are usually feminine: **el desayuno, la cena**.

b Words referring to males and females, such as occupations, must change. Change –o to –a or add –a to the consonant: el secretario – la secretaria, el doctor – la doctora.

c Nouns ending in –ista and many of those ending in –nte do not change: el/la artista, el/la estudiante.

d Some nouns have different male and female forms: **el actor, la actriz.**

e Nouns ending in a vowel form the plural by adding –s: el **libro – los libros.**

f Nouns ending in a consonant add –es: el hotel – los hoteles.

g The masculine plural of some nouns may be used to refer to members of both sexes: **el padre** *father*, **la madre** *mother*, **los padres** *parents*.

5 Adjectives: number, gender and position (Units 1, 8, 10)

a Adjectives must agree in gender (masculine/feminine) and number (singular/plural) with the noun they describe, but generally, those ending in a consonant or in –e change for number but not for gender: **un jersey negro, una camisa negra, unos pantalones negros,** but **un sombrero/una camisa azul, unos zapatos azules.**

b Adjectives of nationality add –a to the consonant: **un amigo español, una amiga española.**

c Adjectives normally follow the noun they describe but for emphasis, or to convey some kind of emotion, they are sometimes placed before the noun: **un hotel caro, un excelente hotel.**

d A few adjectives, among them **bueno, malo,** often precede the noun. Before a masculine singular noun, **bueno** and **malo** become **buen** and **mal,** respectively: **un buen/mal momento** but **una buena/mala educación.** Other adjectives with a shortened form are **primero, tercero, alguno, ninguno: el primer semáforo** but **la primera calle; ningún estudiante** but **ninguna persona.**

e **Grande** normally follows the noun when its meaning is 'big' or 'large', but it goes before it when it means 'great'. Before a *masculine or feminine* singular noun **grande** becomes **gran: un gran hombre/una gran mujer.**

6 Comparative form of adjectives (Unit 8, 10)

a Comparisons such as *smaller, more comfortable*, are expressed with the construction **más ... (que)**: **Mi piso es más pequeño, pero más cómodo que el de Eva.**

b For forms such as '*fastest*', '*most economical*', use **el/la/los/las más ...**: **Este coche es el más rápido y el más económico.**

c To say '*(not) as ... as*' use **(no) tan ... como**: **Madrid no es tan caro como Londres.**

d **Bueno** and **malo** have irregular comparative forms: **mejor(es)**, *better*, **peor(es)**, *worse*, **el/la/los/las mejor(es)**, *the best*, **el/la/los/las peor(es)**, *the worst*.

e The comparative forms for **grande** and **pequeño**, when they refer to age, are **mayor(es)** *older*, **menor(es)** *younger*, **el/la/los/las mayor(es)** *the oldest*, **el/la/los/las menor(es)** *the youngest*.

7 Adverbs (18)

a Many adverbs can be formed by adding **–mente** to the feminine form of the adjective: **rápido – rápidamente**. If the adjective ends in a consonant or **–e** add **–mente**: **fácil – fácilmente, amable – amablemente**.

b Many adverbs are not derived from adjectives: **ahora, aquí, bien**, etc.

8 Subject pronouns (Units 1, 3)

yo	*I*	**nosotros/as**	*we*
tú	*you* (informal, singular)	**vosotros/as**	*you* (informal, plural)
usted	*you* (formal, singular)	**ustedes**	*you* (formal, plural)
él, ella	*he, she*	**ellos, ellas**	*they*

Subject pronouns are usually omitted in Spanish, except for emphasis or to avoid ambiguity (as with **usted, él, ella,** or **ustedes, ellos, ellas,** which share the same verb forms).

Vosotros/as, and all forms related to it, are not used in Latin American Spanish, where **ustedes** is used in formal and informal address.

9 Object pronouns (Units 5, 8, 9, 23, 24)

9.1 Direct and indirect object pronouns

In sentences such as *He gave it to me*, **Él me lo/la dio**, *John sold them to us*, **John nos los/las vendió**, 'it' and 'me', in the first sentence, and 'them' and 'us' in the second one are known as *object pronouns*. 'It' stands for what was given, for example 'the money', while 'them' stands for what was sold, for example 'the books'. 'It' and 'them' are said to be the *direct object pronouns* while 'me' and 'them', the recipients of the giving and the selling are said to be the *indirect objects*. In the first and second person singular and plural there is no distinction between direct and indirect object pronouns:

singular	plural
me *me, to me, for me* **te** *you, to you, for you* (informal)	**nos** *us, to us, for us* **os** *you, to you, for you* (informal)

In the third person singular and plural, direct and indirect object pronouns differ:

Direct object pronouns	Indirect object pronouns
lo/le *you* (formal)/*him/it* (m, sing) **la** *you* (formal)/*her/it* (f, sing) **los/les** *you* (formal)/*them* (m, pl) **las** *you* (formal)/them (f, pl)	**le** *(to) you* (formal)/*him/her/it* (m/f,sing) **les** *(to) you* (formal)/them (m/f, pl)

In many parts of Spain now **le** and **les** are used as direct object pronouns instead of the standard **lo** and **los** to refer to human males, for example **Le llamé** *I called him*, with **lo** and **los** referring to masculine objects, as in **Lo compré** *I bought it*.

As indirect object pronouns, however, **le** and **les** are the norm among most speakers: **Le dije** *I told him/her*.

9.2 Position of direct and indirect object pronouns

a Object pronouns normally precede the verb: **Me invitaron** *They invited me* (literally, *Me they invited*).

b In sentences with two object pronouns, one direct the other indirect, the indirect one comes first: **Te lo/la daré mañana** *I'll give it to you tomorrow* (literally, *To you it I'll give tomorrow*).

c **Le** and **les** become **se** before **lo, la, los, las**: **Se lo/la traigo ahora mismo** *I'll bring it to you right now.*

d In constructions with a main verb followed by an *infinitive* (e.g. **escribir**) or a *gerund* (e.g. **escribiendo**), the object pronoun can either precede the main verb or be attached to the infinitive or gerund: **Voy a escribirle** or **Le voy a escribir** *I'm going to write to him/her.*

e Object pronouns must follow positive *imperative* or *command* forms, but they precede negative ones: **Dígale** *Tell him/her,* **No le diga** *Don't tell him/her.*

10 Reflexive pronouns (Unit 12)

Reflexive verbs, for example, **levantarse** *to get up,* **irse** *to leave,* **divertirse** *to enjoy oneself,* are always accompanied by a reflexive pronoun, the Spanish equivalent of words like 'myself', 'yourself', etc. But note that many Spanish verbs which are used with a reflexive pronoun do not require a reflexive pronoun in English.

Reflexive pronouns are: **me** (for 'yo'), **te** (for 'tú'), **se** (for 'él, ella, Vd.') , **nos** (for 'nosotros/as'), **os** (for 'vosotros/as'), **se** (for 'ellos, ellas, Vds.'): **Me levanto a las 6:30** *I get up at 6.30,* **¿A qué hora te levantas tú?** *What time do you get up?*

The position of reflexive pronouns in the sentence is the same as for object pronouns (see 9.2 above): **(Yo) me levanto a las 7:00.**

11 Pronouns with prepositions (Unit 5)

With prepositions, that is words like **a, para, por, sin,** etc., use the following set of pronouns: **mí** (for yo), **ti** (for tú), and subject pronouns for all other persons, that is, **usted, él, ella, nosotros/as, vosotros/as, ellos, ellas**: **Para mí, una cerveza, para él/ella un café, ¿y para ti?.**

Con 'with' is a special case: **conmigo** with me, **contigo** with you, (inf) but **con él/ella/usted**, etc.

12 Demonstratives (Unit 7)

These are words like **este/esta** this (m/f, sing.), **estos/estas** these (m/f, pl). For the full forms see Unit 7.

13 Possessives (Units 2, 3, 20)

These are words like **mi** my, **tu** your (informal), etc., which are sometimes referred to as *short forms*, as apposed to **mío** mine, **tuyo** yours (informal), which are known as *long forms*. Short forms are treated in Units 2 and 3, and long forms in Unit 20.

14 Uses of 'por' and 'para' (Units 5, 6, 11)

14.1 Por is used:

a To indicate cause or reason: **Lo hago por ti** *I do it for you.*
b With expressions of time: **por la mañana/noche** *in the morning/at night*
c To indicate movement through or along: **Pasé por Sevilla** *We passed **through** Seville,* **Anduvimos por el río** *We walked **along** the river*
c To express means: **por email** *by e-mail*
d To indicate rate: **por hora/día** *per hour/day*
e To express cost or value: **Pagué mucho dinero por él** *I paid a lot of money **for** it*
f To introduce the agent of an action: **América fue descubierta por Colón** *America was discovered **by** Columbus*

14.2 Para is used:

a To indicate direction: **un billete para Ecuador** *a ticket for Ecuador*
b With expressions of time: **una habitación para dos días** *a room for two days,* **Déjalo para mañana** *Leave it **till** tomorrow*
c To express destination: **para una persona** *for one person,* **para mí** *for me*
d To express purpose: **Fue a España para aprender español** *He/she went to Spain **to/in order to** learn Spanish*

For other prepositions see Grammar section in Units 2, 5, 6, 11, 18)

15 Question words (Units 1, 2, 3, 6, 17)

a **¿Cómo?** ¿Cómo te llamas? *What's your name?*, ¿Cómo estás? *How are you?*

b **¿Cuál?** ¿Cuál quieres? *Which one do you want?*, ¿Cuál es tu email? *What's your e-mail?*, ¿Cuáles son sus maletas? *Which are your suitcases?*

c **¿Cuándo?** ¿Cuándo vuelves? *When are you coming back?*

d **¿Cuánto/s?** ¿Cuánto cuesta? *How much does it cost?*, ¿Cuántos hay? *How many are there?*

e **¿Dónde?** ¿Dónde está? *Where is it?*, ¿De dónde eres? *Where are you from?* Note also **¿adónde?** *where(to)?*

f **¿Por qué?** ¿Por qué no vienes conmigo? *Why don't you come with me?*

g **¿Qué?** ¿Qué desea? *What would you like?*

h **¿Quién?** ¿Quién es? *Who is it?*, ¿Quiénes son? *Who are they?*

Verbs

16 Present tense (Units 1, 2, 3, 4, 12, 22)

The *present tense* is used to talk about actions taking place in the present, but it has a number of other uses, among them the following ones: to talk about timeless events and actions taking place regularly, to talk about the immediate future, etc.

¿Qué haces?	*What are you doing?*
Carmen es peruana.	*Carmen is Peruvian.*
Se levantan siempre a las 6:30.	*They always get up at 6.30.*
Nos vamos mañana.	*We're leaving tomorrow.*

For the *present tense forms* see the references above.

16.1 Stem-changing verbs (Units 3, 5, 12)

Some verbs undergo a vowel change in the stem in all persons but **nosotros, vosotros,** but their endings remain the same as for regular verbs. Such verbs are known as *stem-changing* or *radical-changing* verbs. The main types of changes are:

a **e>ie** (empezar, entender, pensar, etc.): **Empiezo a las 9:00** *I start at 9.00.*

b **o>ue** (volver, poder, acostarse, etc.): **Vuelven mañana** *They're coming back tomorrow.*

c **e>i** (seguir, pedir, servir, etc.): **¿Sigo todo recto?** *Shall I go straight on?*

16.2 Irregular verbs (Units 1, 2, 4, 12 and pages 302–5.)

A number of verbs form the present tense in an irregular way. Some, for example **salir** *to leave*, are irregular only in the first person singular, **salgo** *I leave*, while others, like **ser** *to be* or **ir** *to go*, are completely irregular. For a list of irregular verbs see pages 302–5.

17 Preterite tense (Units 15, 16, 17)

The *preterite tense* is used for talking about events which took place at a specific point in the past or which lasted over an extended period but ended in the past.

Ayer hablé con él.	*I spoke to him yesterday.*
Viví dos años allí.	*I lived there for two years.*

For the *preterite tense* forms see the references above.

18 Imperfect tense (Units 17, 18)

The *imperfect tense* is used to describe people, places and things known in the past, to talk about actions which occurred regularly in the past, to say what you were doing and, in place of the present tense, to request something in a polite way.

Era una persona maravillosa.	*She/he was a wonderful person.*
Nos visitaban a menudo.	*They used to visit us often.*
Iba hacia la oficina.	*I was going to the office.*
Quería una habitación.	*I wanted/would like a room.*

For the *imperfect tense* forms see the references above.

19 Future tense (Unit 20)

The *future tense* is used for talking about future events, especially in the written language. It is also used to express probability, certainty and uncertainty with regard to the present or the future, promises and predictions.

Este año iremos a México.	*This year we'll go to Mexico.*
¿Hablarán español?	*I wonder whether they speak Spanish.*
Lo haré esta tarde. Te lo prometo.	*I'll do it this afternoon. I promise you.*
Seguro que vendrá.	*I'm sure he/she will come.*

For the *future tense* forms see the reference above.

20 Conditional tense (Unit 21)

Like the English 'would', the Spanish *conditional tense* is used for expressing conditions. It is also used for politeness, especially with **poder** and **querer**, but also with other verbs.

Yo iría con vosotros, pero no puedo.	*I'd go with you, but I can't.*
¿Podría Vd. volver mañana?	*Could you come back tomorrow?*
¿Querría acompañarme, por favor?	*Would you come with me, please?*

For the *conditional tense* see the reference above.

21 Present subjunctive (Unit 25)

The *present subjunctive*, like the subjunctive as a whole, has several uses, but only three have been discussed in this book: to express requirements with regard to something or someone, to express hope, to express uncertainty or doubt. The subjunctive normally occurs in a construction with a main verb, for example **quiero** I *want*, followed by **que** *that*, *which*, *who* and a subjunctive verb.

Busco una casa que **tenga** garaje.	*I'm looking for a house that has a garage.*
Quiero una persona que **trabaje.**	*I want someone who works.*
Espero que la **encuentres.**	*I hope you find her.*
No creo que **sea** difícil.	*I don't think it will be difficult.*

For the *present subjunctive* forms see the reference above.

22 Perfect tense (Unit 19)

The *perfect tense* is used for talking about the recent past and, generally, about past events which bear some relationship with the present.

He desayunado hace un momento.	*I had breakfast a moment ago.*
He visto esta película dos veces.	*I've seen this film twice* (up until now)

For the *perfect tense* forms see the reference above.

23 Pluperfect tense (Unit 22)

The *pluperfect tense* is used much in the same way as in English, that is, to refer to what one had done or what had happened before another past event or situation.

Me dio un libro, pero yo ya lo había leído.	*He/she gave me a book, but I had already read it.*
Habíamos estado allí dos veces.	*We had been there twice.*

For the *pluperfect tense* forms see the reference above.

24 Imperative or command form (Units 23, 24)

Expressions such as **¿Dígame?** *Hello?* (on the phone), **Deme** *Give me*, **Siga todo recto** *Go straight on*, **Mira** *Look!*, **No nos esperes** *Don't wait for us*, correspond to the *imperative* or *command* form of the verb. Unlike English, Spanish uses different imperative forms depending on who you are talking to - *formal* or *informal form* - and whether you are speaking to one or more than one person, *singular* or *plural form*. In addition to that, the informal imperative has different *positive* and *negative forms*. For formal imperatives see Unit 23; for informal ones see Unit 24.

25 Gerund (Unit 14)

Gerunds are forms like **hablando** *speaking*, **comiendo** *eating*, which are used with **estar** to refer to an action that is or was in progress, for example **Está hablando por otra línea** *He/she is speaking on another line*, **Yo estaba comiendo cuando llegaron** *I was eating when they arrived*. The gerund has a number of other uses which are beyond the scope of this book.

26 Using 'ser' and 'estar' (Unit 1, 2, 3, 4, 6, 7, 10, 14, 16, 17)

26.1 Ser is used:

a to give personal information such as who you are, your nationality, where you are from or your occupation: **Soy español** *I'm Spanish*, **Clara es mexicana** *Clara is Mexican*, **Agustín es estudiante** *Agustín is a student*.

b to describe people, places and things: **Barcelona es una ciudad preciosa** *Barcelona is a beautiful city*.

c with time phrases: **¿Qué hora es?** *What time is it?*, **Mañana es domingo** *Tomorrow is Sunday*.

d to refer to the material something is made of: **Es de algodón** *It is made from cotton*.

e to denote possession: **Es mío** *It's mine*.

f to express cost: **¿Cuánto es?** *'How much is it?* **Son cinco euros** It's five euros.

g to say where an event will take place: **La reunión es aquí** *The meeting is here*.

For other uses of **ser** you may like to refer to a Grammar book.

26.2 Estar is used:

a to express location: **Buenos Aires está en Argentina** *Buenos Aires is in Argentina*.

b to express marital status: **Está soltero** *He's single* (in Latin America also **Es soltero**)

c to ask people how they are: **¿Cómo estás?** *How are you?*

d to denote a temporary state or condition: **Gloria está muy guapa hoy** *Gloria is/looks very pretty today*.

e to express cost when prices fluctuate: **¿A cómo/cuánto está el cambio?** *What is the rate of exchange?*.

f with *past participles*, to denote a condition resulting from an action **La puerta está abierta** *The door is open*.

g with *gerunds*, to talk about actions in progress: **Está lloviendo** *It's raining*.

h with time phrases: **Estamos a 15 de julio** *It's the 15th of July*.

For other uses of **estar** refer to a grammar book.

27 Using 'se' (Unit 3, 9, 12)

Se is used with the third person of the verb:

a to form impersonal sentences: **¿Cómo se va al aeropuerto?** *How do you/does one get to the airport?*

b to convey the idea that something 'is done': **Aquí se habla español** *Spanish is spoken here.*

c with reflexive verbs: **Se levantan tarde** *They get up late.*

d in place of **le** or **les** before **lo/la/los/las**: **Ahora mismo se lo traigo** *I'll bring it to you right now.*

irregular verbs

The following list includes only the most common irregular verbs. Only irregular forms are given (verbs marked with an asterisk are also stem- or radical-changing).

abrir *to open*
past participle: abierto

andar *to walk*
preterite: anduve, anduviste, anduvo, anduvimos, anduvisteis, anduvieron

conducir *to drive*
present indicative: (yo) conduzco
present subjunctive: conduzca, conduzcas, conduzca, conduzcamos, conduzcáis, conduzcan
preterite: conduje, condujiste, condujo, condujimos, condujisteis, condujeron

dar *to give*
present indicative: (yo) doy
preterite: di, diste, dio, dimos, disteis, dieron
present subjunctive: dé, des, dé, demos, deis, den

decir* to say
present indicative: (yo) digo
present subjunctive: diga, digas, diga, digamos, digáis, digan
preterite: dije, dijiste, dijo, dijimos, dijisteis, dijeron
future: diré, dirás, dirá, diremos, diréis, dirán
conditional: diría, dirías, diría, diríamos, diríais, dirían
imperative (familiar, singular): di *(formal, singular)*: diga
gerund: diciendo
past participle: dicho

escribir *to write*
past participle: escrito

estar *to be*
present indicative: estoy, estás, está, estamos, estáis, están
present subjunctive: esté, estés, esté, estemos, estéis, estén
preterite: estuve, estuviste, estuvo, estuvimos, estuvisteis,
   estuvieron
imperative (familiar, singular): está

hacer *to do, make*
present indicative: (yo) hago
present subjunctive: haga, hagas, haga, hagamos, hagáis,
   hagan
preterite: hice, hiciste, hizo, hicimos, hicisteis, hicieron
future: haré, harás, hará, haremos, haréis, harán
conditional: haría, harías, haría, haríamos, haríais, harían
imperative: (Vd.) haga, (tú) haz
past participle: hecho

ir *to go*
present indicative: voy, vas, va, vamos, vais, van
present subjunctive: vaya, vayas, vaya, vayamos, vayáis, vayan
imperfect: iba, ibas, iba, íbamos, ibais, iban
preterite: fui, fuiste, fue, fuimos, fuisteis, fueron
imperative: (Vd.) vaya, (tú) ve
gerund: yendo

leer *to read*
preterite: (él, ella, Vd.) leyó, (ellos, ellas, Vds.) leyeron
gerund: leyendo

oír *to hear*
present indicative: oigo, oyes, oye, oímos, oís, oyen
present subjunctive: oiga, oigas, oiga, oigamos, oigáis, oigan
preterite: (él, ella, Vd.) oyó, (ellos, ellas, Vds.) oyeron
imperative: (Vd.) oiga, (tú) oye
gerund: oyendo

poder* *to be able to, can*
preterite: pude, pudiste, pudo, pudimos, pudisteis, pudieron
future: podré, podrás, podrá, podremos, podréis, podrán
conditional: podría, podrías, podría, podríamos, podríais,
   podrían

poner *to put*
present indicative: (yo) pongo
present subjunctive: ponga, pongas, ponga, pongamos,
    pongáis, pongan
preterite: puse, pusiste, puso, pusimos, pusisteis, pusieron
future: pondré, pondrás, pondrá, pondremos, pondréis,
    pondrán
conditional: pondría, pondrías, pondría, pondríamos,
    pondríais, pondrían
imperative: (Vd.) ponga, (tú) pon
past participle: puesto

querer* *to want, love*
preterite: quise, quisiste, quiso, quisimos, quisisteis, quisieron
future: querré, querrás, querrá, querremos, querréis, querrán
conditional: querría, querrías, querría, querríamos, querríais,
    querrían

saber *to know*
present indicative: (yo) sé
present subjunctive: sepa, sepas, sepa, sepamos, sepáis, sepan
preterite: supe, supiste, supo, supimos, supisteis, supieron
future: sabré, sabrás, sabrá, sabremos, sabréis, sabrán
conditional: sabría, sabrías, sabría, sabríamos, sabríais, sabrían
imperative: (Vd.) sepa

salir *to go out*
present indicative: (yo) salgo
present subjunctive: salga, salgas, salga, salgamos, salgáis, salgan
future: saldré, saldrás, saldrá, saldremos, saldréis, saldrán
conditional: saldría, saldrías, saldría, saldríamos, saldríais,
    saldrían
imperative: (Vd.) salga, (tú) sal

ser *to be*
present indicative: soy, eres, es, somos, sois, son
present subjunctive: sea, seas, sea, seamos, seáis, sean
preterite: fui, fuiste, fue, fuimos, fuisteis, fueron
imperfect indicative: era, eras, era, éramos, erais, eran
imperative: (Vd.) sea, (tú) sé

tener* *to have*
present indicative: (yo) tengo
present subjunctive: tenga, tengas, tenga, tengamos, tengáis,
    tengan
preterite: tuve, tuviste, tuvo, tuvimos, tuvisteis, tuvieron

future: tendré, tendrás, tendrá, tendremos, tendréis, tendrán
conditional: tendría, tendrías, tendría, tendríamos, tendríais,
  tendrían
imperative: (Vd.) tenga, (tú) ten

traer *to bring*
present indicative: (yo) traigo
present subjunctive: traiga, traigas, traiga, traigamos, traigáis,
  traigan
preterite: traje, trajiste, trajo, trajimos, trajisteis, trajeron
imperative: (Vd.) traiga
gerund: trayendo

venir* *to come*
present indicative: (yo) vengo
present subjunctive: venga, vengas, venga, vengamos, vengáis,
  vengan
preterite: vine, viniste, vino, vinimos, vinisteis, vinieron
future: vendré, vendrás, vendrá, vendremos, vendréis, vendrán
conditional: vendría, vendrías, vendría, vendríamos, vendríais,
  vendrían
imperative: (Vd.) venga, (tú) ven
gerund: viniendo

ver *to see*
present indicative: (yo) veo
present subjunctive: vea, veas, vea, veamos, veáis, vean
imperfect indicative: veía, veías, veía, veíamos, veíais, veían
imperative: (Vd.) vea
past participle: visto

volver* *to come back*
past participle: vuelto

Introductory unit

Activity 1.1

- ¡Hola!
- Hola, buenos días.

- Hola, ¿qué tal?
- ¡Hola!

- Buenas tardes.
- Hola, buenas tardes.

- Hola, buenas noches.
- Buenas noches.

Unit 1

Activity 2

a Me llamo Silvia, soy española. Soy de Barcelona. Hablo español y catalán.
b Me llamo Cristóbal, soy argentino. Soy de Buenos Aires. Hablo español e inglés.
c Me llamo Sofía, soy norteamericana. Soy de California. Hablo inglés, italiano y un poco de español.

Unit 2

Activity 5

– ¿Dónde vive usted, Silvia?
– En Barcelona. Vivo en el Barrio Gótico, en la Plaza del Rey.

– ¿Dónde vives, Ana?
– Vivo en la Ciudad de México, en el Paseo de la Reforma.

– Y tú Julio, ¿dónde vives?
– Vivo en la calle de la Libertad.

Activity 7

a – Cero, cero, tres, información.
   – Por favor, ¿el teléfono del hotel Sancho?
   – El hotel Sancho tiene el número 965 12 20 18.
   – Muchas gracias.
   – De nada.
b – Informacción, ¿qué número desea?
   – El número de teléfono del señor Martín Ramos, por favor.
   – Martín Ramos. Un momento, por favor.
   – Es el 947 925 436.
   – Gracias.

Unit 3

Activity 2

a – ¿La habitación del señor Luis García, por favor?
   – Es la número cuarenta y ocho.
b – Por favor, ¿el despacho de la señorita Sáez?
   – El treinta y seis.
c – Buenos días, ¿cuál es la habitación de los señores Silva, por favor?
   – Un momentito, por favor. Los señores Silva tienen la habitación número cien.

Unit 4

Activity 5

a

Señora	Por favor, la avenida del Mar, ¿está muy lejos?
Señor	Está a unos diez minutos de aquí. Sigue todo recto y luego toma la cuarta calle a la derecha. La avenida del Mar está al final de la calle.

b

Señor 1	¿Para ir a la playa, por favor?
Señor 2	Está un poco lejos. En el autobús, entre diez y quince minutos. La parada del autobús está en la esquina, enfrente de la iglesia.

c

Señora 1	Perdone, señora, ¿sabe usted dónde está Correos?
Señora 2	Lo siento, no lo sé. No soy aquí. No conozco muy bien la ciudad.
Señora 1	Por favor, señor, Correos, ¿dónde está?
Señor	Está en la calle de Picasso, al lado del museo. Sube usted por esta calle y coge la primera a la izquierda. Está a unos cinco minutos de aquí.

d

Señor	Los teléfonos, por favor, ¿dónde están?
Señorita	Están en la segunda planta, enfrente de los servicios. La escalera está al fondo del pasillo.

Unit 5

Activity 2

a Oiga, ¿nos trae otra botella de vino tinto, por favor?
b ¿Me pasas la sal?
c Por favor, ¿me traes dos aguas minerales sin gas del supermercado?
d ¿Me trae más azúcar, por favor?
e Por favor, ¿nos trae otros dos cafés y un té?
f ¿Me pasas una servilleta?

Activity 4

Camarero	Buenas noches. ¿Qué van a tomar?
Ramón	¿Qué tapas tiene?
Camarero	Hay champiñones, gambas, calamares y tortilla de patatas.
Ramón	¿Qué vas a tomar tú, Sofía?
Sofía	Para mí, una de calamares y una cerveza.
Ramón	¿Y para ti, Clara?
Clara	Yo quiero un bocadillo.
Camarero	Tenemos de jamón, queso, salchichón y chorizo.
Clara	De queso.
Camarero	¿Y para beber?
Clara	Un cortado.
Camarero	¿Y para usted?
Ramón	Yo, champiñones y un vino blanco.
Camarero	¿Algo más?
Ramón	No, nada más.

Unit 6

Activity 3

Buenos días. Soy Inés Suárez, de Iberiatur. Llamo para confirmar su vuelo a Lima, Perú, para el jueves diecisiete. El avión sale de Madrid a las veintitrés treinta y llega a Lima el viernes a las diez menos veinte de la mañana, hora local. La hora de presentación en el aeropuerto es a las veintiuna treinta.

Unit 7

Activity 4

Clienta	¿Cuánto es todo?
Vendedor	Son tres euros con veinte las fresas ..., un euro con noventa las manzanas ..., dos euros con diez las naranjas ..., tres euros con sesenta las uvas ..., un euro con setenta y cinco el melón y sesenta céntimos los ajos. Son trece euros con quince.

Unit 8

Activity 4

Dependienta	Hola, buenos días. ¿Qué desea?
Carmen	Por favor, quería ver esos zapatos.
Dependienta	¿Cuáles? ¿Esos?
Carmen	Sí, esos.
Dependienta	¿Qué número?
Carmen	Treinta y ocho.
Dependienta	¿De qué color?
Carmen	Los prefiero en negro.
Dependienta	En negro del número treinta y ocho no los tengo. Los tengo en marrón y en rojo solamente.
Carmen	Los prefiero en rojo.
Dependienta	Aquí tiene. ¿Quiere probárselos?
Carmen	No me quedan bien. ¿Tiene un número más grande?
Dependienta	Un momento, por favor.

Unit 9

Activity 1

– Buenos días. Quisiera cambiar libras a euros. ¿A cómo está el cambio? Tengo billetes.
– El cambio de la libra está a ... un euro con cuarenta. ¿Cuánto quería cambiar?
– Ciento setenta y cinco libras.

– ¿Dígame?
– Buenas tardes. Tengo unos cheques de viaje en francos suizos y quería cambiarlos a euros. ¿A cuánto está el cambio?
– Francos suizos ... un momento, por favor. Sí, mire, está a sesenta céntimos.
– Quiero cambiar doscientos cincuenta.
– Bien, ¿me permite su pasaporte, por favor?

– Por favor, quisiera cambiar ciento veinte coronas suecas a euros. ¿Puede decirme a cuánto está el cambio?
– La corona sueca está a diez céntimos.

Unit 10

Activity 4

Hola, me llamo Rodrigo Mora, soy ingeniero, tengo cuarenta y nueve años. Estoy casado y tengo cuatro hijos. El mayor, Raúl, tiene veintiocho años y la menor, Gloria, tiene veintiuno. Mi mujer se llama Pilar y tiene cuarenta y seis años.

Hola, yo soy Rosa, soy abogada, tengo treinta y dos años. Estoy divorciada y vivo con mi madre y mi hijo Rafael, que tiene siete años.

Unit 11

Activity 3

– ¿A qué te dedicas, Alfonso?
– Soy recepcionista. Trabajo en un hotel.
– ¿Cuánto tiempo hace que estás allí?
– Hace un año y medio.
– ¿Qué horario tienes?
– Bueno, durante el día hay dos turnos, uno de 8:00 de la mañana a 3:00 de la tarde y el otro de 3:00 a 10:00 de la noche.
– ¿Qué turno prefieres tú?
– Prefiero el turno de la mañana, porque durante la tarde tengo más tiempo para estar en casa, ver a mis amigos, hacer deportes...
– Y los sábados, ¿es igual?
– Sí, los sábados se trabaja igual, pero no trabajo los domingos.
– ¿Y cuántas semanas de vacaciones tienes al año?
– Tengo sólo quince días.

Unit 12

Activity 3

Los sábados suelo levantarme sobre las diez, me ducho y después tomo un café y unas tostadas y salgo a hacer la compra para la semana. A veces almuerzo fuera con algún amigo y por la tarde juego al tenis cerca de casa. Por la noche salgo con amigos al cine o al teatro, o a algún concierto. Los sábados me acuesto siempre muy tarde.

Los domingos por la mañana normalmente voy a algún museo para ver alguna exposición y a veces voy a casa de mi hermano que vive en el campo. Paso el día con él y su familia y vuelvo a casa por la noche. Ceno algo ligero y me acuesto.

Unit 14

Activity 2

Voz	¿Dígame?
Raquel	¿Está Lorenzo, por favor?
Voz	Está duchándose en este momento. ¿De parte de quién?
Raquel	Soy Raquel.
Voz	¿Quieres dejarle algún recado?
Raquel	Sí, dile que tengo las entradas para el concierto de esta noche.
Voz	Vale.

Activity 5

Voz	¿Dígame?
Sandra	Buenos días. Llamo por el anuncio para el puesto de diseñadora gráfica. Quería solicitar una entrevista.
Voz	Un momento, por favor. ¿Puede usted venir el lunes a las nueve y media?
Sandra	Sí, a las nueve y media me va bien.
Voz	Dígame, por favor, su nombre y su número de teléfono.

Unit 15

Activity 5

a Me llamo María, nací en México el 24 de julio de 1975. Llegué a España en 1998. Hace cinco años conocí a Antonio, un español con quien me casé.

b Me llamo Rafael, nací en Galicia el 4 de junio de 1935. Hace cincuenta años emigré a Argentina con mi mujer. Nuestros hijos nacieron en Argentina.

c Yo soy Fátima, nací en Marruecos el 16 de noviembre de 1986. Mis padres llegaron a España hace quince años. Estudié secretariado bilingüe en Barcelona y llevo un año trabajando.

d Me llamo José, nací en Argentina el 18 de mayo de 1979 y llegué a trabajar a España hace tres años. Primero trabajé en un bar y ahora estoy trabajando en un restaurante argentino. Llevo un año y medio allí. Estoy soltero y vivo con un amigo español.

Unit 16

Activity 7

Buenos Aires tuvo ayer un día de sol con temperaturas que llegaron a nueve grados la mínima y dieciséis la máxima. Para hoy se anunció nublado y lluvia por la tarde, con temperaturas extremas probables de cinco y doce grados. Perspectivas para mañana miércoles quince de julio, lluvia y fuerte viento por la mañana, y sol después del mediodía, con una temperatura mínima probable de siete grados y una máxima de catorce.

Unit 17

Activity 4

Roberto era un amigo extraordinario. Nos conocimos hace muchos años en un viaje a África y desde entonces fuimos amigos inseparables. Roberto era arquitecto y era un excelente profesional. Tenía una gran capacidad de trabajo y era muy creativo. Era un verdadero artista. Era alegre y extrovertido y tenía una muy buena relación con su familia y los amigos. Hace dos años Robertó dejó su trabajo, su familia y sus amigos y se fue del país. Un día me llegó una carta suya. Estaba en el Tíbet...

Unit 18

Activity 4

Begoña	¿A qué te dedicabas antes, Esteban?
Esteban	Trabajaba en un restaurante. Era camarero.
Begoña	Y ahora, ¿qué haces?
Esteban	Soy programador. Trabajo en una empresa de programación.
Begoña	Y tú Víctor, ¿qué hacías antes de llegar a España?
Víctor	Era estudiante. Estudiaba lenguas. Ahora soy intérprete y trabajo para la Unión Europea. ¿Y tú, Begoña?
Begoña	Yo era maestra. Trabajaba en un colegio, pero ahora estoy sin trabajo.

Unit 19

Activity 1

Buenos días. Soy María Bravo de México. Llamaba para informarles que ha sido imposible encontrar un vuelo para el 28 de marzo. Todos los vuelos están completos. He tenido que aplazar el viaje para el martes 2 de abril. Viajo en el vuelo 732 de Aeroméxico, que llega allí el miércoles a las once y media de la mañana. He reservado una habitación en el Hotel Intercontinental. Adiós, gracias.

Activity 3

Laura	Buenas tardes.
Recepcionista	Buenas tardes, señora. ¿Qué desea?
Laura	Mire, mi marido y yo hemos pedido una habitación con vistas al mar, y usted nos ha dado una con vistas al aparcamiento. ¡Esto no puede ser! Además, la habitación no tiene ni baño completo ni terraza. Y el hotel no está a cien metros de la playa como ponía en el anuncio. Y no tiene piscina ni solarium. ¡Esto es el colmo! Hemos venido aquí varias veces y esta es la primera vez que nos pasa algo así.
Recepcionista	Perdone usted, señora, pero ha sido una equivocación de su agencia de viajes. No es culpa nuestra. Yo no puedo hacer nada.
Laura	¡Es increíble!

Unit 20

Activity 2

a Hola Mónica, soy María. Te llamaba para confirmar que salgo de Madrid esta tarde en el tren de las 5:00. Llego a Sevilla a las 7:30. ¿Vendrás a la estación a recogerme? Tengo mucho equipaje. Hasta luego. Un beso.

b Mónica, soy Mark. Te llamo de Londres. Tengo un problema en el trabajo y me será imposible viajar el miércoles como tenía planeado. He cambiado el vuelo para el domingo. Saldré de Londres a las 9:30 de la mañana y llegaré allí al mediodía. Iré directamente a tu casa en un taxi. Adiós.

Unit 21

Activity 3

a – Oye, Lucía, ¿quieres venir a tomar una copa conmigo después del
       trabajo?
   – Imposible, he quedado con María para ir de compras. Otro día,
       ¿qué te parece?
   – Vale. Otro día.

b – Buenas tardes, señor Flores. Esta tarde hay un cóctel para darle
       la bienvenida al nuevo director. ¿Quiere usted venir?
   – Lo siento, pero no puedo. Tengo hora con el dentista.

c – Hola Mario. ¿Tienes algún plan para el martes por la noche?
   – No, ninguno.
   – ¿Por qué no vienes a mi fiesta de cumpleaños? Voy a celebrarlo en
       casa.
   – Encantado gracias.

Unit 23

Activity 2

Al salir del hotel tome la calle Palacio que está aquí enfrente y doble a
la derecha en la calle Triunfo. Siga por la calle Triunfo hasta la Plaza
de Armas, cruce la plaza y después tome la calle Garcilaso. El hostal
está una calle más arriba, a la izquierda.

Unit 24

Activity 2

a

Doctor   ¿Qué le pasa?

Señora   Me siento muy cansada, doctor, y no duermo bien por la
          noche. Estoy constantemente nerviosa, intranquila. No sé
          qué hacer, doctor.

Doctor   Usted parece estar estresada. Tiene que descansar. Tómese
          unos días de vacaciones. Eso es lo que necesita.

b

Señor   Doctora, no sé qué me pasa. Desde hace dos días tengo un
          dolor de estómago horrible. No puedo comer nada. Me
          encuentro muy mal, doctora.

Doctora   A ver ... ¿Le duele aquí?

Señor	Ay, sí, doctora, me duele muchísimo.
Doctora	¿Ha tenido vómitos?
Señor	Sí, he tenido vómitos y fiebre.
Doctora	Bueno, probablemente se trata de una infección estomacal. Le voy a recetar unas pastillas. Tome dos cada seis horas. Con esto se le pasará.

Unit 25

Activity 6

Teresa	Veamos qué tipo de persona necesitamos para relaciones públicas.
Julio	Pues, tiene que ser alguien que sepa relacionarse bien con la gente. Eso es fundamental. Y que tenga dos o tres años de experiencia como mínimo. Que sepa idiomas.....
Teresa	Sí, sí, claro, que hable inglés y preferiblemente algo de francés.
Julio	Sí, creo que eso es muy importante. Y, por supuesto, que tenga conocimientos de informática y que tenga carnet de conducir. Queremos una persona que sea dinámica, creativa....
Teresa	Sí, claro, y que esté dispuesta a trabajar en equipo. Espero que encontremos a alguien.
Julio	No creo que sea difícil.

key to the activities

Introductory unit

1.2 a Hola, ¿qué tal? **b** Buenos días. **c** Buenas tardes. **d** Buenas noches.

2.4 a Me llamo (*your name*). ¿Y tú?/Y tú, ¿cómo te llamas? **b** Me llamo (*your name*). ¿Y usted?/Y usted, ¿cómo se llama?/¿Cómo se llama usted?

3.2 a ¿Qué significa *habitación*? **b** Más despacio, por favor. **c** Perdón/Perdone, no entiendo. ¿Puede repetir, por favor? **d** Perdone, no hablo muy bien español. ¿Habla usted inglés?

4.2 a Adiós (, buenas tardes). **b** Hasta luego. **c** Chao.

Check what you have learnt llama – llamo – usted – entiendo – puede – hablo – habla.

Unit 1

Dialogues

1.2 ¿De dónde eres?
2.1 a F **b** F **c** F **d** V
2.2 a Usted es español, ¿verdad? **b** ¿De dónde es usted?
3.1 a No. **b** Spanish.
3.2 a ¿Habla Vd. ...? **b** Hablo ...
 4 Catalan, Spanish and some English

Practice

 1 a-6-E, b-4-D, c-5-F, d-7-G, e-1-C, f-3-B, g-2-A
 2 a Española. Barcelona. Español y catalán. **b** Argentino. Buenos Aires. Español e inglés. **c** Norteamericana. California. Inglés, italiano y un poco de español.

3 **a** Me llamo Boris. Soy de Moscú. Hablo ruso. **b** ... Paco. ... de Granada. ... español. **c** ... Ingrid. ... de Berlín. ... alemán. **d** ... Marguerite. ... de París. ... francés. **e** ... Mark. ... de Nueva York. ... inglés. **f** ... Mª Ángeles. ... de Monterrey, México. ... español.
4 Me llamo ... soy ... Soy ..., hablo.
5 *Follow Activity 4.*
6 **a** Palma. **b** Guillermo. **c** Córdoba, España.
7 ¿Cómo se llama Vd.?/Me llamo ..., ¿de dónde es Vd.?/Soy de ... ¿Habla Vd. inglés?/Sí, hablo un poco de español.

Unit 2

Dialogues

1.1 Are you Mr Peña?; Yo soy Cristina Dueñas.
1.3 a ¿Es usted el señor Santana? Yo soy (*name*). Encantado/a *or* Mucho gusto.
2.1 ¿Cómo está?, Muy bien, gracias. ¿Y usted?
2.2 Le presento a (*name*), Esta es la señora (*name*).
3.1 ¿Cómo estás?, ¿Y tú?, Te presento a ...
3.2 a Te presento a Luis/a, mi marido/mujer. **b** Esta es Isabel, una compañera de trabajo.
4.1 Home Tel. number: 981 54 63 72. Mobile phone: 696 00 19 82.
4.2 a ¿Cuál es tu número de teléfono? El teléfono de mi casa es el (*number*) **b** ¿Tienes correo electrónico?

Practice

1 **a** eres/soy/soy/estás. **b** es/es/está/está/es.
2 **a** – **b** la **c** la **d** el **e** – **f** una **g** un
3 ¿Vd. es el señor Barrios?/Yo soy .../ Encantado/a, señor Barrios./Le presento a John, un compañero de trabajo.
4 **a** Te presento a mi marido/mujer. **b** ... mi novio/a. **c** ... mi padre/madre. **d** ... mi hermano/a. **e** Esta es ... **f** Este es ... **g** Este es ... **h** Esta es ...
5 **a** la Ciudad de México, en el Paseo de la Reforma. **b** ... la calle de la Libertad. **c** ... Barcelona, en el Barrio Gótico, en la Plaza del Rey.
7 **a** 965 12 20 18 **b** 947 92 54 36.

8 **a** Vivo en (*city*). **b** Vivo en (*area*). **c** Vivo en la calle (*name of street*). **d** (*Your telephone Nº*). **e** Sí/No tengo teléfono. **f** (*Telephone Nº at work*). **g** Sí/No tengo. **h** (*Extension Nº*) **i** Es el (*number*)/No tengo teléfono móvil/celular. **j** Es (*your e-mail*)/No tengo correo electrónico/email.

9 *Horizontales*: 1 tiene 2 tienes 3 usted 4 vivo 5 eres
Verticales: 1 vive 2 mi 3 tengo 4 su 5 tu

Unit 3

Dialogues

1.1 She wants a single room for six nights.

1.2 Para dos personas. Una habitación doble. Para tres noches.

2.1 They want a double room with two beds. The rooms have a bathroom. television and air conditioning.

2.2 Somos dos, - Quisiéramos una habitación doble con cama de matrimonio. - Sí, claro, (tienen) baño, teléfono, aire acondicionado, televisión y minibar. - Sí, está incluido.

3.2 **a** Tenemos una habitación reservada. **b** ¿A qué nombre? **c** Tienen la habitación treinta y cinco. **d** Pueden cambiar aquí mismo.

Practice

1 Treinta y seis, cuarenta y cinco, cincuenta y nueve, sesenta y cuatro, setenta y seis, ochenta y ocho, noventa y tres.

2 **a** Habitación 48. **b** Despacho 36. **c** Habitación 100.

3 a-5 b-1 c-6 d-3 e-4 f-2

4 C: Buenas tardes/noches. Quisiéramos una habitación doble con baño, por favor. R: ¿Para cuántas noches? C: Para cinco noches. ¿Está incluido el desayuno? R: No, es sin desayuno. El desayuno es aparte. C: Vale. ¿Se puede aparcar en el hotel? R: Sí, claro. Sus pasaportes, por favor. Gracias. Tienen la habitación setenta y ocho.

5 **a** tengo **b** tienen **c** son **d** tienen **e** tiene/tenemos **f** son/somos.

6 **a** Air conditioning, dining room and bar, telephone, bar, fire exit. **b** individual safe-deposit box. **c** In four- and five-star hotels/In all hotels.

8 Check alphabet on page 40.

9 Check alphabet on page 40.

Unit 4

Dialogues

1.1 She's looking for a bureau de change and a hotel. ¿Hay una oficina de cambio por aquí? ¿Y dónde hay un hotel?

1.3 **a** ¿Hay un banco por aquí? **b** Hay uno en la calle Bandera, la cuarta a la izquierda, al lado de la oficina de turismo.

2.1 It's at the end of this street, on the right, five minutes away.

2.2 **a** ¿Sabe (Vd.) dónde está la catedral? **b** Lo siento, no (lo) sé. No conozco muy bien Granada. **c** Está lejos. Al final de la calle, a la izquierda, está la parada del autobús.

3.1 ¿Dónde están los servicios?

3.2 They are on the first floor. Go straight on to the end, then take the corridor on the left and go up the stairs. The toilets are opposite the cafe.

Practice

1 **a** hay **b** está **c** hay **d** está **e** están **f** hay

2 **a** ¿Hay un restaurante por aquí cerca? **b** ¿ ... una librería ...? **c** ¿ ... una tienda de ropa ...? **d** ¿ ... una tienda de comestibles ...? **e** ¿Dónde está la estación de autobuses? **f** ¿ ... la iglesia? **g** ¿ ... la biblioteca? **h** ¿ ... la plaza Mayor?

3 sabes; sé; conozco; conozco; conoces; conozco.

4 *Possible answers*: **a** Hay dos, uno detrás de la plaza de la Luz y otro detrás del cine. **b** Hay uno en la esquina, al lado de un restaurante. **c** Está entre el museo y la estación de metro. **d** Hay dos, uno delante de la gasolinera y otro delante de la estación de metro. **e** Está en la primera calle, a la derecha, al final de la calle. **f** Hay una al lado de la parada de autobuses, a la izquierda. **g** Hay una en la primera calle, a la derecha, al lado de un restaurante. **h** Está detrás de la iglesia/Correos.

5 **a** The avenida del Mar is about ten minutes from here. Go straight on and then take the fourth street on the right. The avenida del Mar is at the end of the street. **b** The beach is a bit far. On the bus, between ten and fifteen minutes. The bus stop is at the corner, opposite the church. **c** (The first person doesn't know where the post office is, as she's not from there and doesn't know the city very well) It's on calle Picasso, next to the museum. Go up this street and take the first (turning) on the left. It's about five minutes from here. **d** The telephones are on the second floor, opposite the toilets. The stairs are at the end of the corridor.

6 *Possible answers*: **a** Está en (*name of street/area*). **b** Hay una parada de autobús a cinco minutos de mi casa. **c** Hay un supermercado, tiendas de ropa, una panadería, etc. **d** Hay un museo, una biblioteca, un parque.

Unit 5

Dialogues

1.1 a Gazpacho, and grilled hake and salad. **b** Peas and ham, and chicken and chips. **c** Still mineral water. **d** Red wine.

1.2 Queremos el menú del día. Para mí ... , ¿Y para usted ...?, De primero/segundo.

2.1 Javier wants some more bread, and Ángeles another mineral water. Ángeles orders a chocolate ice cream and Javier a creme caramel and coffee.

2.2 a ¿Nos trae (un poco) más (de) vino? **b** ¿Me trae otro café? **c** ¿Nos trae la cuenta?

3.1 Silvia: b, e **Gloria** c, f **Paco** a, d.

3.2 a-3, b-1, c-2.

Practice

1 **R:** para – de – de – de – con. **C:** para. **F:** de – con – de – a – con. **C:** para. **F:** de. **C:** con – sin. **F:** con – sin.

2 **a** Vd. **b** tú **c** tú **d** Vd. **e** Vd. **f** tú.

3 **Tú:** Queremos el menú del día, por favor. **P:** Yo quiero una ensalada mixta de primero, y de segundo quiero paella. **Tú:** Para mí sopa, y de segundo quiero cordero asado con puré de patatas. **Tú:** Vino tinto para mí, por favor. ¿Y para ti Pepe? ¿Qué quieres beber? **P:** Quiero un vaso de vino blanco. **Tú:** ¿Nos trae también una botella de agua (mineral) sin gas? **Tú:** ¿Qué tiene(n) de postre? **P:** Yo quiero fresas con nata. **Tú:** Arroz con leche para mí. ¿Y nos trae dos cafés y la cuenta, por favor?

4 **Sofía:** squid/a beer. **Clara:** cheese sandwich/white coffee (with a dash of milk). **Ramón:** mushrooms/white wine.

5 **Pescado:** atún, merluza. **Carne:** pollo, cordero, cerdo. **Verdura:** lechugas, ajos, cebollas. **Fruta:** piñas, uvas, manzanas. **Utensilios:** cuchillo, cuchara, tenedor, plato.

6 **a** F **b** F **c** V **d** F.

Unit 6

Dialogues

2.1 a 9.15 a.m., 11.30 a.m., 2.30 p.m., 4.15 p.m. **b** a single ticket **c** business class.

2.2 a Quería hacer una reserva para Barcelona, para el sábado. **b** Hay un tren que sale a las trece cuarenta y cinco, otro a las quince quince y otro a las diecisiete veinte. **c** El tren de las quince quince, ¿a qué hora llega a Barcelona? **d** Quiero un billete de ida y vuelta. **e** ¿Cuánto cuesta la clase turista? **f** Ciento treinta y cinco euros.

3.1 a They run every hour. **b** An hour and a half. **c** It leaves in half an hour (9.05) and it arrives in Ronda at 10.35. **d** She gets a return ticket.

3.2 a cada hora **b** El próximo sale ... **c** ¿Cuánto tarda el viaje? **d** ¿Cuánto es?

Practice

1 ¿Qué hora es en (*name of city*)? **a** Son las seis de la tarde. **b** Son las cinco de la tarde. **c** Es la una de la mañana. **d** Son las nueve de la mañana. **e** Es la una de la tarde. **f** Son las doce/Es mediodía.

2 a A las ocho menos diez, a las doce y veinte, a las siete menos veinte de la tarde. **b** A las once menos dos, a las cuatro y diecisiete minutos de la tarde, a las diez y tres minutos de la noche.

3 *Destination*: Lima, Perú *Departure*: Thursday 17th, 11.30 p.m. *Arrival*: Friday, 9.40 a.m., local time. 21.30 at airport.

4 100, 299, 500, 900, 3500, 100.000, 1.000.000, 2.000.000.

5 Doscientos cuarenta euros – trescientos veintiocho euros – novecientos euros – mil cuatrocientos setenta y siete euros – novecientos treinta y tres euros – mil doscientos seis euros – mil seiscientos noventa y tres euros.

6 Buenos días. Quería hacer una reserva para Cartagena para el viernes por la mañana. ¿A qué hora hay vuelos? – ¿A qué hora llega a Cartagena? – Para el domingo por la noche. ¿A qué hora sale el último vuelo de Cartagena? - ¿Cuánto cuesta el billete/boleto (LAm) de ida y vuelta? – Está bien. Deme un billete/boleto de ida y vuelta, por favor.

Unit 7

Dialogues

1.2 One kg bananas, one and a half kg oranges, 2 kg tomatoes, one lettuce, 2 kg potatoes.

1.3 **a** ¿Qué quería? **b** ¿Cuánto cuestan estas ...? **c** ¿(Quiere) algo más?, ¿Alguna cosa más? **d** ¿Cuánto es todo?

2.1 **a** quarter kg cheese, one hundred and fifty grams of ham, half kg olives, one packet of butter, a tin of tuna fish, a loaf of bread, half a dozen eggs, one litre bottle of olive oil.

2.2 **a** doscientos gramos de jamón serrano **b** un kilo de azúcar **c** un paquete de galletas de chocolate **d** una lata de salmón **e** un cuarto de chorizo **f** una barra de pan integral.

Practice

1 1-d 2-e 3-a 4-f 5-b 6-c
2 Quería un kilo y medio de tomates. - ¿Cuánto cuestan/valen las fresas? *or* ¿A cómo/cuánto están las fresas? – Me da/pone un kilo. *or* Deme/Póngame un kilo. - ¿Tiene pimientos verdes? – Quiero cuatro. – Sí, quiero perejil también. – Eso es todo, gracias.
3 **a** plato **b** botella **c** lata.
4 **a** 3.20 € **b** 1.90 € **c** 2.10 € **d** 3.60 € **e** 1.75 € **f** 0.60 €
5 **a** i esto ii estas iii este iv esta v estos **b** i esas ii ese iii eso iv esos v esa.

Unit 8

Dialogues

1.1 1-c 2-f 3-d 4-a 5-e 6-b. She's buying a (red) jacket and a (black) sweater.

1.2 **a** ¿De qué color la quiere? **b** La prefiero en rojo. **c** Me queda grande. **d** ¿Tiene una más pequeña? **e** Esta me queda bien. **f** Me la llevo.

2.1 He's buying (grey) trousers and a (medium size white) shirt.

2.2 **a** forty-six, for the trousers and medium for the shirt. **b** at the back, on the right **c** ¿Puedo probármelos? **d** ¿Cómo le quedan? **e** Me quedan muy bien. Me los llevo.

Practice

1 **a** (*See model*) **b** ... esos zapatos marrones - ¿Estos? – Sí, esos - ¿... probármelos? - ¿... le quedan? – Me quedan pequeños. **c** ... esa camiseta amarilla - ¿Esta? – Sí, esa - ¿... probármela? - ¿... queda? - Me queda ancha. **d** ... ese vestido gris - ¿Este? – Sí, ese - ¿... probármelo? - ¿... queda? – Me queda estrecho.

2 **a** más corta **b** más baratas **c** más pequeña **d** más largos **e** más anchos **f** más grande.

3 **a** ¿Puedo probármelos? **b** Me lo llevo. **c** Me quedan bien. Me las llevo. **d** Me los llevo. **e** ¿Puedo probármela? **f** No me queda bien. No me lo llevo.

4 **a** size 38 **b** black **c** brown and red **d** red **e** They don't fit well. She wants a larger size.

Unit 9

Dialogues

1.1 She's changing 250 dollars. The rate of exchange is 0.79 cents.

1.2 ¿Qué desea? – Quería cambiar ... – ¿Tiene cheques de viaje ...? – Tengo billetes. ¿A cómo está ...? – Está a 540 ... ¿Cuánto quería cambiar? – Cien dólares – Muy bien. ¿Tiene su pasaporte? – Sí, aquí tiene. – ¿Cuál es su dirección aquí? – Calle Moneda 842.

2.1 **a** F **b** F **c** V **d** F.

2.2 19 € per day.

2.3 **a** ¿Qué nos recomienda? **b** Les recomiendo ... **c** Se lo recomiendo. **d** ¿Podemos pagar ...?

3.1 She wants to go to the airport and she wants the taxi right now.

3.2 Quería un taxi para ir a la Estación de Atocha, por favor. ¿Me lo puede enviar a las 11:00?/Lo quiero para las 11:00. Pues, se lo envío a las 11:00. (*No other changes in dialogue apart from address and telephone number*).

Practice

1 Libras: 1.45 €, 175 pounds; Swiss francs: 0.60 €, 250 Swiss francs; Swedish crowns: 0.10 €, 120 Swedish crowns.

2 **Tú** Quisiera cambiar dólares a pesos. ¿A cuánto/cómo está el cambio? **E** ¿Tiene billetes? **Tú** No, tengo cheques de viaje. **E** Está a once pesos por dólar. ¿Cuánto quiere cambiar? **Tú** Quisiera/ Quería cambiar doscientos dólares./Y el cambio de la libra, ¿a cuánto/cómo está? **E** La libra está a 15 pesos. **Tú** Quisiera/Quería cambiar 180 libras. **E** ¿Qué dirección tiene en México? **Tú** (*address*).

3 me – le – lo – lo – lo.

4 (*Possible questions*) **a** Queríamos un coche económico. ¿Qué (coche) nos recomienda? **b** ¿Cuánto es/cuesta el alquiler? **c** ¿Está incluido el seguro obligatorio?/El seguro obligatorio, ¿está incluido? **d** Y los impuestos, ¿están incluidos?/¿Están incluidos los impuestos? **e** ¿Va con gasolina o con gasóleo? **f** ¿Podemos pagar con tarjeta de crédito?/¿Se puede pagar con ...? **g** ¿Podemos llevarlo ahora mismo?/¿Lo podemos llevar ahora mismo?

5 **a** Queríamos/Quisiéramos el desayuno en la habitación, por favor. Estamos en la habitación 12. **b** ¿Puede enviárnoslo ahora mismo?/¿Nos lo puede enviar ...? Queremos un té y un café, un zumo/jugo (LAm.) de piña y un zumo/jugo (LAm.) de naranja, y pan integral. **c** ¿Puede enviarnos un periódico inglés?/¿Nos puede enviar ...? **d** También quisiéramos/queríamos un taxi para ir al aeropuerto. **e** El avión sale a las doce y media. Lo queremos para las diez y media. **f** ¿Nos da la cuenta, por favor? Quisiéramos/Queríamos pagar con tarjeta de crédito.

6 *Horizontales:* 1 efectivo 2 alquilar 3 quisiera 4 tarjeta 5 incluidos 6 gasolina 7 recomiendo *Verticales:* 1 alquiler 2 cuánto 3 firmar 4 cambiar 5 billetes 6 viaje 7 casa (LAm usage).

Unit 10

Dialogues

1.1 a F b V c V d F.

1.2 **a** Estás casada, ¿verdad? **b** Tú estás soltero, ¿no? **c** Tengo veintidós años. **d** el mayor/la menor.

2.1 bathroom, neighbourhood/area, heating, kitchen, bedroom/room, flat, sitting room; **a** It's not bad. It has four bedrooms, a large sitting room, a fitted kitchen, two bathrooms, and it's very bright. **b** It's very good and quieter than the centre. **c** His flat is not as big as María's but it's very comfortable. It has three bedrooms, a sitting room, a large kitchen, independent heating.

2.2 **a** Gracia **b** Génova.

Practice

1 **a** llamo **b** tengo **c** estoy **d** vivo **e** padres **f** mayor **g** llama **h** tiene **i** que **j** menor

2 **a** se llama **b** tiene **c** está **d** Vive con su madre, sus tres hermanos y su abuela. **e** Sus padres ... **f** Él es el menor. **g** llama **h** tiene **i** que **j** menor es su hermana ...

3 *Possible answer*: Me llamo Luisa, tengo cuarenta y cinco años, estoy casada. Mi marido se llama Pedro y tiene cuarenta y siete años. Tengo tres hijos. La mayor se llama Teresa y tiene veintitrés años, después viene Raquel, que tiene veinte, y el menor es mi hijo Felipe, que tiene diecisiete años.

4 **a** Tiene cuarenta y nueve. **b** Tiene cuatro. **c** El mayor tiene veintiocho y la menor veintiuno. **d** Tiene cuarenta y seis. **e** Tiene treinta y dos. **f** Está divorciada. **g** Vive con su madre y con su hijo de siete años.

5 *Follow models*: dialogue 1, key to Activity 3, and transcript for Activity 4.

6 **a** Tiene dos. **b** Es estupendo, mucho mejor que el anterior y más barato. **c** Es muy tranquilo. **d** Tiene calefacción y aparcamiento.

7 **a** *See example.* **b** El piso de la calle Lorca es más grande que el piso de la avenida Salvador. **c** ... Salvador es más céntrico que ... Lorca. **d** ... Lorca es tan cómodo como ... Salvador. **e** ... Lorca es más seguro que ... Salvador. **f** ... Lorca es tan tranquilo como ... Salvador.

8 Use Elena's letter in Activity 6 as a model.

Unit 11

Dialogues

1.1 Elena is a nurse and works in a hospital. Álvaro is a student. He's studying history.

1.2 a Cristina **b** Cristóbal **c** Ángeles.

1.3 a ¿Qué estudias? **b** Trabajo en un hospital. **c** ¿Cuánto tiempo hace que trabajas allí? **d** Doy clases de inglés **e** Estoy jubilada **f** Estoy sin trabajo.

2.1 a He works from 8.30 to 1.00 and from 2.30 to 6.30, Monday to Friday. He doesn't work on Saturdays. **b** Three weeks. **c** She works at home.

2.2 Isabel: Trabajo de 9:00 a 5:00 (de la tarde), de lunes a viernes, y de 10:00 a 2:00 (de la tarde) los sábados. Tengo un mes de vacaciones. **Hugo** Trabajo de 9:00 a 2:00 y de 4:00 a 7:00 de la tarde, de lunes a sábado.

Practice

1 a-4 b-9 c-6 d-1 e-8 f-7 g-3 h-10 i-5 j-2

2 a-2 b-4 c-1 d-3

3 a Es recepcionista. Trabaja en un hotel. **b** Un año y medio **c** Durante el día hay dos turnos, uno de 8:00 a 3:00 de la tarde y otro de 3:00 a 10:00 de la noche, de lunes a sábado. **d** Prefiere el turno de la mañana. **e** Quince días.

4 a Mónica **b** Victoria **c** María Ángeles **d** Juan Carlos **e** Eugenio **f** Adela.

5 *Follow Activity 4 as a model.*

6 a ¿Cuánto tiempo hace que estás aquí? Estoy aquí desde hace dos meses y medio *or* Hace dos meses y medio que estoy aquí. **b** ¿ ... que estudias inglés? Estudio inglés desde hace ... /Hace ... que estudio inglés. **c** ¿ ... que vives en este barrio? Vivo en este barrio desde hace .../Hace ... que vivo en este barrio. **d** ¿ ... que conoces a Paul? Conozco a Paul desde hace .../Hace ... que conozco a Paul.

7 *Possible answers*: **a** Soy (*occupation*), Trabajo en (*place of work*), Trabajo allí desde hace (*number of months/years*), Trabajo de (*time*) a (*time*), de (lunes) a (viernes). Tengo tres semanas de vacaciones al año. **b** Estudio (*lenguas*) en (*un colegio/una universidad*), Hace (*un año*) que estudio español, Tengo clases de (9.00 a 1.00) de (lunes) a (viernes)/No tengo un horario regular.

Unit 12

Dialogues

1.1 **a** siete **b** nueve **c** una hora/la oficina **d** autobús/el coche **e** un restaurante/la oficina **f** cinco/seis **g** once/once y media.

1.2 te levantas/me levanto, empiezo, tardo, vas/voy, almuerzas/almuerzo, sales/salgo, vuelvo, te acuestas/me acuesto.

1.3 **a** Me levanto a las siete y cuarto. **b** Empiezo a trabajar a las nueve y media. **c** Voy al trabajo en tren. **d** Almuerzo en la oficina. **e** Nunca salgo de la oficina antes de las cinco y media.

2.1 **Joaquín:** a, b, d, f, g **Amaya y Ramiro:** i, j, l, n

Practice

1 **a** 2, 6, 8, 9 **b** 3, 4 7 **c** 1, 5

2 **a** Me levanto a las seis. **b** Me ducho. **c** Me afeito. **d** Me lavo los dientes. **e** Me peino. **f** Me visto/pongo la ropa. **g** Desayuno. **h** Leo el periódico.

3 **a** She takes a shower, has a coffee and toast and goes out to do the week's shopping. **b** She plays tennis near her home. **c** She goes out with friends to the cinema, theatre, or a concert . **d** She normally goes to a museum to see an exhibition.

4 **a** ¿A qué hora te levantas? **b** ¿Cómo vas al trabajo? **c** ¿A qué hora empiezas a trabajar? **d** ¿Dónde almuerzas? **e** ¿A qué hora sales del trabajo? **f** ¿Qué haces por la noche?

5 *Use dialogues and Activities in the Practice section as a model, including the transcript of the listening comprehension text for Activity 3.*

6 **a** Completely quiet. He doesn't accept any engagement and does absolutely nothing. He stays at home, he rehearses, studies, reads ... **b** He eats a very light meal, a little bit of chicken or some veal and soup. **c** Eight hours on a normal day, but when he has a performance he sleeps up to eleven hours. **d** Most of the time by the seaside.

Unit 13

Dialogues

1.1 Nieves, 3. Miguel, 2, Eduardo, 1.
1.2 a Voy a ir al cine. b ¿Vas a salir? c ¿Te gusta el cine? d Me gusta mucho. e A Raquel le encanta bailar.
2.1 1-c, 2-e, 3-a, 4-f, 5-b, 6-d.
2.2 Eduardo: 1, 2, 3. Nieves: 4, 5, 6.
2.3 a New York b She likes it very much c Travelling by plane d They are going to spend ten days in Ibiza.

Practice

1 vamos, pensamos, quieres, vamos a ir, me encanta, le gusta.
2 *Follow Activity 1 as a model.*
3 a ¿Adónde vas a ir este verano? b ¿Con quién vas a ir? c ¿Cuánto tiempo vas a quedarte? d ¿Dónde vas a alojarte? e ¿Qué te gusta hacer en tus vacaciones? f ¿Te gusta nadar? g ¿Cuándo vas a volver?
4 *Examples:* Me encanta escuchar música, me gusta ir al cine, no me gusta (nada) trabajar, detesto realizar tareas domésticas.
5 me gusta - me encanta – detesto - me fascina - me gusta - me gusta - nos gusta - nos encanta - le gusta - no me gusta nada.
6 a Cristina b Elvira c Daniel d Cristina e Elvira f David g Daniel h David.
7 *Follow models above.*

Unit 14

Dialogues

1.1 He's speaking on another line.
1.2 Sí, ¿díga? - ¿Está María? – No, no está en este momento. ¿De parte de quién? – De José Luis. - ¿Quieres dejarle algún recado? – No, luego la llamo.
2.1 a Quisiera hablar con ... b Su extensión no es esta. c Es la tres, sesenta y ocho. d ¿Me puede poner con ...?
3.1 a For tomorrow b Thursday c 9.30 a.m. or 4.15 p.m. d 9.30 a.m.

3.2 **a** Quisiera pedir hora con el/la dentista para el lunes. **b** No hay hora disponible hasta el miércoles a las diez y veinte o por la tarde a las tres menos cuarto. **c** A las tres menos cuarto me va bien.

Practice

1 ¿Está Leonor? – ¿De parte de quién?/¿Quién la llama? – ¿Quiere dejarle algún recado?

2 **a** 3 **b** She says she's got the tickets for tonight's concert.

3 ¿Dígame? – La señora Smith no puede ponerse en este momento. Está almorzando con un cliente. ¿De parte de quién?/¿Quién la llama? – ¿Quiere dejarle algún recado? – Muy bien, señor Calle. Le daré su recado. – Sí, el señor Roberts está. No se retire, por favor. En seguida se pone.

4 **a** pones – necesita **b** atendiendo – quiere **c** se pone **d** se retire – pongo **e** cuelgue **f** comunicando.

5 **a** Llamo por el anuncio para el puesto de diseñadora gráfica. **b** Quería solicitar una entrevista. **c** Sí, a las nueve y media me va bien.

Unit 15

Dialogues

1.1 **a** I arrived in December 1997. **b** I met her a year and a half ago. **c** We got married in October of last year.

2.1 She's been there for three years. She lived and worked in Seville before.

2.2 **a** Llevo cinco años en España. **b** Trabajé dos años en Salamanca. **c** Estudié español allí.

3.1 She was born in Santander on 15th March 1983.

3.2 **a** Nací en (place). **b** Nací el (date).

Practice

1 a-6, b-3, c-1, d-4, e-2, f-5.

2 terminé – trabajé – me trasladé – ingresé – desempeñé – ocupé – perdí.

3 **a** ¿Dónde nació? **b** ¿Cuándo nació? **c** ¿Qué estudió? **d** ¿Cuándo terminó sus estudios? **e** ¿Dónde trabaja ahora? **f** ¿Cuánto tiempo lleva trabajando allí? **g** ¿Dónde trabajó antes?

4.1 a-4, b-2, c-1, d-3.

4.2 a ¿Cuánto tiempo llevas viviendo en Londres? – Llevo dos años (viviendo en Londres). **b** ¿... estudiando inglés? – Llevo un año y medio... **c** ¿... haciendo atletismo? – Llevo tres años ... **d** ¿... trabajando como enfermera? – Llevo un año ...

5 a María: 24th July 1975; Rafael: 4th June 1935; Fátima: 16th November 1986; José: 18th May 1979. **b** five years ago **c** fifty years ago **d** in Argentina **e** fifteen years go **f** one year **g** three years ago **h** He worked in a bar and now he's working in an Argentinian restaurant.

6 Antonio Banderas; nació – filmó – dejó – triunfó – se casó – tuvieron – fue – realizó – actuó – obtuvo.

7 nació – llegó – es – está – tiene – estudió – terminó – conoció – se casaron – su (primer hijo) – su (hija Francisca) – su (marido).

Unit 16

Dialogues

1.1 b, c, e.

1.2 estuve/estuvimos, pasé, gustó, hicisteis/hice, fuiste/fui, fueron, encantó, me quedé, pareció.

1.3 interesantísimo, muchísimo.

2.1 The weather seemed very pleasant to her. It's not very warm, although in July it often rains. They were lucky because it only rained once.

2.2 no hace mucho calor, llueve a menudo, sólo llovió una vez, hizo muchísimo calor.

Practice

1 salió – fue – hice – cené – me acosté – tuve – estuve – me gustó – fui – hice – vinieron – fuimos – pasé – conocí – parecieron.

2 a-3, salió **b**-5, fue **c**-1, nadó **d**-4, conoció **e**-6, hizo **f**-2, tomó

3 **a** fuimos **b** estuvimos **c** vimos **d** anduvimos/nos parecieron **e** hicimos **f** tuvimos.

4 **a** ¿Dónde fuiste? **b** ¿Cuánto tiempo estuviste allí? **c** ¿Te quedaste con amigos? **d** ¿Qué hiciste allí? **e** ¿Qué te pareció el lugar? **f** ¿Hizo mucho calor?

5 Follow the models in the previous activities.

6.1 a-6, b-2, c-8, d-1, e-7, f-4, g-3, h-5.

6.2 **a** Hace sol. **b** Hace viento y está nublado. **c** Está lloviendo/llueve. **d** Está nublado.

8 **a** It was a sunny day **b** It will be cloudy in the morning and there'll be rain in the afternoon. **c** There'll be rain and strong wind in the morning. **d** It will be sunny after midday. **e** Minimum temperature, 7 degrees, maximum, 14.

Unit 17

Dialogues

1.2 **a** Rocío's boss: insoportable, agresivo, antipático, feo, horrible. **b** Santiago: guapo, inteligente, divertido, irresponsable, machista; Daniel's mother: reservada, tímida, trabajadora, generosa, estricta. **c** mis compañeros de trabajo, todo lo contrario, un gran sentido del humor.

2.1 Hotel Don Quijote.

2.2 It was very good. It was a 4-star hotel, a hundred metres from the beach, it had a swimming pool, a good restaurant, seaview and parking. The rooms were comfortable and they had air conditioning and cable TV.

Practice

1 a-3, b-4, c-6, d-1, e-2, f-5.

2 **a** aburrido **b** alegre **c** tímido **d** inteligente **e** arrogante **f** descortés **g** pesimista **h** antipático **i** débil **j** agradable **k** perezoso **l** responsable **m** maduro **n** inseguro

4 **a** They met while travelling in Africa. **b** He was an architect. **c** He had great capacity for work and was very creative. He was a real artist. He was cheerful and extrovert and had a good relationship with his family and friends. **b** He left his job, family and friends and left the country to go to Tibet.

6 **a** era **b** era **c** tenía **d** estaban **e** estaban **f** había **g** habían **h** estaba **i** era **j** había **k** eran **l** era.

Unit 18

Dialogue

1.1 She was there for five years. She worked as a sales manager in a travel agency.

1.2 antes de llegar, vivía en, trabajaba en..., compartía un piso.

2.1 She had good friends there and used to see them practically everyday. They used to go out for drinks or to dinner, and at weekends they used to go dancing.

2.2 The job wasn't bad. She didn't earn much: El sueldo no estaba mal. No ganaba mucho.

Practice

1. 1-e me levantaba, 2-c iba a la escuela, 3-f comía con mi madre, 4-a dormía la siesta, 5-d hacía los deberes, 6-b jugaba con mi pelota.

2. vivía, trabajaba, iba, empezaba, salía, ganaba, estaba, tenía, se llamaba, nos veíamos, dábamos, hablábamos.

3. *Example:* Vivía en... Mi padre era *(occupation)* y trabajaba en *(place)*. Mi madre era ... y ... trabajaba en ... Mi madre me llevaba a la escuela. Me gustaba/encantaba ir a la escuela. Pasaba mis vacaciones en ... Allí nadaba, jugaba, salía con mis amigos, etc.

4. **Esteban:** c trabajaba/era, f es/trabaja; **Víctor:** e era/estudiaba, a es/trabaja; **Begoña:** b era/trabajaba, e está.

5. **a** Contestaban ... **b** Leían ... **c** Mandaban ... **d** Trabajaban ... **e** Atendían ... **f** Servían ...

6. **a** Contestábamos... **b** Leíamos ... **c** Mandábamos ... **d** Trabajábamos ... **e** Atendíamos ... **f** Servíamos ...

7. **a** ¿A qué se dedicaba antes?/¿En qué trabajaba antes?/¿Qué hacía antes? **b** ¿Cuánto tiempo trabajó allí? **c** ¿Cuánto ganaba? **d** ¿Por qué dejó su trabajo?

Unit 19

Dialogues

1.1 a He estado dos veces aquí. **b** Es la primera vez que vengo. **c** He ido al museo, pero todavía no he visto la catedral. **d** Por la tarde he salido con unos amigos a comer.

1.2 a Esta es la segunda vez que vengo a España. **b** Hoy he ido al mercado. **c** Todavía no he visto las ruinas. **d** Me han dicho que son muy interesantes.

2.1 It's a blue checked umbrella.

2.2 He comido aquí, ¿Es este su paraguas?, Sí, es ese.

3.1 They had asked for an outward-facing room and they have been given one facing a central patio. The air conditioning doesn't work and there aren't enough towels.

3.2 llamo de..., no funciona, usted perdone, ahora mismo les doy otra habitación.

Practice

1 María Bravo from Mexico has phoned. She says it has been impossible to find a flight for the 28th of March. All flights are full. She has had to put off her journey until Tuesday 2nd of April. She's flying on Aeromexico flight 732, which arrives on Wednesday at 11.30 a.m. She has booked a room at the Intercontinental hotel.

2 a ha hecho **b** han pasado **c** ha viajado **d** ha vuelto **e** se han mudado **f** me he quedado **g** hemos pintado **h** han abierto

3.1 Hotel Condes

3.2 a V **b** F **c** F

4 a The heating, the air conditioning, the television, the hot/cold tap … isn't working. **b** The toilet, the wash basin, the bath … is blocked. **c** There isn't any soap, shampoo, toilet paper. **d** There aren't enough towels.

5 a La calefacción no funciona. **b** El lavabo está atascado. **c** Falta/No hay jabón en el baño. **d** Necesito más mantas en mi cama.

6 She left a briefcase with some documents. She says it is a black leather briefcase.

7 *Possible answers*: Perdone, he estado aquí al mediodía y he olvidado/dejado un libro de español/un jersey gris de manga larga/un bolso negro.

8 a See example. **b** See example. **c** ¿Ha pedido hora con …? Sí, ya la he pedido. **d** ¿Ha escrito a …? Sí, ya les he escrito. **e** ¿Ha hecho el pedido de …? No, todavía no lo he hecho. **f** ¿Ha visto a …? Sí, ya la he visto. **g** ¿Ha abierto la …? No, todavía no la he abierto.

Unit 20

Dialogues

1.1 He's leaving this afternoon and will be arriving in Madrid at 8.30 tomorrow.

1.2 a She offers to pick him up at the airport. **b** Rafael's, because her car is too small. **c** He'll phone Ana. **d** Seguro que mañana hará calor.

2.1 a Llamaba por ... **b** una reserva a nombre de ... **c** No podremos viajar. **d** Tendremos que cancelarla.

2.2 Buenas tardes/noches. Llamaba por una reserva que hice a nombre de ..... para el 20 de agosto. No podré viajar en esa fecha y tendré que anularla. Lo siento mucho.

Practice

1 saldré, llegaré, me quedaré, llamaré, llevaré.

2 **a** María is calling to confirm that she's leaving Madrid this afternoon on the 5.00 o'clock train and will be arriving in Seville at 7.30. She asks Mónica whether she can come to the station to pick her up, as she has a lot of luggage.
b Mark is phoning from London to say that it will be impossible for him to travel on Wednesday as planned. He has changed his flight for Sunday. He will leave London at 9.30 in the morning and will arrive there at midday. He will go straight to Mónica's house in a taxi.

3 **a** – 4, **b** – 5, **c** – 1, **d** – 2, **e** – 3.

4 **a** See example, **b** ... te entrevistarán, **c** ... te lo ofrecerán, **d** ... será muy bueno **e** ... te lo darán.

5 **a** See example, **b** ... vendrá solo, **c** ... tendrá nuestra dirección, **d** ... sabrá cómo llegar aquí, **e** ... entenderá algo de español.

6 **a** su – mío - el mío, **b** sus – mías – las mías.

Unit 21

Dialogues

1.1 a She suggests going to the cinema tonight. **b** In front of the cinemam, about 9.30. **c** Because he has to work.

1.2 a ¿Qué te parece si vamos al teatro mañana? **b** Me gustaría ver ... **c** He visto la obra, pero me encantaría verla otra vez. **d** Podríamos quedar aquí mismo sobre las ocho menos cuarto.

2.1 Antonio accepts it: Yo, encantado, gracias. Santiago doesn't accept it: A mí me encantaría, pero no puedo. Tengo un compromiso. ¿Otro día quizá?

2.2 **a** ¿Queréis/Os gustaría venir a mi casa el sábado? Tengo una fiesta y he invitado a otros amigos. **b** Me encantaría, pero no puedo. Tengo un compromiso con unos/algunos amigos de la oficina. ¿La próxima vez, quizá?

Practice

1 **a** haría **b** lavaría **c** escribiría **d** llamaría **e** saldríamos **f** veríamos **g** tendríamos **h** podríamos

2 Soy (*your name*). ¿Tienes algún plan para esta noche? ¿Qué te parece si vamos al teatro? Me gustaría ver (*play*). ¿La has visto? La ponen en el Olimpia y empieza a las 7:00. Podríamos quedar en el café enfrente del teatro a las 6:30. ¿Qué te parece?

3 **Lucía** is being invited to have a drink with someone after work. She doesn't accept the invitation because she's going shopping with María. **Señor Flores** is being invited to a cocktail party to receive the new Director, but he can't accept because he has an appointment with the dentist. **Mario** is being invited to a birthday party, and he accepts the invitation.

4 He's inviting me to see Joaquín Cortés and he suggests we meet in the bar next to the theatre at 7:30.

5 *Follow Activity 4 as a model.*

6 The Chamber of Commerce of Santa Cruz has pleasure in inviting you to the inauguration ceremony for our new offices. The opening ceremony, which will be attended by the local authorities will take place/be held on Avenida del Libertador, 52, on Tuesday 25th May at 19.30.

Unit 22

Dialogues

1.1 **a** She had never been to Mérida. **b** She thinks it is a very beautiful city.

1.2 **a** ¿Había estado en España antes? **b** Había estado en Barcelona, pero nunca había venido a Granada. **c** ¿Qué le parece el hotel? **d** Me gusta. Es un hotel buenísimo/muy bueno.

2.1 **a** buenísimo **b** delicioso **c** un poco más **d** un poco más de

2.2 **a** La paella está buenísima. **b** El pollo está delicioso. **c** ¿Le sirvo un poco más de postre? **d** ¿Quiere un poco más de café?

3.1 **1** c,d **2** a,b.

3.2 **a** ¡Qué tarde es! **b** Debo irme. **c** Gracias for haber venido. **d** ¡Que tenga un buen viaje!

Practice

1 1-d: había aprendido 2-c: había viajado 3-e: había hecho 4-f: había estudiado 5-a: había escrito 6-b: había terminado.

2 **a**-2 **b**-4 **c**-1 **d**-3.

3 No había estado nunca aquí antes. Es un país muy bonito. /Los mariscos están buenísimos./Están deliciosos./Sí, pero sólo un poco./No, gracias./¿De verdad?/Sí, de verdad, gracias. No puedo beber más porque tengo que conducir.

4 *Possible answers:* **a** ¿Le sirvo otra taza de café?/¿Quiere otro café? **b** ¿Quiere/Le sirvo un poco más de tarta? **c** ¿Quiere/Le sirvo un poco más de coñac? **d** ¿Quiere/Le sirvo más agua mineral?

5 **a** *por* tu regalo **b** *ha* sido **c** mucho *de* **d** conocer*la*.

6 agradecer – marido – estancia – placer – poder – visita.

Unit 23

Dialogues

1.1 He's looking for the post office. He needs to go straight on and when he reaches Mijas Avenue, the fourth on the right, he has to turn right. The post office is on Bailén Street, the second on the left.

1.2 ¿Podría decirme dónde está el museo? – Siga todo recto y al llegar a la calle (de) Cervantes gire a la izquierda. El museo está en la avenida San Alfonso, la tercera a la derecha.

2.1 **a** F **b** V **c** F.

2.2 por – hasta – de.

3.1 **a** de 9:00 a 11:30 de la mañana y por la tarde de 4:00 a 6:00 **b** al 952 642 21 09 **c** 952 759 55 32.

3.2 **a** marque **b** llame **c** indique **d** haga.

Practice

1 1-d 2-g 3-a 4-f 5-h 6-c 7-e 8-b
2 He/she is staying at Hotel Monasterio and is looking for the Hostal Los Marqueses.
3 siga – gire – tome – siga – suba – pregunte
4 Sí, siga todo recto/de frente y tome/coja la tercera (calle) a la izquierda, luego tome/coja la primera a la derecha y siga todo recto/de frente hasta el final de la calle. El banco está enfrente de la estación.
5 *Possible answer:* Siga todo recto/Siga por la calle San Antonio, después tome/coja la primera (calle) a la izquierda y luego la primera a la derecha. Esa es la avenida de Bailén. La estación está pasada la avenida de Mijas a la izquierda.
6 a Envíelo b Llámela c No lo haga d Pásemelas e No lo conteste f Enséñemelo

Unit 24

Dialogues

1.1 a tráeme b tengo c espera
1.2 a ¿Qué te pasa? b Vuelvo en seguida.
2.1 a She's not feeling well. b Because she's too hot. c To rest for a while, to try to sleep and not to get up.
2.2 a No me encuentro bien. b Me duele la cabeza. c Por favor, abre la ventana. d ¿Por qué no descansas ...?

Practice

1 Germany, the Netherlands (Low Countries) and Spain.
2 a Fatiga, ansiedad/insomnio/problemas digestivos. b To rest and take a holiday/Some tablets, two every six hours.
3 a me encuentro/siento b me duele c tengo dolor d tengo e me duele f me siento
4 No me encuentro/siento bien. – Tengo un dolor de cabeza horrible y tengo fiebre. – Por favor, tráeme un vaso de agua mineral. Tengo mucha sed. – ¿ Podrías abrir la puerta? Tengo mucho calor. – No, gracias, no tengo hambre.
5 Isabel: She doesn't manage to lose weight. Sometimes she goes on a diet for a few days and loses a few kilos, but she's not persevering and so gains weight again. Ricardo:

At the end of the day he suffers from terrible headaches which prevent him from doing anything. He also has nausea which usually ends up in vomiting.

6 **Isabel:** b, c, f. **Ricardo:** a, d, e.

Unit 25

Dialogues

1.1 She's looking for a flat near the centre, with three or four bedrooms, and not too expensive. She doesn't want to pay more than 800 euros. And she prefers it furnished.

1.2 The one which costs 650 € *or* the one which costs 700 €.

1.3 *Example:* Busco una casa que esté cerca de la playa, que tenga dos o tres dormitorios, que tenga garaje y jardín, y que no cueste más de 1200 €. La prefiero sin amueblar.

2.1 a V b F c V d F.

2.2 Espero que encuentres a alguien, No creo que sea fácil.

2.3 *Example:* Quiero una persona que sea joven/mayor, que sea estudiante o profesional, que sea tranquila, que tenga sentido del humor y que le gusten los deportes (como a mí).

Practice

1.1 a 93 330 16 87 b 977 894 69 05 c Luisa d 93 357 26 71 e Begoña f Carlota.

1.2 973 44 04 57.

2 viva – alquile – haya – puedan – esté.

3 *Follow activities 1 and 2 as a model.*

4 a sea b esté c sepa d tenga e le gusten f se lleve.

5 a to know languages, to have a driving licence, to have experience, to be able to relate to people well/sepa, tenga, tenga, sea. b to be creative and dynamic, to be presentable, to have finished higher education/sea, tenga, haya. c to be familiar with computers, to have own vehicle/car, to be willing to travel, to be able to join the company immediately/tenga, cuente, esté, pueda.

6.1 sepa relacionarse ... , tenga experiencia, sepa idiomas, tenga conocimientos de ... , tenga carnet de ... , sea dinámica, sea creativa y que esté dispuesta a trabajar en equipo.

7 **a** He did Business Studies in Madrid and has a Master's degree from a university in the United States. He also speaks and writes English and French perfectly. **b** He's extrovert and nice. **c** He has been to the Department of Employment many times, he has sent his curriculum dozens of times, and he has read hundreds of job advertisements in the newspapers. **d** Some companies require experience, others tell him that with his qualifications they can't pay him an appropriate salary. **e** He doesn't know what to do, he's desperate.

For reasons of space this Spanish–English vocabulary does not include all words in the book. A small dictionary may be sufficient to look up words which are not listed here. Abbreviations used include *(AmE)* for American English, *(LAm)* for Latin America, *(m)* for masculine, *(f)* for feminine, *(sing)* for singular, *(pl)* for plural, *(adj)* for adjective, *(esp)* for especially, *(inf)* for informal.

a   *on, to, at*
abierto/a   *open*
abrigo (m)   *coat*
abrir   *to open*
absolutamente   *absolutely*
abuelo/a   *grandfather/grandmother*
abundante   *plenty, generous*
aburrido/a   *boring*
acabar en   *to end up in*
acampar   *to camp, to go camping*
acción (f)   *action*
aceite de oliva (m)   *olive oil*
aceptar   *to accept*
acostarse (o>ue)   *to go to bed*
actuar   *to act*
acuáticos: deportes ___ (m)   *water sports*
acuerdo: de ___   *fine, all right*
además   *besides*
adicto/a   *addicted*
adiós   *goodbye,* (AmE) *so long*
administración pública (f)   *civil service,* (AmE) *public administration*
administrativo/a   *clerk, office worker*
afectar   *to affect*

afeitarse   *to shave*
afueras (f)   *outskirts*
agencia de viajes (f)   *travel agency*
agradable   *pleasant*
agradecer   *to thank, be grateful*
agrícola   *agricultural*
agua (f)   *water*
ahora   *now;* ___ mismo   *right away/now*
aire acondicionado (m)   *air conditioning*
ajo (m)   *garlic*
albaricoque (m)   *apricot*
alegrarse   *to be glad*
alegre   *happy*
alemán (m) (language)   *German*
alemán/alemana   *German*
Alemania   *Germany*
algo   *something, anything;* ¿___más?   *anything else?*
alguien   *someone, somebody*
algún   *some, any* (before a sing, m noun)
alguna: ¿___ cosa más?   *anything else*
alguna vez   *ever*

alguno/a, algunos/as *some, any*
alimentación: tienda de ___ (f)
  grocer´s, (AmE) *grocery*
alimento (m) *food*
allí *there*
almorzar (o>ue) *to have lunch*
almuerzo (m) *lunch*
alquilar *to hire*, (AmE) *rent*
alquiler (m) *hire, hiring*, (AmE)
  renting
alto/a *high*
ama de casa (f) *housewife*
amable *kind*
ambiente (m) *atmosphere,*
  environment
amueblado/a *furnished*
amueblar *to furnish*
ancho/a *loose, loose-fitting*
andar *to walk*
anoche *last night*
ansiedad (f) *anxiety*
anteayer *the day before yesterday*
anterior *previous*
antes *before*
antes de ayer *the day before*
  yesterday
anticuado/a *old-fashioned*
antipático/a *unpleasant*
anunciar *to announce*
anuncio (m) *advertisement*
año (m) *year*
aparcamiento (m) *car park*, (AmE)
  parking lot
aparcar *to park*
aparecer *to appear*
apartamento (m) *flat*, (AmE)
  apartment
aparte *separate;* ___ de *apart from*
apellidarse *to be called* (surname)
apellido (m) *surname*, (AmE) *last*
  name
apetecer *to feel like, fancy*
aplazar *to postpone*
apreciar *to appreciate, notice*
aprender *to learn*
aquí *here;* ___mismo *right here;* ___
  tiene *here you are*
arquitecto/a *architect*
arriba: más ___ *further up*
arroz (m) *rice*
artículo (m) *article*

asado/a *roast; grilled*, (AmE) *broiled*
ascensor (m) *lift*, (AmE) *elevator*
aseo (m) *toilet*, (AmE) *rest room*
así *like this*
atascado/a *blocked*
atención (f) *kindness, attention*
atender *to see, serve, deal with*
atentamente *yours sincerely*, (AmE)
  sincerely yours
atletismo (m) *athletics*
atún (m) *tuna fish*
audaz *bold, audacious*
aumentar *to increase*
aun *even*
aún *still, yet*
aunque *although, even though*
auto (m) (LAm) *car*
autobús (m) *bus*
autoridad (f) *authority*
avenida (f) *avenue*
avería (f) *breakdown*
avión (m) *aeroplane*, (AmE) *airplane*
ayer *yesterday*
ayudar *to help*
azafata (f) *air hostess, stewardess,*
  (AmE) *flight attendant*

bailar *to dance*
bajar *to go down*
bajar(se) (Internet) *to unload*
bajo/a *low*
baloncesto (m) *basketball*
banco (m) *bank*
bañarse *to have a bath, bathe*
bañera (f) *bath, bathtub*
baño (m) *toilet*, (esp AmE)
  bathroom
barato/a *cheap*
barco (m) *boat, ship*
barra de pan (f) *loaf of bread*
barrio (m) *area, district*, (AmE)
  neighborhood
bastante *quite, rather*
beber *to drink*
belga (m/f) *Belgian*
beso (m) *kiss*
bibliotecario/a *librarian*
bien *well, fine*
billete (m) *ticket; banknote*, (AmE)
  bill
blusa (f) *blouse*

bocadillo (m) *sandwich*
boleto (m) (LAm) *ticket*
bolso (m) *bag, handbag,* (AmE)
  purse
bonito/a *pretty*
botas (f) *boots*
botella (f) *bottle*
brasileño/a *Brazilian*
breve *brief*
británico/a *British*
buen *good (before a sing, m noun)*
bueno/a *good, well*
bueno: hace ___ *the weather is good*
buscar *to look for*

cabeza (f) *head*
cada *every, each*
café (m) *coffe, cafe;* ___solo *black
  coffee;* ___con leche *white coffee,*
  (AmE) *regular coffee*
caja (f) *box*
caja fuerte (f) *safe, strong-box*
calamar (m) *squid*
calcetines (m) *socks*
calefacción (f) *heating*
caliente *hot*
calle (f) *street*
calor: hace ___ *it´s hot/warm;* tener
  ___ *to be hot*
cama (f) *bed ;* ___ de matrimonio (f)
  double bed
camarero/a *waiter/waitress*
cambiar *to change*
cambio (m) *exchange rate*
camión (m) *lorry,* (AmE) *truck*
camisa (f) *shirt*
camiseta (f) *T shirt, vest,* (AmE)
  undershirt
campo (m) *country*
cancelar *to cancel*
cansado/a *tired*
cantar *to sing*
cantidad (f) *quantity, amount*
capacidad (f) *capacity*
carácter (m) *character*
cargo (m) *post, job*
Caribe (m) *Caribbean*
carne (f) *meat*
carnet de conducir (m) *driving
  license,* (AmE) *driver´s license*
caro/a *expensive*

carpeta (f) *file*
carpintero/a *carpenter*
carrera (f) *career; race*
carretera nacional (f) *A-road,* (AmE)
  state highway
carta (f) *letter; menu*
cartel: en ___ *(film, show) showing*
cartera (f) *briefcase;* (LAm) *bag,
  handbag,* (AmE) *purse*
cartero/a *postman/postwoman,*
  (AmE) *mailman/mailwoman*
casa (f) *house*
casa de cambio(s) (f) (LAm) *bureau
  de change*
casado/a *married*
casarse *to marry, get married*
casi *almost*
caso: en ___ de *in case of*
catalán (m) *(language) Catalan*
catalán/catalana *Catalan, Catalonian*
causar *to cause*
cebolla (f) *onion*
celebrar *to celebrate*
celular (m): (LAm) el teléfono ___
  mobile/cell phone
cena (f) *dinner*
cenar *to have dinner*
céntimo (m) *cent*
céntrico/a *central*
centro (m) *centre,* (AmE) *center*
cerca *near*
cercano/a *near, nearby, close to*
cerdo (m) *pork*
cerrar (e>ie) *to close, shut*
cerveza (f) *beer*
champiñón (m) *mushroom*
champú (m) *shampoo*
chaqueta (f) *jacket*
chatear *(Internet) to chat*
cheque (m) *cheque,* (AmE) *check*
cheques de viaje (m) *traveller´s
  cheques,* (AmE) *traveler´s checks*
chico/a *boy/girl*
cierto *true*
cine (m) *cinema,* (AmE) *movie
  theater*
cinturón (m) *belt*
cita (f) *appointment, date*
ciudad (f) *city*
claro *certainly, of course, sure*
clase particular (f) *private lesson*

coche (m) *car*
cocina (f) *kitchen;* ___ equipada
fitted, equipped kitchen
cocinar *to cook*
coger *to take, catch*
colegio (m) *school*
colgar (o>ue) *to hang up*
coliflor (f) *cauliflower*
comedor (m) *dining-room*
comer *to eat*
comestibles (m, pl) *food*
comida (f) *meal, lunch;* (LAm)
dinner
como *as*
cómo *how?, what?;* ¿cómo (dice)?
pardon me?
comodidad (f) *comfort*
cómodo/a *comfortable*
compañero/a de clase *classmate*
compañero/a de trabajo *colleague*
compartido/a *shared*
compartir *to share*
completo/a *full*
compra (f) *shopping*
comprar *to buy*
compromiso (m) *engagement*
computador, computadora (LAm)
computer
común *common*
con *with*
conducir *to drive*
conductor/a *driver*
confirmado/a *confirmed*
confirmar *to confirm*
conmigo *with me*
conocer *to know, meet* (for the first
time)
conocimiento (m) *knowledge*
consecuencia (f) *consequence*
construcción (f) *construction*
consulta (f) *surgery, practice*
consumidor (m) *consumer*
consumir *to consume*
contable (m/f) *accountant*
contar (o>ue) *to tell*
contar (o>ue) con *to have*
contestar *to answer, reply*
contigo *with you* (inf, sing)
continuar *to continue*
contrario: todo lo ___ *on the contrary*
coñac (m) *brandy, cognac*

copa (f) *drink; glass*
coraje (m) *courage*
corazón (m) *heart;* revista del ___
true romance magazine
cordero (m) *lamb*
corona sueca (f) *Swedish crown*
correo electrónico (m) *e-mail*
correos: la oficina de ___ (f) *post
office*
correspondencia (f) *post,* (AmE) *mail*
corresponder *to repay, return*
cortado (m) *coffee with a dash of
milk*
cortés *courteous*
corto/a *short*
cosa (f) *thing*
costar (o>ue) *to cost*
creativo/a *creative*
creer *to think;* creo que sí *I think so*
crucero (m) *cruise*
crucigrama (m) *crossword puzzle*
cruzar *to cross*
cuadros: de ___ *checked*
cuál/cuáles *what?, which?*
cualquier/a *any*
cuándo *when?*
cuánto tiempo *how long?*
cuánto/a *how much?*
cuánto: ¿a ___ está/n? *how much is
it/are they?*
cuántos/as *how many?*
cuarto (m) *quarter; room*
cuarto/a *fourth*
cubierto: estar ___ *to be overcast*
cuchara (f) *spoon*
cuchillo (m) *knife*
cuelgue: no ___ *don't hang up*
cuenta (f) *bill,* (AmE) *check*
cuerpo (m) *body*
cuidar *to look after*
culpa (f) *fault;* no es ___ nuestra *it's
not our fault*
culto/a *cultured, well educated*
cumpleaños (m) *birthday*
cumplir (age) *to be*
curso (m) *course*
cuyo/a *whose*

damasco (m) (LAm) *apricot*
dar *to give;* ___ clases *to teach;* ___
a *to face*

dar un recado *to pass on a message*
dato (m) *information*
deber *to have to, must*
deberes (m, pl) *homework*
décimo/a *tenth*
decir (e>i) *to say, tell*
dedicarse a: ¿a qué se/te dedica/s?
what do you do (for a living)?
dejar *to leave, leave behind*
dejar un recado *to leave a message*
delante *in front*
delicioso/a *delicious*
demasiado *too, very, too much*
deme *give me*
dentro de *within*
departamento (m) (LAm) *flat,
apartment*
dependiente/a *shop assistant, (AmE)
salesclerk*
deporte (m) *sport*
deportivo/a (adj) *sport*
depositar *to deposit*
depto. (abb. `departamento´) (m)
section, division
derecha (f) *right*
desayunar *to have breakfast*
desayuno (m) *breakfast*
desde *from, since*
desear *to want, wish*
desempeñar (job) *to hold*
desesperado/a *desperate*
despacho (m) *office*
despacio *slowly*
despierto/a *sharp, awake*
después *then, afterwards*
destino (m) *destination*
desviación (f) *diversion*
detestar *to detest, loathe*
detrás *behind*
devastador/a *terrible*
día (m) *day*
dibujar *to draw*
diciembre *December*
diente (m) *tooth*
dieta (f) *diet*
difícil *difficult*
¿dígame?/¿diga? (on the phone) *hello?*;
(in a shop) *can I help you?*
digestivo/a *digestive*
dinero (m) *money*
dirección (f) *address, direction*
disponer de *to have*

disponibilidad (f) *availability*
dispuesto/a a *willing to*
distancia (f) *distance*
Distinguido/a señor/señora *Dear
Sir/Madam*
distribuidor/a *distributor*
divertido/a *funny, amusing*
divertirse (e>ie) *to enjoy oneself*
doblar *to turn*
doble (m) *double*
docena (f) *dozen*
documentación (f) *documents*
doler (o>ue) *to hurt, feel pain*
dolor (m) *pain, ache*
dónde *where?*
dormir (o>ue) *to sleep*
dormitorio (m) *bedroom*
ducha (f) *shower*
ducharse *to shower*
duele: me ___ la cabeza/el estómago *I
have a headache/stomach ache*
durante *during*
durazno (m) (LAm) *peach*

e *and* (before `i´)
echar una siesta *to have a siesta/nap*
ecuatoriano/a *Ecuadoran*
edad (f) *age*
edificio (m) *building*
efectivo: en ___ *cash*
egipcio/a *Egyptian*
ejemplar (m) *copy*
ejemplo: por ___ *for example*
el *the* (m, sing.)
elegir (e>i) *to choose*
empezar (e>ie) *to start, begin*
empleo (m) *job, employment*
empresa (f) *company, firm*
empresariales: ciencias ___ (f)
business studies
empresario/a
businessman/businesswoman
en *in, on, at*
en seguida *straightaway*
encantado/a *pleased to meet you;*
(accepting something) *I'll be delighted*
encantar *to love* (something/doing
something)
encanto (m) *charm*
encargado/a *person in charge,
manager*
encargar *to order*

encender (e>ie) *to turn/switch on*
encontrar (o>ue) *to meet, find*
encontrarse (o>ue) bien/mal *to feel well/unwell*
encuentro (m) *encounter, meeting*
enfermero/a *nurse*
enfrente de *opposite*
ensalada (mixta) (f) *mixed salad*
entender (e>ie) *to understand*
entonces *then*
entrada (f) (show, game) *ticket*
entrar *to start, enter*
entre *between, among*
entrevista (f) *interview*
entrevistar *to interview*
enviar *to send*
época (f) *time*
equipaje (m) *luggage,* (AmE) *baggage*
equipo (m) *team*
equivocación (f) *mistake*
equivocado: se ha ___ (de número) *you've got the wrong number*
escalera (f) *stairs*
escaparate (m) *shop window,* (AmE) *store window*
escribir *to write, spell*
escrito: por ___ *in writing*
escuchar *to listen to*
escuela (f) *school;* ___de lenguas *language school*
espalda (f) *back*
español (m) *Spanish language*
español/a *Spanish*
especialidad (f) *speciality,* (AmE) *specialty*
esperar *to hope, wait, expect*
espinaca (f) *spinach*
esposo/a *husband/wife* (formal)
esquiar *to ski*
esquina (f) *corner*
estación (f) *station*
estado civil (m) *marital status*
estar *to be*
estilo (m) *style*
Estimado/a Carlos/María *Dear Carlos/María*
estrecho/a *tight*
estrenarse (film, etc.) *to be shown for the first time*
estrés (m) *stress*
estricto/a *strict*
estudiante (m/f) *student*

estudiar *to study*
estudios superiores (m) *higher education*
estupendamente *great*
estupendo/a *great*
Europa *Europe;* ___ del Este *Eastern Europe*
evitable *avoidable, preventable*
exceso *excess*
exigir *to demand, require*
éxito: tener ___ *to succeed, to be successful*
exposición (f) *exhibition*
exterior *facing the street*
extranjero (m) *abroad*
extranjero/a *foreign*
extraño/a *strange*

fábrica (f) *factory*
fácil *easy*
falda (f) *skirt*
faltar *to be lacking, not to be enough*
famoso/a *famous*
farmacia (f) *chemist's,* (AmE) *drugstore*
fascinar *to love* (something/doing something)
fatiga (f) *fatigue, tiredness*
fecha (f) *date*
feo/a *ugly*
fiebre: tener ___ *to have a fever, be feverish*
filmar *to film*
fin de semana (m) *weekend*
fin: poner ___ a *to put an end to*
final: al ___ de *at the end of*
firmar *to sign*
flan (m) *caramel custard*
folleto (m) *brochure*
fondo: hasta el ___ *to the end*
fontanero/a *plumber*
forma (f) *way, form*
forma: de igual ___ *in the same way*
francés (m) (language) *French*
francés/francesa *French*
franco suizo (m) *Swiss franc*
frecuentemente *frequently*
fregar (e>ie) *to wash up, to wash the dishes*
frente: seguir de ___ *to go straight on*
fresa (f) *strawberry*
fresco/a *fresh*

frío (m)   *cold*; hace ___ *it´s cold*
frito/a   *fried*
fruta (f)   *fruit*
frutilla (f)   (LAm) *strawberry*
fuera   *out, outside*; ___ de *away
from*
fuerte   *strong*
fumador/a   *smoker*
fumar   *to smoke*
función (f)   *performance, show*
funcionar   *to work*; no funciona *it
doesn't work*
futbolista (m/f)   *football player*

galleta (f)   *biscuit*, (AmE) *cookie*
gamba (f)   *prawn*, (AmE) *shrimp*
ganar   *to earn*
gasóleo (m)   *diesel*
gasolina (f)   *petrol*, (AmE) *gas(oline)*
gasto (m)   *expense*
gato (m)   *cat*
gazpacho (m)   *Andalusian cold soup*
generoso/a   *generous*
gente (f)   *people*
gerente (m/f)   *manager*
gimnasio (m)   *gym*
girar   *to turn*
gobierno (m)   *government*
grado (m)   *degree*
gramo (m)   *gram*
grande   *large, big*
grandes almacenes (m, pl)
department store
grasa (f)   *fat*
gratis   *free*
grato: me es muy ___ *I have pleasure
in*
grifo (m)   *tap*, (AmE) *faucet*
grupo (m)   *group*
guantes (m)   *gloves*
guapo/a   *good-looking, pretty*
guerra (f)   *war*
guisantes (m, pl.)   *peas*
gustar   *to like*
gusto (m)   *pleasure*

habitación (f)   *room*
habitante (m/f)   *inhabitant*
habla: persona de ___ inglesa/española
English/Spanish speaking person
hablar   *to speak*
hace (un año)   *(a year) ago*

hace: ¿cuánto tiempo ___? *how long
is it?*
hace: desde ___ (un año) *for (a year)*
hacer   *to do, make*
hacer bien   *to do good*
harina (f)   *flour*
hasta   *up to*
hay   *there is/are, is/are there?*
hay: no ___ de qué   *you're welcome*
helado (m)   *ice cream*
hermano/a   *brother/sister*
hijo/a   *son/daughter*
hilo musical (m)   *piped music*
hispanoamericano/a   *Spanish
American, Latin American*
historia (f)   *history*
hola   *hello*
hombre (m)   *man*
hora (f)   *time, hour*; ___local *local
time*; a la ___ *on time*
hora: pedir ___   *to ask for an
appointment* (with doctor,
hairdresser, etc.)
hora: tener ___   *to have an
appointment* (with doctor,
hairdresser, etc)
horario (m)   *timetable*, (AmE);
schedule ; ___ de trabajo *working
hours*
horario fijo (m)   *fixed working hours*
horas de oficina (f)   *office hours*
hostal (m)   *small family-run hotel*
hostelería (f)   *hotel and catering*
hoy   *today*

ida/ida y vuelta (f)   (ticket)
single/return, (AmE) *one-way/round
trip*
idioma (m)   *language*
iglesia (f)   *church*
igual   *same*; al ___ que *as well as*
ilimitado/a   *unlimited*
imaginar(se)   *to imagine*
imponente   *imposing*
importar: si no te/le importa   *if you
don't mind*
impresora (f)   *printer*
impuesto (m)   *tax*
incapacitar   *to incapacitate*
incluido/a   *included*
incluir   *to include*
incluso   *even*

indemnización (f) *compensation*
indicar *to indicate, signal*
indio/a *Indian*
individual *single* (room)
individual: calefacción ___
 independent heating
industria (f) *industry*
infección (f) *infection*
inferior *lower*
informar *to inform*
informática (f) *computing*
informe (m) *report*
ingeniero/a *engineer*
Inglaterra *England*
inglés (m) *English* (language)
inglés/inglesa *Englishman/woman*
ingresar *to join*
inmaduro/a *immature*
inmediato: de ___ *immediately*
inseguro/a *insecure*
insomnio (m) *insomnia*
insoportable *unbearable*
instituto (m) *secondary school,*
 (AmE) *high school*
interesante *interesting*
interesar *to be interested in*
interrumpir *to interrupt*
invierno (m) *winter*
invitar *to invite*
ir *to go*
irse *to leave*
IVA (m) *vat*
izquierda (f) *left*

jabón (m) *soap*
jamón (m) *ham;* ___ serrano *cured*
 ham
jardín (m) *garden*
jefe/a *boss*
jersey/jersei (m) *sweater, pullover,*
 jumper
jitomate (m) (Mex) *tomato*
joven *young*
jubilado/a *retired*
judías verdes (f, pl.) *green beans*
jueves (m) *Thursday*
jugar (u>ue) *to play*
jugo (m) (LAm) *juice*
junto a *next to*
juntos/as *together*

labores domésticas (f) *domestic work*
lado: al ___ de *next to;* al otro ___ de
 on the other side of
largo/a *long*
lástima (f) *pity, shame*
lavabo (m) *washbasin; bathroom,*
 washroom; (public place) *toilet,*
 restroom
lavandería (f) *launderette,* (AmE)
 laundromat
lavarse *to wash (oneself)*
lavarse los dientes *to brush one´s*
 teeth
lechuga (f) *lettuce*
leer *to read*
lejos *far*
lengua (f) *language*
levantarse *to get up*
libra esterlina (f) *pound sterling*
libre *available, free*
libre: trabajar por ___ *to work*
 freelance
librería (f) *bookshop,* (AmE)
 bookstore
libro (m) *book*
licencia (f) de conducir *driving*
 license, (AmE) *driver´s license*
licenciado/a *graduate*
ligero/a *light*
limón (m) *lemon*
limpieza (f) *cleaning*
línea (f) (telephone) *line*
línea aérea (f) *airline*
litro (m) *litre*
llamar *to phone, call up*
llamarse *to be called*
llave (f) *key*
llegada (f) *arrival*
llegar *to arrive, get*
llevar *to carry, contain, take*
llevarse bien *to get on well*
llover (o>ue) *to rain*
loco/a *crazy*
lograr *to manage*
Londres *London*
luego *then, afterwards*
lugar (m) *place*
lujo (m) *luxury*
luminoso/a *bright*
lunes (m) *Monday*

machista *male chauvinist(ic)*
madre (f) *mother*
mal *bad, badly*
maleta (f) *suitcase*
maletín (m) *brief case, attaché case*
mandar *to send*
manera *manner, way*
manta (f) *blanket*
manzana (f) *apple*
mañana *tomorrow*
mañana (f) *morning*
mapa (m) *map*
maquillarse *to put on make-up*
maravilloso/a *wonderful*
marcar *to dial*
marido (m) *husband*
más *more, most, else;* ¿qué ___? *what else?*
material de oficina (m) *office supplies, stationery*
mayor *older, larger, greater*
mayoría (f) *majority*
me *(to, for) me, myself*
media (f) *average*
media hora *half an hour*
mediano/a *medium (size)*
medianoche (f) *midnight*
medias (f) *stockings*
médico/a *doctor*
medio/a *half*
mediodía (m) *midday*
mejor *better;* el/la ___ *the best*
melocotón (m) *peach*
melón (m) *melon*
memoria (f) *memory*
menor *younger*
menos *less*
mensaje (m) *message*
mensual *per month, monthly*
menú del día (m) *day´s menu*
menudo: a ___ *often*
mercado (m) *market*
mercancías (f) *goods, merchandise*
merecer *to deserve*
merluza (f) *hake*
mes (m) *month*
metro (m) metre: ___ cuadrado *square metre*
mexicano/a, mejicano/a *Mexican*
miedo: tener ___ *to be afraid*
mientras *while*

miércoles (m) *Wednesday*
mínimo/a *minimum*
mirada (f) *look*
mire/a *look* (formal/inf)
miseria (f) *misery*
mitad (f) *half*
molestar *to bother*
momento (m) *moment*
moneda (f) *currency, coin*
montar en bicicleta *to ride a bicycle*
móvil (m): el teléfono ___ *mobile phone,* (AmE) *cell phone*
mucho gusto *pleased to meet you*
mudarse *to move (house)*
muebles (m) *furniture*
mujer (f) *woman, wife*
mundo (m) *world*
museo (m) *museum*
Muy señor/señora mío/a *Dear Sir/Madam*

nacer *to be born*
nacionalidad (f) *nationality*
nada *nothing;* de ___ *you´re welcome;* ___ más *nothing else*
naranja (f) *orange;* (adj) *orange (colour)*
narrador (m) *narrator*
Navidad (f) *Christmas*
necesitar *to need*
negocio (m) *business*
negro/a *black*
neogótico/a *neogothic*
nervioso/a *nervous*
nevar (e>ie) *to snow*
ni ..... ni *neither ..... nor*
niebla (f) *fog*
nieto/a *grandson/granddaughter*
ningún *no, none* (before a sing, m noun)
ninguno/a *no, none*
niño/a *child*
nivel (m) *level*
noche (f) *night*
nombre (m) *name*
nombre: ¿a qué ___? *in what name?;* a ___ de *in the name of*
nominado/a *nominated*
normalmente *normally*
norteamericano/a, americano/a *American*

nota (f) *note*
noveno/a *ninth*
novio/a *boyfriend/girlfriend*
nublado: estar___ *to be cloudy*
nuestro(s)/nuestra(s) *our, ours*
nuevamente *again*
nuevo/a *new*; de nuevo *again*
número (m) *number*; (shoes) *size*; ___ de teléfono *telephone number*
nunca *never*

obligatorio/a *compulsory*
obra de teatro (f) *play*
ocupado/a *occupied*
ocupar *to occupy*
ocurrir *to occur, happen*
oficina (f) *office*; ___ de cambio *bureau de change*; ___ de turismo *tourist office*
ofrecer *to offer*
oiga *excuse me!* (form.)
olvidar *to forget*
oportunidad (f) *opportunity, occasion*
ordenador (m) *computer*
ordinario/a *ordinary*
origen (m) *origin*
orilla del mar (f) *seashore*
oscuro/a *dark*
otra vez *again*
otro/a, otros/as *another, others*

paciencia (f) *patience*; tener ___ *to be patient*
padre/s (m) *father/parents*
pagar *to pay*
país (m) *country*
Países Bajos (m, pl) *the Netherlands*
palabra (f) *word*
palacio (m) *palace*
pan (m) *bread*
pan integral *wholemeal bread*
panadería (f) *baker's (shop), bakery*
pantalón/pantalones (m) *trousers*, (AmE) *pants*
papa (f) (LAm) *potato*
papel (m) *role*
papel higiénico (m) *toilet paper*
papelería (f) *stationer's (shop)*
paquete (m) *packet*
paquistaní (m/f) *Pakistani*

para *for, in order to, to*
parada de autobuses (f) *bus stop*
paraguas (m) *umbrella*
parecer *to seem*
pariente (m/f) *relative*
paro (m) *unemployment*; en ___ *unemployed*
parrilla: a la ___ *grilled*, (AmE) *broiled*
parte: ¿de ___ de quién? (on the phone) *who's calling?*
parte: la mayor ___ *most of them*
participar *to take part, participate*
partir: a ___ de *starting in/on/at; from*
pasa: ¿qué te ___? *what's wrong with you?*
pasado mañana *the day after tomorrow*
pasado/a *past*
pasado: el año ___ *last year*
pasaporte (m) *passport*
pasar *to happen, pass, hand in,* (time) *spend*
pasarlo bien *to have a good time*
pasarse *to stop, cease*
pasatiempo (m) *pastime, hobby*
paseo (m) *avenue, walk*; dar un ___ *to go for a walk/stroll*
pasillo (m) *corridor*
patata (f) *potato*; ___ s fritas *chips, crisps*
pedido: hacer un ___ *to place an order*
pedir *to ask for*
peinarse *to comb*
película (f) *film*, (AmE) *movie*
pelota (f) *ball*
peluquería (f) *hairdresser's*
pensar (e>ie) *to think, be thinking of*
peor *worse*; el/la ___ *the worst*
pepino (m) *cucumber*
pequeño/a *small, young*
pequeño/a: de ___ *when I was young*
perder (e>ie) *to lose*
perdón/perdone *excuse me, I'm sorry, pardon me*
perejil (m) *parsley*
periódico (m) *newspaper*
periodista (m/f) *journalist*
permitir *to allow*
pero *but*

perro (m) *dog*
peruano/a *Peruvian*
pescado (m) *fish*
pescar *to fish*
peso (m) *LAm currency (Chile, Cuba, Mex, etc)*
peso (m) *weight;* bajar de ___ *to lose weight*
pie (m) *foot*
piel (f) *leather*
pies (m) *feet*
pimiento (verde/rojo) (m) *(green/red) pepper*
pintura (f) *painting*
piña (f) *pineapple*
piscina (f) swimming pool
piso (m) *floor, storey; flat, apartment*
placer (m) *pleasure*
plancha: a la ___ *grilled*
planchar *to iron*
plano (m) *plan*
planta (f) *floor, storey;* ___ baja *ground floor, (AmE) first floor*
planta (f) *plant*
plátano (m) *banana*
plato (m) *plate, dish, course (meal)*
playa (f) *beach*
pleno: en ___ centro *right in the centre*
plomero/a (LAm) *plumber*
poco/a (quantity) *little*
poco: un ___ de *a little, some*
poder (o>ue) *to be able to, can*
pollo (m) *chicken*
poner *to put, give (see 'póngame');* (film) *to show*
ponerse *to put on;* ___ al teléfono *to come to the phone*
póngame (from 'poner' *to put*) *give me*
pongo: ¿qué le ___? *what shall I give you?*
pongo: ahora/en seguida le pongo *I'll put you through straight away*
por aquí *around here*
por qué *why?*
por supuesto *certainly, of course*
porque *because*
posible: a ser ___ *if possible*
postre (m) *dessert*
practicar *to practise, (AmE) practice*

precioso/a *beautiful*
preferente: clase ___ (f) *business class*
preferentemente *preferably*
preferiblemente *preferably*
preferir (e>ie) *to prefer*
prefijo (m) *(dialling) code, (AmE) area code*
preguntar *to ask*
preparar *to prepare*
prepararse *to prepare oneself*
presencia: tener buena ___ *to have a good appearance*
presentación (f) *introduction*
presentar *to introduce*
primero/a *first*
primero: de ___ *as a first course*
primo/a *cousin*
principalmente *mainly*
probador (m) *fitting-room*
probarse *to try on*
prodigioso/a *prodigious, marvellous*
profesor/a *teacher*
programa (m) *programme, (AmE) program*
programador/a *programmer*
prometer *to promise*
propio/a *own*
provecho: (LAm) buen ___ *enjoy your meal, bon appétit, (AmE) enjoy*
próximo/a *next*
prudente *careful*
psicología (f) *psychology*
psicólogo/a *psychologist*
pueblo (m) *town, village*
puerro (m) *leek*
puerta (f) *door*
pues *well, then*
puesto (m) *job, post*
puntualmente *on time, punctually*
puré (m) *mashed potatoes*

que *that, which, who*
qué *what?, which?*
quedar *to fit; to meet, arrange to meet*
quedarse *to stay*
queja (f) *complaint*
querer (e>ie) *to want, love*
quería (from 'querer') *I'd like (lit. I wanted)*
querido/a *dear*

queso (m) *cheese*
quién/quiénes *who?* (sing/pl)
quinto/a *fifth*
quiosco (m) *kiosk*
quisiera (from `querer´ *to want*) *I would like*
quizá(s) *perhaps*

ración (f) *portion, plate*
rato (m) *while*
razón (f) *reason;* tener ___ *to be right*
realizar *to carry out, do*
realmente *truly, really*
recado (m) message
recibir *to receive*
reclamación (f) *complaint*
recoger *to pick up*
recomendar *to recommend*
reconocer *to recognize*
recordar (o>ue) *to remember*
recto: todo ___ *straight on*
referencias (f) *references*
reformado/a *converted, renovated, restored*
regalo (m) *present, gift*
régimen: ponerse a *to go on a diet*
regresar *to come back, return*
regular *average, so-so*
Reino Unido (m) *United Kingdom*
relación (f) *relationship*
relación: con ___ a *with regard to, in connection with*
relacionarse *to relate, get on*
repartir *to deliver*
repetir (e>i) *to repeat*
reserva (f) *reservation*
reservado/a *booked*
reservar *to book, reserve*
resfriado/a: estar ___ *to have a cold*
responder *to answer*
respuesta (f) *answer*
retrasarse *to be delayed*
reunirse *to meet*
revisar *to check*
revista (f) *magazine*
rico/a *rich, wealthy*
río (m) *river*
rojo/a *red*
ropa (f) *clothes*
ruido (m) *noise*

ruidoso/a *noisy*
ruso (m) (language) *Russian*
ruso/a *Russian*

saber *to know;* ___ de memoria *to know by heart*
salida (f) *exit;* ___ de incendio *fire exit;* departure
salir *to leave, go out*
salón (m) *living-room, lounge; hall*
salón comedor (m) *sitting room-dining-room*
saludar *to greet*
sandalias (f) *sandals*
sandía (f) *watermelon*
satisfactorio/a *satisfactory*
secretariado bilingüe *bilingual secretarial course*
sed: tener ___ *to be thirsty*
seguida: en ___ *right away*
seguir (e>i) *to go on, continue*
segundo/a *second;* de ___ *as a second course*
seguridad (f) *safety*
Seguridad Social (f) *Social Security*
seguro *sure, surely*
seguro (m) *insurance*
seguro/a *safe*
seleccionar *to choose*
semáforo (m) *traffic light*
semana (f) *week*
semanal *weekly*
sentarse (e>ie) *to sit*
sentido del humor (m) *sense of humour*
sentir (e>ie) *to be sorry*
sentirse (e>ie) *to feel*
señal (f) *signal*
separado/a *separated*
ser *to be*
servicio militar *military service*
servicios (m, pl) *toilets,* (AmE) *restrooms*
servicios: sector ___ (m) *the public service sector*
servilleta (f) *serviette, napkin*
servir *to serve*
si *if;* si no *otherwise*
sí *yes*
siempre *always*
siéntese *sit down* (formal)

siento: lo ___ *I´m sorry*
siga todo recto *go straight on*
siglo (m) *century*
significar *to mean*
siguiente (m/f) *following*
simpático/a (for people) *nice*
sin *without*
sin embargo *however*
sitio (m) *place*
situado/a *situated*
sobre *about, around, on, above*
socio/a *partner*
sol (m) *sun, light;* hace ___ *it´s sunny*
solamente *only*
soleado/a *sunny*
soler (o>ue) *to usually (do something)*
solicitar *to request*
sólo *only*
solo/a(s) *alone*
soltero/a *single*
solución (f) *solution*
sombrero (m) *hat*
sopa (f) *soup*
sorpresa (f) *surprise*
subir *to go up*
suegro/suegra *father/mother-in-law*
sueldo (m) *salary*
sueño: tener ___ *to be sleepy*
suerte (f) *luck;* tener___ *to be lucky*
suficiente *enough, sufficient*
sugerir (e>ie) *to suggest*
súper *really*
superficie (f) *area*
superior *upper*
supermercado (m) *supermarket*
suponer *to suppose*
supuesto: por ___ *of course*

talla (f) (clothes) *size*
tamaño (m) *size*
también *also*
tampoco *not...either, neither*
tan *so;* tan ... como *as ... as*
tanto ..... como ..... *as well as .....*
tapa (f) *tapa, bar snack*
tardar (time) *to take*
tarde *late*
tarde (f) *afternoon*
tareas domésticas (f, pl) *housework,*

household chores
tarjeta de crédito (f) *credit card*
tarta (f) *cake*
taxista (m/f) *taxi driver*
taza (f) *cup*
te *(to, for) you, yourself* (inf)
té (m) *tea*
teatro (m) *theatre, theater*
Telefónica: compañía ___ (f) *telephone company*
teleserie (f) *TV series*
tema (m) *theme, subject, topic*
temprano *early*
tendero/a *shopkeeper,* (AmE), *storekeeper,* (for food) *grocer*
tenedor *(m)* fork
tener (e>ie) *to have, to be*
tener que *to have to*
terminar *to finish*
ternera (f) *veal*
terraza (f) *balcony*
terror: película de ___ (f) *horror film*
tiempo (m) *time*
tiempo (m) *weather:* hace buen/mal ___ *the weather is good/bad*
tienda (f) *shop,* (AmE) *store*
tímido/a *shy*
tío/a *uncle/aunt*
típico/a *typical, traditional*
toalla de mano/baño (f) *hand/bath towel*
tocar *to play* (an instrument)
todavía *still, yet*
todo/a *all, whole*
tomar (food and drink) *to have; to take*
tomar el sol *to sunbathe*
tonto/a *fool*
torcer (o>ue) *to turn*
tormenta (f) *storm*
tortilla (f) *omelette*
tostada (f) *toast*
trabajador/a *worker* ; ___ extranjero/a *foreign worker*
trabajador/a (adj) *hard working*
trabajar *to work*
traductor/a *translator*
traer *to bring*
tranquilidad (f) *peace*
tranquilo/a *quiet*

trasladarse *to move*
tren (m) *train*
tribunal (m) *law court*
triste *sad*

u *or* (before `o´)
último/a *last*
un/a *a*
urgentemente *urgently*
urna (f) *box*
utilizar to use
uva (f) *grape*

vacaciones (f, pl) *holidays, vacations*
vale *OK* (inf)
valer *to cost*
vaqueros (m) *jeans*
varios/as *several*
vaso (m) *glass*
váter (m) *lavatory, W.C.,* (AmE) *restroom*
veces: a ___ *sometimes*
vecino/a *neighbour*
vehículo (m) *vehicle*
vela: hacer ___ *to sail*
vender *to sell*
venir (e>ie) *to come*
venta (f) *sale;* en ___ *for sale*
ver *to watch, see*
verano (m) *summer*
verdad *true;* de ___ *sure*
verdad: ¿de ___? *really*
verdura (f) *vegetable*
vergüenza: tener ___ *to be ashamed*
verse *to see one another*

vestido (m) *dress*
vestirse (e>i) *to get dressed*
vez (f) *time;* una ___ *once*
vez: de ___ en cuando *from time to time*
viajar *to travel*
viaje (m) *travel, journey, trip;* ___ de negocios *business trip*
viajero/a *traveller*
viento (m) *wind;* hace ___ *it´s windy*
viernes (m) *Friday*
vino (m) *wine;* ___ tinto/blanco *red/white wine*
visita (f) *visit*
visitante (m/f) *visitor*
visitar *to visit*
vista(s) al mar (f) *seaview*
vivir *to live*
volver (o>ue) *to come back, return*
vuelo (m) *flight*
vuelta (f) *return;* dar la ___ *to turn round*

y *and*

zanahoria (f) *carrot*
zapatero/a *shoemaker*
zapatillas (f) *trainers, sneakers*
zapatos (m) *shoes*
zona (f) *area, zone*
zumo (m) *juice*

accommodation *alojamiento* (m)
accountant *contable* (m), (LAm) *contador* (m)
actress *actriz*
address *dirección* (f)
advertisement *anuncio* (m)
aeroplane *avión* (m)
after *después de*
afternoon *tarde* (f)
afterwards *después, luego*
again *otra vez, nuevamente, de nuevo*
age *edad* (f)
air conditioning *aire acondicionado* (m)
air hostess *azafata* (f)
airline *línea aérea* (f)
airplane (AmE) *avión* (m)
airport *aeropuerto* (m)
allow: to ___ *permitir*
almost *casi*
alone *solo/a*
already *ya*
also *también*
always *siempre*
American *americano/a, norteamericano/a, estadounidense*
among *entre*
amusing *divertido/a*
and *y*, (before i, hi) *e*
another *otro/a*
answer *respuesta* (f)
apartment *piso* (m), *apartamento* (m), (LAm) *departamento* (m)
appear: to ___ *aparecer*
apple *manzana* (f)
appointment *cita (f)*, (with doctor) *hora*

apricot *albaricoque* (m), (LAm) *damasco* (m)
April *abril*
Arabic *árabe*
architect *arquitecto/a*
area *barrio* (m); ___ code (AmE) *prefijo* (m)
around *alrededor*
arrival *llegada* (f)
arrive: to ___ *llegar*
as *como*
as ..... as *tan ..... como*
as far as *hasta*
ask: to ___ *preguntar*; to ___ for *pedir* (e>i)
at *en*
attend: to ___ *asistir*
August *agosto*
aunt *tía*
avocado *aguacate* (m), (S. Cone) *palta* (f)

back *espalda* (f)
bad *malo/a*
bag *bolsa* (f)
baggage (AmE) *equipaje* (m)
banana *plátano* (m)
bank *banco* (m)
banknote *billete* (m)
barber's *peluquería* (f)
basketball *baloncesto* (m), *basquetbol* (m)
bath *baño* (m); to have a ___ *bañarse*
bathe: to ___ *bañarse*
bathroom *baño* (m)
be: to ___ *ser, estar*
beach *playa* (f)

beautiful *bonito/a, hermoso/a,* (LAm)
lindo/a

because *porque*

bed *cama* (f)

bedroom *dormitorio* (m), *habitación*
(f)

beer *cerveza* (f)

before *antes, delante*

behind *detrás*

belt *cinturón* (m)

besides *además*

better *mejor*

between *entre*

bicycle *bicicleta* (f), (short) *bici*

big *grande,* (before a noun) *gran*

bill (money) *billete* (m); (restaurant)
cuenta (f)

birthday *cumpleaños* (m, sing)

biscuit *galleta* (f)

black *negro/a*

blanket *manta* (f), (LAm) *cobija* (f),
frazada (f)

blouse *blusa* (f)

blue *azul*

boarding house *hostal* (m), *pensión*
(f)

boarding house *hostal* (m), *casa de
huéspedes* (f), *pensión* (f)

boat *barco* (m)

body *cuerpo* (m)

book *libro* (m)

bookshop *librería* (f)

bookstore *librería* (f)

boots *botas* (f)

boring *aburrido/a*

born: to be ___ *nacer*

boss *jefe/a*

bother: to ___ *molestar*

bottle *botella* (f)

boyfriend *novio*

bread *pan* (m)

breakfast *desayuno* (m); to have ___
desayunar

briefcase *cartera* (f), *portadocumentos*
(m, sing)

bring: to ___ *traer*

British *británico/a*

broiled *a la plancha, a la parrilla*

brother *hermano*

brother-in-law *cuñado*

brothers and sisters *hermanos*

brown *marrón,* (LAm) *café*

buenas noches *good evening/night*

building *edificio* (m)

bureau de change *oficina de cambio*
(f), (LAm) *casa de cambio(s)* (f)

bus (esp Spain) *autobús* (m), (LAm)
colectivo (m), *micro* (m), (Mex)
camión

bus stop *parada* (f), (LAm) *paradero*

businessman/woman *empresario/a*

but *pero*

butter *mantequilla* (f)

buy: to ___ *comprar*

by *por*

call *llamada* (f)

call: to ___ *llamar; llamar por
teléfono, telefonear*

can *lata* (f)

can *poder* (o>ue)

cancel: to ___ *anular, cancelar*

car *coche* (m), (LAm) *carro* (m),
auto (m)

car park *aparcamiento* (m), *garaje*
(m), (LAm) *estacionamiento* (m)

card *tarjeta* (f); credit ___ *tarjeta de
crédito*

carrot *zanahoria* (f)

carry: to ___ *llevar*

cash *efectivo* (m)

cat *gato* (m)

cauliflower *coliflor* (f)

celery *apio* (m)

cell phone (AmE) *móvil* (m)

center (AmE) *centro* (m)

centre *centro* (m)

cerdo (m) *pork*

certainly *claro, por supuesto*

change *cambio* (m)

change: to ___ *cambiar*

chat: to ___ (Internet) *chatear*

check (AmE) *cheque* (m); (restaurant)
cuenta (f); traveller's __ *cheque* (m)
de viaje

cheese *queso* (m)

chemist's *farmacia* (f)

cheque *cheque* (m)

cherry *cereza* (f)

chicken *pollo* (m)

children *hijos*

chips *patatas* (f) *fritas,* (LAm)
papas___

choose: to ___ *elegir* (e>i)

cinema *cine* (m)
city *ciudad* (f)
civil service *administración pública* (f)
clean: to ___ *limpiar*
cleaning *limpieza* (f)
clerk *administrativo/a, empleado/a*
close: to ___ *cerrar* (e>ie)
clothes *ropa* (f)
cloudy *nublado*
coat *chaqueta* (f), *americana* (f),
  (LAm) *saco* (m); (long coat) *abrigo*
  (m)
coffee *café* (m); black ___ *café solo;*
  white/regular ___ *café con leche*
cold *frío/a*; it´s ___ *hace* ___
colleague *compañero/a (de trabajo)*
comb: to ___ *peinarse*
come: to ___ *venir* (e>ie); ___ back
  volver (o>ue), *regresar*
comfortable *cómodo/a*
computer *ordenador* (m), (LAm)
  computadora (f), *computador* (m)
computing *informática* (f)
concert *concierto*
continue: to ___ *continuar, seguir*
  (e>i)
cook: to ___ *cocinar*
cookie (AmE) *galleta* (f)
corner *esquina* (f)
corridor *pasillo* (m)
cost: to ___ *costar* (o>ue), *valer*
country *país* (m), (countryside) *campo*
  (m)
course *curso* (m)
cousin *primo/a*
crisps *patatas* (f) *fritas,* (LAm) *papas*
  (f) ___
cucumber *pepino* (m)
cup *taza* (f)
currency *moneda* (f)

dance: to ___ *bailar*
date *fecha* (f); (arrangement to meet)
  cita (f)
daughter *hija*
day *día* (m)
day before yesterday: the ___ *anteayer,*
  antes de ayer
dear *querido/a*
December *diciembre*
degree *título* (m)
dentista *dentista* (m/f)

departure *salida* (f)
dessert *postre* (m)
dial: to ___ *marcar*
different *diferente*
difficult *difícil*
dining-room *comedor* (m)
dinner *cena* (f), *comida* (f); to have
  ___ *cenar, comer*
dish *plato* (m)
district *barrio* (m)
divorced *divorciado/a*
doctor *doctor/a*
dog *perro* (m)
dollar *dólar* (m)
door *puerta* (f)
download: to ___ (Internet) *bajar,*
  bajarse
dozen *docena* (f)
dress *vestido* (m)
drink *copa* (f); to have a ___ *tomar*
  una copa
drink: to ___ *beber*
drive: to ___ *conducir,* (LAm) *manejar*
driver´s license *permiso/carnet* (m) *de*
  conducir
driving license (AmE) *permiso/carnet*
  (m) *de conducir*
drugstore (AmE) *farmacia* (f)

each *cada*
eat: to ___ *comer*
education *educación* (f)
egg *huevo* (m)
electronic mail *correo* (m) *electrónico*
elevator *ascensor* (m) , (Mex)
  elevador (m)
else *más*; what ___? *¿qué más?*
employee *empleado/a*
end *fin* (m), *final* (m): at the ___ of
  al final de
engineer *ingeniero/a*
England *Inglaterra*
English *inglés/inglesa*
English (language) *inglés* (m)
enjoy (AmE) *buen provecho*
evening *tarde* (f), *noche* (f)
every *todos/todas, cada*
example *ejemplo* (m)
excuse me (sorry) *perdón,* (formal)
  perdone, (inf) *perdona*
executive *ejecutivo/a*
expect: to ___ *esperar*

expensive *caro/a*
eye *ojo* (m)

factory *fábrica* (f)
family *familia* (f)
family name *apellido* (m)
far *lejos*
father *padre*
father-in-law *suegro*
faucet (AmE) *grifo* (m)
February *febrero*
feel: to ___ (well/unwell) *sentirse*
 (e>ie), *encontrarse* (o>ue) (*bien/mal*)
feet *pies* (m)
few *pocos/pocas*
fever *fiebre* (f); to have a ___ *tener*
 fiebre
film *película* (f), *film* (m)
first *primero/a, primer* (before a sing,
 m noun)
first floor (AmE) *planta* (f) baja
fish *pescado* (m)
fish: to ___ *pescar*
fitting-room *probador* (m)
fizzy (mineral water) *con gas*
flat *piso* (m), *apartamento* (m), (LAm)
 departamento (m)
flight *vuelo* (m)
flight attendant (AmE) *azafata* (f)
floor (storey) *piso* (m), *planta* (f);
 ground ___ , (AmE) first ___ *planta*
 baja
fog *niebla* (f)
food *alimento* (m)
foot *pie* (m)
football *fútbol* (m)
for *por, para*
forget: to ___ *olvidar*
fourth *cuarto/a*
France *Francia*
freeway *autopista* (f)
French *francés/francesa*; (language)
 francés (m)
Friday *viernes*
fried *frito/a*
friend *amigo/a*
from *de, desde*
front: in ___ of *enfrente de, frente a*
fruit *fruta* (f)
furnished *amueblado/a*, (LAm)
 amoblado/a
garden *jardín* (m)

garlic *ajo* (m)
gas(oline) (AmE) *gasoline*
gas station *gasolinera* (f), *estación* (f)
 de servicio
German *alemán/alemana*; (language)
 alemán (m)
Germany *Alemania*
get up: to ___ *levantarse*
gift *regalo* (m)
girlfriend *novia*
give: to ___ *dar*
glad: to be ___ *alegrarse*
glass *vaso* (m)
gloves *guantes* (m)
go to bed: to ___ *acostarse* (o>ue)
go: to ___ *ir*; to ___ down *bajar*; to
 ___ up *subir*
good *bueno/a, buen* (before a sing, m
 noun)
good afternoon *buenas tardes*
good evening *buenas tardes/noches*
good morning *buenos días*
goodbye *adiós, hasta luego,* (LAm)
 chao/chau (inf)
good-looking *guapo/a*
grandfather *abuelo*
grandmother *abuela*
grapes *uva(s)* (f)
Great Britain *Gran Bretaña*
great! *estupendo*
green *verde*
green beans *judías* (f) *verdes*
green pepper *pimiento* (m) *verde*
grey *gris*
grilled *a la plancha, a la parrilla*
grocer´s (shop) *tienda* (f) *de*
 comestibles
grocery *tienda* (f) *de comestibles*
ground floor *planta* (f) *baja*
guest house *hostal* (m), *pensión* (f),
 casa (f) *de huéspedes*

hair *pelo* (m), *cabello* (m)
hairdresser´s *peluquería* (f)
half *medio/a; mitad* (f)
ham *jamón* (m)
hand *mano* (f)
handbag *bolso* (m), (LAm) *cartera* (f)
happen: to ___ *pasar, ocurrir, suceder*
happy *alegre, feliz, contento/a*
hardworking *trabajador/a*
hat *sombrero* (m)

have: to __ *tener* (e>ie); to __ to *tener que*; (auxiliary verb) *haber*

he *él*

head *cabeza* (f)

headache *dolor de cabeza* (m)

heating *calefacción* (f); central __ *calefacción central*

hello *hola*; (on the phone) *¿dígame?*, (LAm) *¿aló?*, (Mex) *¿bueno?*

help: to __ *ayudar*

her *la, le*

high school (AmE) (esp Spain) *instituto* (m) *(de enseñanza secundaria)*

highway *carretera* (f)

him *lo, le*

hire: to __ *alquilar*, (LAm) *arrendar*, (Mex) *rentar*

hiring *alquiler* (m)

holiday *vacaciones* (f)

home *casa* (f)

homework *deberes* (m, pl)

hope: to __ *esperar*

hour *hora* (f)

housewife *ama* (f) *de casa*

how many? *¿cuántos/cuantas?*

how much? *¿cuánto/cuánta?*

hunger *hambre* (m)

hungry: to be __ *tener* (e>ie) *hambre*

hurt: to __ *doler* (o>ue)

husband *marido* (m), (formal, esp LAm) *esposo* (m)

I *yo*

ice *hielo* (m)

ice-cream *helado* (m)

if *si*

impolite *descortés*

in *en*

increase: to __ *aumentar*

Indian *indio/a*

insurance *seguro* (m)

interview *entrevista* (f)

interview: to __ *entrevistar*

introduce: to __ *presentar*

iron: to __ *planchar*

jacket *chaqueta* (f) *americana* (f), (LAm) *saco* (m)

jam *mermelada* (f)

January *enero*

jeans *vaqueros, jeans* (m, pl)

job *puesto* (m), *cargo* (m)

jogging *footing* (m), *jogging* (m)

join: to __ *ingresar*

journalist *periodista* (m/f)

journey *viaje* (m)

juice *zumo* (m), (LAm) *jugo*

July *julio*

June *junio*

key *llave* (f)

kitchen *cocina* (f)

knife *cuchillo* (m)

know: to __ (fact) *saber*, (people and places) *conocer*

knowledge *conocimiento* (m)

lamb *cordero* (m)

language *lengua* (f), *idioma* (m)

large *grande*, (before a noun) *gran*

last *último/a*; __ name *apellido* (m)

last: __ week *la semana pasada*; __ month/year *el mes/año pasado*

Latin America *Latinoamérica*

launderette *lavandería* (f)

laundromat (AmE) *lavandería* (f)

law *derecho* (m)

lawyer *abogado/a*

lazy *perezoso/a*

learn: to __ *aprender*

leave: to __ *salir, irse, dejar*

left *izquierdo/a*

lemon *limón* (m)

less *menos*

letter *carta* (f)

lettuce *lechuga* (f)

level *nivel* (m)

librarian *bibliotecario/a*

library *biblioteca* (f)

lift *ascensor* (m), (Mex) *elevador* (m)

light *luz* (f); (meal) *ligero/a*

like *as*

like: to __ *gustar, apetecer*; to __ a lot *encantar, fascinar*

line *línea* (f)

listen: to __ to *escuchar*

little (amount) *poco/a*; (size) *pequeño/a*

live: to __ *vivir*

loaf *barra* (f)

London *Londres*

long *largo/a*

look: to __ *mirar*; to __ for *buscar*;

to ___ after *cuidar*
lorry *camión* (m)
lose: to ___ *perder* (e>ie)
lounge *salón* (m), *sala* (f) *de estar*,
(LAm) *living* (m)
love: to ___ *querer* (e>ie); (to love
something) *encantar, fascinar*
low *bajo/a*
luck *suerte* (f)
lucky: to be __ *tener* (e>ie) *suerte*
luggage *equipaje* (m)
lunch *almuerzo* (m), *comida* (f); to
have ___ *almorzar, comer*

madam *señora*
magazine *revista (f)*
mail (AmE) *correspondencia* (f)
mailman/woman (AmE) *cartero/a*
man *hombre*
manager *gerente* (m/f), *encargado/a*
map *mapa* (m)
March *marzo*
marital status *estado* (m) *civil*
market *mercado* (m)
married *casado/a*
marvellous *maravilloso/a*
May *mayo*
meal *comida* (f)
meat *carne* (f)
meet: to ___ (for the 1st time)
conocer; (by arrangement) *quedar*
(con)
melon *melón* (m)
menu: set ___ *menú* (m) *del día*,
(Mex) *comida* (f) *corrida*
message *recado* (m), *mensaje* (m)
midday *mediodía* (m)
midnight *medianoche* (f)
milk *leche* (f)
mineral water *agua* (f) *mineral* (but *el
agua mineral*)
minute *minuto* (m)
miss *señorita*
mistake *equivocación* (f), *error* (m)
mister *señor*
mixed salad *ensalada* (f) *mixta*
Monday *lunes*
money *dinero* (m)
month *mes* (m)
monthly *mensual*
more *más*; more ..... than *más..... que*
morning *mañana* (f); in the ___ *por la*

mañana; (LAm) *en la* ___
Moroccan *marroquí*
most: the ___ *el/la/los/las más*
mother *madre*
motorway *autopista* (f)
move house: to___ *mudarse de casa*
movie (AmE) *película* (f), *film* (m),
filme (m); ___ theater *cine* (m)
museum *museo* (m)
mushroom *champiñón* (m)
music *música* (f)
must *deber, tener* (e>ie) *que*

name *nombre* (m)
name: first/Christian ___ *nombre* (m)
de pila; surname/last ___ *apellido* (m)
napkin *servilleta* (f)
nationality *nacionalidad* (f)
near *cerca*
need: to ___ *necesitar*
neighbour *vecino/a*
neighbourhood *barrio* (m)
neither *tampoco*
nephew *sobrino*
never *nunca*
news *noticia* (f)
newspaper *periódico* (m), *diario* (m)
next *próximo/a*
next to *junto a, al lado de*
nice *bonito/a, agradable,* (character)
simpático/a
niece *sobrina*
night *noche* (f); at ___ *por la noche*,
(LAm) *en* ___ ; last ___ *anoche*
noisy *ruidoso/a*
noon *mediodía* (m)
normally *normalmente, generalmente*
not ... either *tampoco*
nothing *nada*
November *noviembre*
now *ahora*; right ___ *ahora mismo*
número *number* (m)
nurse *enfermero/a*

O.K. *vale* (esp Spain), *de acuerdo*,
(LAm) *OK*
October *octubre*
of *de*
of course *claro, por supuesto*
offer: to ___ *ofrecer*
office *oficina* (f), *despacho* (m)
often *a menudo*

oil *aceite* (m); olive ___ *aceite de oliva*

old *viejo/a*

older *mayor*

olive *aceituna* (f)

omelette *tortilla* (f)

on *en*

one-way ticket *billete* (m) or (LAm) *boleto* (m) *de ida*

onion *cebolla* (f)

only *sólo, solamente*

open *abierto/a*

open: to ___ *abrir*

opposite *enfrente de, frente a*

or *o,* (before o) *u*

orange (colour) *naranja*

orange (fruit) *naranja* (f)

order *pedido* (m)

order: in __ to *para*

others *otros/otras*

out *fuera*

outskirts *afueras* (f, pl)

overcast *cubierto, nublado*

overcoat *abrigo* (m)

own *propio/a*

paint: to ___ *pintar*

painting *pintura* (f)

Pakistani *paquistaní*

pants (AmE) *pantalón* (m, sing), *pantalones* (m, pl)

parents *padres*

park *parque* (m)

parking lot *aparcamiento* (m), (LAm) *estacionamiento* (m), *aparcadero* (m)

park: to ___ *aparcar,* (esp LAm) *estacionar*

parsley *perejil* (m)

past *pasado/a*

pay: to ___ *pagar*

pea *guisante* (m), (LAm) *arveja/alverja* (f), (Mex) *chícharo*

peach *melocotón* (m), (LAm) *durazno* (m)

pear *pera* (f)

people *gente* (f, sing)

pepper *pimienta* (f)

pepper: red ___ *pimiento* (m) *rojo*

per *por, al*

performance *función* (f)

perhaps *quizá(s), tal vez, a lo mejor*

petrol station *gasolinera* (f), *estación* (f) *de servicio*

phone:to ___ *llamar (por teléfono), telefonear*

pineapple *piña* (f), (LAm) *ananá* (f)

pink *rosa ,* (LAm) *rosado*

place *lugar* (m), *sitio* (m)

play: to ___ *jugar* (u>ue); (music) *tocar*

pleasant *agradable*

please *por favor*

plumber *fontanero* (m), (LAm) *plomero*

poetry *poesía* (f)

polite *cortés, amable*

population *población* (f)

pork *cerdo* (m)

port *puerto* (m)

portion: a ___ of *una ración de*

post (letter) *correspondencia* (f)

post (job) *puesto* (m), *cargo* (m)

post office *oficina* (f) *de correos*

postman/woman *cartero/a*

postpone: to ___ *aplazar*

potato *patata* (f), (LAm) *papa* (f)

pound (sterling) *libra* (f) *esterlina*

practice to___ (AmE) *practicar*

practice (doctor's) *consulta* (f)

prawn *gamba* (f)

prefer: to ___ *preferir* (e>ie)

present *regalo* (m)

pretty *bonito/a, hermoso/a,* (LAm) *lindo/a*

price *precio* (m); what's the ___? *¿qué precio tiene?*

program (AmE) *programa*

proud *orgulloso/a*

public administration (AmE) *administración pública* (f)

pulse *legumbre* (f)

purchase *compra* (f)

purse *bolso* (m), (LAm) *cartera*

put: to ___ *poner*; to put on (clothes) *ponerse*; (telephone) to ___ through *poner (con)*

quiet *tranquilo/a*

radish *rábano* (m)

railway *ferrocarril* (m)

rain *lluvia* (f)

rain: to ___ *llover* (o>ue)
read: to ___ *leer*
reading *lectura* (f)
really *de verdad*; really? *¿de verdad?*
receive: to ___ *recibir*
red *rojo/a*; (wine) *tinto*
regret: to ___ *lamentar*
remember: to ___ *acordarse* (o>ue),
recordar (o>ue)
rent: to ___ *alquilar*, (LAm) *arrendar*,
(Mex) *rentar*
renting *alquiler* (m)
repair: to ___ *reparar*
request: to ___ *solicitar*
reservation *reserva* (f), (LAm)
reservación
rest: to ___ *descansar*
restroom *servicio* (m), *aseo* (m) *baño*
(m)
retired *jubilado/a*
return ticket *billete* (m)/(LAm) *boleto*
(m) *de ida y vuelta*
rice *arroz* (m)
right *derecho/a*; on the ___ *a la
derecha*
right away *ahora mismo, en seguida,
inmediatamente, de inmediato*
river *río* (m)
road *carretera* (f)
roast *asado/a*
room *habitación* (f), *cuarto* (m), (esp
LAm) *pieza* (f), (Mex) *recámara* (f)
room: double ___ *habitación* (f)
doble; single ___ *habitación* (f)
individual
rooming house *hostal* (m), *pensión* (f),
casa (f) *de huéspedes*

sad *triste*
safe deposit box *caja* (f) *fuerte*
sail: to ___ *hacer vela*
salad *ensalada* (f)
salary *sueldo* (m)
sale *venta* (f)
sales assistant *dependiente/a,
empleado/a, vendedor/a*
salesclerk (AmE) *dependiente/a,
empleado/a, vendedor/a*
salesman/woman *vendedor/a,
dependiente/a*
salesperson *vendedor/a, dependiente/a*
salt *sal* (f)

same *igual*
sandals *sandalias* (f)
sandwich *bocadillo* (m), (esp LAm)
sándwich (m)
Saturday *sábado*
sausage *salchichón* (m), *chorizo* (m)
schedule *horario* (m)
school *colegio* (m), *escuela* (f)
sea *mar* (usually m)
seat *asiento* (m)
second *segundo/a*
secondary school (esp Spain) *instituto*
(m) *(de enseñanza secundaria)*
secretary *secretario/a*
security *seguridad* (f)
see: to ___ *ver*
seem: to ___ *parecer*
sell: to ___ *vender*
send: to ___ *enviar, mandar*
September *septiembre, setiembre*
service station *estación* (f) *de servicio,
gasolinera* (f)
several *varios/varias*
shave: to ___ *afeitarse*
she *ella*
ship *barco* (m)
shirt *camisa* (f)
shoe shop/store *zapatería* (f)
shoes *zapatos* (m)
shop assistant *dependiente/a,
vendedor/a*
shop *tienda* (f)
shop window *escaparate* (m)
shopping: to do the __ *hacer la
compra*
short *corto/a*
show: to ___ *enseñar, mostrar* (o>ue)
shower *ducha* (f); to have a ___, to
shower *ducharse*
shrimp *gamba* (f)
shy *tímido/a*
sign: to ___ *firmar*
signal *señal* (f)
silly *tonto/a*
sincerely yours (AmE) *atentameate*
single *soltero/a*
single (ticket) *(billete/(LAm) boleto) de
ida*; (room) *(habitación) individual*
sir *señor*
sister *hermana*
sitting-room *salón* (m), *sala* (f) *de
estar*, (LAm) *living* (m)

size (clothes) *talla* (f); (general)
 tamaño (m)
skirt *falda* (f)
sleep: to ___ *dormir* (o>ue)
slice *trozo* (m)
small *pequeño/a*
smoker *fumador/a*; non ___ *no
 fumador/a*
snack (in a bar, esp Spain) *tapa* (f)
snow: to ___ *nevar* (e>ie)
soap *jabón* (m)
soap opera *telenovela* (f)
socks *calcetines* (m)
soft drink *refresco* (m)
so long (AmE) *adiós*
sol *sun* (m)
solicitor *abogado/a* (m)
some *algunos/algunas*
someone *alguien*
something *algo*
sometimes *a veces*
son *hijo*
sore throat *dolor de garganta* (m)
sorry: I'm ___ *perdón,
 perdone/perdona* (formal/inf)
soup *sopa* (f)
South America *América* (f) *del Sur,
 Sudamérica, Suramérica*
Spanish *español/española*
Spanish (language) *español* (m)
spare time *tiempo* (m) *libre*
speak: to ___ *hablar*
speciality *especialidad* (f)
specialty (AmE) *especialidad* (f)
spell: to ___ *deletrear*
spend: to ___ (time) *pasar*; (money)
 gastar
spinach *espinaca* (f)
spoon *cuchara* (f)
sport *deporte* (m)
square *plaza* (f)
stairs *escalera* (f)
stamp *sello* (m), (LAm) *estampilla* (f)
star *estrella* (f)
start: to ___ *empezar* (e>ie), *comenzar*
 (e>ie)
starting on *a partir de*
state highway (AmE) *carretera
 nacional*
station *estación* (f)
stationer's *papelería* (f)
stationery store *papelería* (f)

stay: to ___ *quedarse*
steak *bistec* (m)
stewardess *azafata,* (LAm) *aeromoza*
still *todavía, aún*
still (mineral water) *sin gas*
stockings *medias* (f)
stomach ache *dolor* (m) *de estómago*
stop: bus ___ *parada* (f) or (LAm)
 paradero (m)
stop: to ___ *parar*
store (AmE) *tienda* (f)
store window (AmE) *escaparate* (m)
storm *tormenta* (f)
straight on *todo recto, todo de frente,*
 (LAm) *derecho*
strange *extraño/a*
stranger *extraño/a*
strawberry *fresa* (f), (LAm) *frutilla* (f)
street *calle* (f)
strong *fuerte*
study: to ___ *estudiar*
subway *metro* (m)
succeed: to ___ *tener* (e>ie) *éxito*
success *éxito* (m)
sugar *azúcar* (m or f)
suit *traje* (m)
Sunday *domingo*
sunny *soleado/a*
supermarket *supermercado* (m)
supper *cena* (f)
suppose: to ___ *suponer*
surely *seguramente*
surgery *consulta* (f)
surname *apellido* (m)
sweater (Spain) *jersey, jersei* (m),
 (LAm) *suéter* (m)
swim: to ___ *nadar*
swimming *natación* (f)
swimming pool *piscina* (f), (Mex)
 alberca

T shirt *camiseta* (f)
table *mesa* (f)
tablet *pastilla* (f), *píldora* (f)
take: to ___ (general) *tomar,*
 (transport) *coger*
tap *grifo* (m)
tax *impuesto* (m)
tea *té* (m)
teach: to ___ *enseñar, dar clases*
teacher *profesor/a, maestro/a*
technician *técnico* (m)

telephone *teléfono* (m); ___ call
  llamada (f) (*telefónica*)
television *televisión* (f), (inf) *tele* (f)
tennis *tenis* (m)
tent *tienda* (f)
terrace *terraza* (f)
terrible *terrible*
thing *cosa* (f)
think: to ___ *pensar* (e>ie), *creer*
third *tercero/a*, (before a sing, m
  noun) *tercer*
thirst *sed* (f)
thirsty: to be ___ *tener* (e>ie) *sed*
this *este/esta*; (neuter) *esto*
those *esos/esas, aquellos/aquellas*
though *aunque*
throat *garganta* (f)
through *a través de, por*
Thursday *jueves*
ticket *billete* (m), (LAm) *boleto*;
  (show) *entrada* (f)
tie *corbata* (f)
tight *estrecho/a*
time *tiempo* (m), *hora* (f)
timetable (AmE) *horario* (m)
tin *lata* (f)
tired *cansado/a*
toast *tostadas* (f, pl)
today *hoy*
toilet *servicio* (m), *wáter* (m), *lavabo*
  (m), (esp LAm) *baño*
toilet paper *papel* (m) *higiénico*
tomato *tomate* (m), (Mex) *jitomate*
tomorrow *mañana*
too much (adj) *demasiado/a*
toothache *dolor* (m) *de muelas*
tourist office *oficina* (f) *de turismo*
towel *toalla* (f)
town *ciudad* (f), (small town) *pueblo*
  (m)
traffic light *semáforo* (m)
train *tren* (m)
trainers *zapatillas* (f)
translator *traductor/a*
travel agent´s *agencia* (f) *de viajes*
travel: to ___ *viajar*
traveler´s check *cheque* (m) *de viaje*
traveller´s cheque *cheque* (m) *de viaje*
trip *viaje* (m): one-way/round ___
  (AmE) *viaje de ida/de ida y vuelta*
trousers *pantalones* (m, pl), *pantalón*
  (m, sing)

truck (AmE) *camión* (m)
true *verdad* (f)
try: to ___ to *tratar de*; to ___ on
  probarse (o>ue)
Tuesday *martes*
tuna fish *atún* (m)
turn: to ___ *girar, doblar, torcer*
  (o>ue)
TV series *teleserie* (f)

ugly *feo/a*
umbrella *paraguas* (m)
uncle *tío*
underground railway *metro* (m)
undershirt (AmE) *camiseta* (f)
understand: to ___ *entender* (e>ie),
  comprender
United States *Estados Unidos (abbrev.
  EE.UU.)* (m, pl)
until *hasta*
use: to ___ *utilizar, usar*
usually *generalmente, normalmente*

vacations *vacaciones* (f)
veal *ternera* (f)
vegetable *verdura* (f)
very *muy*
vest *camiseta* (f)
visitor *visitante* (m/f), *visita* (f)

wait: to ___ *esperar*
waiter *camarero*, (LAm) *mesero*
waitress *camarera*, (LAm) *mesera*
walk *paseo* (m); to go for a ___ *dar
  un paseo*
walk: to ___ *andar, caminar*
want *querer* (e>ie), *desear*
warm: it is ___ *hace calor*
wash up: to ___ *fregar* (e>ie), *lavar
  (los platos)*
wash: to ___ *lavar*, (oneself) *lavarse*
washbasin *lavabo* (m), *lavamanos* (m)
washroom *lavabo* (m) *lavamanos* (m)
watch: to ___ *mirar*
water *agua* (f) (but *el agua*)
water-melon *sandía* (f)
Wednesday *miércoles*
week *semana* (f)
weekend *fin* (m) *de semana*
weekly *semanal, por semana*
weight *peso* (m)

welcome: you´re ___ *de nada, no hay de qué, (gracias) a usted.*
well *bien*
what else? *¿qué más?*
when? *¿cuándo?*
where? *¿dónde?*
which? *¿cuál/cuáles?*
while *rato* (m); (conjunction) *mientras*
white *blanco/a*
who? *¿quién/quiénes?*
why? *¿por qué?*
wide *ancho/a*
wife *mujer,* (formal, esp LAm) *esposa*
wind *viento* (m)
window *ventana* (f)
windy: it´s ___ *hace viento*
wine *vino* (m); red ___ *vino tinto;* white ___ *vino blanco*
winter *invierno*(m)
with *con*
without *sin*
woman *mujer*
wonderful *maravilloso/a*
word *palabra* (f)
work *trabajo* (m)
work: to ___ *trabajar*
worker *trabajador/a, obrero/a*
working hours *horario* (m) *de trabajo*
world *mundo* (m)
write: to ___ *escribir*
wrong *equivocado/a*

year *año* (m)
yellow *amarillo/a*
yes *sí*
yesterday *ayer;* the day before ___ *antes de ayer, anteayer*
yet *todavía, aún*
young *joven*
younger *menor, más joven*
yours sincerely *atentamente*
youth hostel *albergue* (m) *juvenil*

index to grammar

teach® yourself

From Advanced Sudoku to Zulu, you'll find everything you need in the **teach yourself** range, in books, on CD and on DVD.

Visit **www.teachyourself.co.uk** for more details.

Advanced Sudoku and Kakuro
Afrikaans
Alexander Technique
Algebra
Ancient Greek
Applied Psychology
Arabic
Aromatherapy
Art History
Astrology
Astronomy
AutoCAD 2004
AutoCAD 2007
Ayurveda
Baby Massage and Yoga
Baby Signing
Baby Sleep
Bach Flower Remedies
Backgammon
Ballroom Dancing
Basic Accounting
Basic Computer Skills
Basic Mathematics
Beauty
Beekeeping
Beginner's Arabic Script
Beginner's Chinese Script
Beginner's Dutch

Beginner's French
Beginner's German
Beginner's Greek
Beginner's Greek Script
Beginner's Hindi
Beginner's Italian
Beginner's Japanese
Beginner's Japanese Script
Beginner's Latin
Beginner's Mandarin Chinese
Beginner's Portuguese
Beginner's Russian
Beginner's Russian Script
Beginner's Spanish
Beginner's Turkish
Beginner's Urdu Script
Bengali
Better Bridge
Better Chess
Better Driving
Better Handwriting
Biblical Hebrew
Biology
Birdwatching
Blogging
Body Language
Book Keeping
Brazilian Portuguese

Bridge
British Empire, The
British Monarchy from Henry VIII, The
Buddhism
Bulgarian
Business Chinese
Business French
Business Japanese
Business Plans
Business Spanish
Business Studies
Buying a Home in France
Buying a Home in Italy
Buying a Home in Portugal
Buying a Home in Spain
C++
Calculus
Calligraphy
Cantonese
Car Buying and Maintenance
Card Games
Catalan
Chess
Chi Kung
Chinese Medicine
Christianity
Classical Music
Coaching
Cold War, The
Collecting
Computing for the Over 50s
Consulting
Copywriting
Correct English
Counselling
Creative Writing
Cricket
Croatian
Crystal Healing
CVs
Czech
Danish
Decluttering
Desktop Publishing
Detox

Digital Home Movie Making
Digital Photography
Dog Training
Drawing
Dream Interpretation
Dutch
Dutch Conversation
Dutch Dictionary
Dutch Grammar
Eastern Philosophy
Electronics
English as a Foreign Language
English for International Business
English Grammar
English Grammar as a Foreign Language
English Vocabulary
Entrepreneurship
Estonian
Ethics
Excel 2003
Feng Shui
Film Making
Film Studies
Finance for Non-Financial Managers
Finnish
First World War, The
Fitness
Flash 8
Flash MX
Flexible Working
Flirting
Flower Arranging
Franchising
French
French Conversation
French Dictionary
French Grammar
French Phrasebook
French Starter Kit
French Verbs
French Vocabulary
Freud
Gaelic

Gardening
Genetics
Geology
German
German Conversation
German Grammar
German Phrasebook
German Verbs
German Vocabulary
Globalization
Go
Golf
Good Study Skills
Great Sex
Greek
Greek Conversation
Greek Phrasebook
Growing Your Business
Guitar
Gulf Arabic
Hand Reflexology
Hausa
Herbal Medicine
Hieroglyphics
Hindi
Hindi Conversation
Hinduism
History of Ireland, The
Home PC Maintenance and
   Networking
How to DJ
How to Run a Marathon
How to Win at Casino Games
How to Win at Horse Racing
How to Win at Online Gambling
How to Win at Poker
How to Write a Blockbuster
Human Anatomy & Physiology
Hungarian
Icelandic
Improve Your French
Improve Your German
Improve Your Italian
Improve Your Spanish
Improving Your Employability

Indian Head Massage
Indonesian
Instant French
Instant German
Instant Greek
Instant Italian
Instant Japanese
Instant Portuguese
Instant Russian
Instant Spanish
Internet, The
Irish
Irish Conversation
Irish Grammar
Islam
Italian
Italian Conversation
Italian Grammar
Italian Phrasebook
Italian Starter Kit
Italian Verbs
Italian Vocabulary
Japanese
Japanese Conversation
Java
JavaScript
Jazz
Jewellery Making
Judaism
Jung
Kama Sutra, The
Keeping Aquarium Fish
Keeping Pigs
Keeping Poultry
Keeping a Rabbit
Knitting
Korean
Latin
Latin American Spanish
Latin Dictionary
Latin Grammar
Latvian
Letter Writing Skills
Life at 50: For Men
Life at 50: For Women

Life Coaching
Linguistics
LINUX
Lithuanian
Magic
Mahjong
Malay
Managing Stress
Managing Your Own Career
Mandarin Chinese
Mandarin Chinese Conversation
Marketing
Marx
Massage
Mathematics
Meditation
Middle East Since 1945, The
Modern China
Modern Hebrew
Modern Persian
Mosaics
Music Theory
Mussolini's Italy
Nazi Germany
Negotiating
Nepali
New Testament Greek
NLP
Norwegian
Norwegian Conversation
Old English
One-Day French
One-Day French – the DVD
One-Day German
One-Day Greek
One-Day Italian
One-Day Portuguese
One-Day Spanish
One-Day Spanish – the DVD
Origami
Owning a Cat
Owning a Horse
Panjabi
PC Networking for Small
  Businesses

Personal Safety and Self
  Defence
Philosophy
Philosophy of Mind
Philosophy of Religion
Photography
Photoshop
PHP with MySQL
Physics
Piano
Pilates
Planning Your Wedding
Polish
Polish Conversation
Politics
Portuguese
Portuguese Conversation
Portuguese Grammar
Portuguese Phrasebook
Postmodernism
Pottery
PowerPoint 2003
PR
Project Management
Psychology
Quick Fix French Grammar
Quick Fix German Grammar
Quick Fix Italian Grammar
Quick Fix Spanish Grammar
Quick Fix: Access 2002
Quick Fix: Excel 2000
Quick Fix: Excel 2002
Quick Fix: HTML
Quick Fix: Windows XP
Quick Fix: Word
Quilting
Recruitment
Reflexology
Reiki
Relaxation
Retaining Staff
Romanian
Running Your Own Business
Russian
Russian Conversation

Russian Grammar
Sage Line 50
Sanskrit
Screenwriting
Second World War, The
Serbian
Setting Up a Small Business
Shorthand Pitman 2000
Sikhism
Singing
Slovene
Small Business Accounting
Small Business Health Check
Songwriting
Spanish
Spanish Conversation
Spanish Dictionary
Spanish Grammar
Spanish Phrasebook
Spanish Starter Kit
Spanish Verbs
Spanish Vocabulary
Speaking On Special Occasions
Speed Reading
Stalin's Russia
Stand Up Comedy
Statistics
Stop Smoking
Sudoku
Swahili
Swahili Dictionary
Swedish
Swedish Conversation
Tagalog
Tai Chi
Tantric Sex
Tap Dancing
Teaching English as a Foreign
    Language
Teams & Team Working
Thai
Theatre
Time Management
Tracing Your Family History
Training

Travel Writing
Trigonometry
Turkish
Turkish Conversation
Twentieth Century USA
Typing
Ukrainian
Understanding Tax for Small
    Businesses
Understanding Terrorism
Urdu
Vietnamese
Visual Basic
Volcanoes
Watercolour Painting
Weight Control through Diet &
    Exercise
Welsh
Welsh Dictionary
Welsh Grammar
Wills & Probate
Windows XP
Wine Tasting
Winning at Job Interviews
Word 2003
World Faiths
Writing Crime Fiction
Writing for Children
Writing for Magazines
Writing a Novel
Writing Poetry
Xhosa
Yiddish
Yoga
Zen
Zulu

| teach yourself | **spanish conversation**
angela howkins & juan kattán-ibarra |

- Do you want to talk with confidence?
- Are you looking for basic conversation skills?
- Do you want to understand what people say to you?

Spanish Conversation is a three-hour, all-audio course which you can use at any time, whether you want a quick refresher before a trip or whether you are a complete beginner. The 20 dialogues on CDs 1 and 2 will teach you the Spanish you will need to speak and understand, without getting bogged down with grammar. CD 3, uniquely, teaches skills for listening and understanding. This is the perfect accompaniment to **Beginner's Spanish** and **Spanish** in the **teach yourself** range: www.teachyourself.co.uk.

teach
yourself

spanish grammar
juan kattán-ibarra

- Are you looking for an accessible guide to Spanish grammar?
- Do you want a book oyu can use either as a reference or as a course?
- Would you like exercises to reinforce your learning?

Spanish Grammar explains the most important structures in a clear and jargon-free way, with plenty of examples to show how they work in context. Use the book as a comprehensive reference to dip in and out of or work through it to build your knowledge.

teach yourself

improve your spanish
juan kattán-ibarra

- Is your Spanish rusty?
- Do you want to get up to speed quickly?
- Are you looking for more than the simplest way of expressing yourself?

Improve your Spanish is an ideal way to extend your language skills. You will build on your existing knowledge and improve your spoken and written Spanish so that you can communicate with confidence in a range of situations.

| teach yourself | **spanish dictionary** |

- Do you want to extend your vocabulary?
- Do you need help with written and spoken Spanish?
- Does your pronunciation need improving?

This **Spanish Dictionary** will give you everything you need to
check and improve your Spanish, for both written and spoken
use. It contains 55,000 key words and phrases, 80,000
translations, up-to-date coverage of modern Spanish (including
the latest terminology), abbreviations, acronyms, proper nouns
and a pronunciation table. With clear and concise instructions
in both languages, it is designed for ease of use and immediate
application.

teach
yourself

spanish verbs
maría rosario hollis

- Do you want a handy reference guide to check verb forms?
- Are you finding tenses difficult?
- Do you want to see verbs used in a variety of contexts?

Spanish Verbs is a quick-and-easy way to check the form and meaning of over 3000 verbs. The clear layout makes the book very easy to navigate and the examples make the uses clear at the same time as building your vocabulary.